Racism, Sexism, and the World-System

Recent Titles in
Contributions in Economics and Economic History
Series Editor: Robert Sobel

Friedrich A. Sorge's *Labor Movement in the United States*: A History of the American Working Class from 1890 to 1896
Kai Schoenhals, translator

The Coming of Age of Political Economy, 1815–1825
Gary F. Langer

The Reconstruction of Economics: An Analysis of the Fundamentals of Institutional Economics
Allan G. Gruchy

Development Finance and the Development Process
Kempe Ronald Hope

Bridging the Gap Between Rich and Poor: American Economic Development Policy Toward the Arab East, 1942–1949
Nathan Godfried

Rethinking the Nineteenth Century: Contradictions and Movements
Francisco O. Ramirez, editor

Textiles in Transition: Technology, Wages, and Industry Relocation in the U.S. Textile Industry, 1880–1930
Nancy Frances Kane

Threats of Quotas in International Trade: Their Effect on the Exporting Country
Gerard Lawrence Stockhausen

A Slippery Slope: The Long Road to the Breakup of AT&T
Fred W. Henck and Bernard Strassburg

The Suppression of the Automobile: Skulduggery at the Crossroads
David Beasley

New Perspectives on Social Class and Socioeconomic Development in the Periphery
Nelson W. Keith and Novella Zett Keith, editors

World Population Trends and Their Impact on Economic Development
Dominick Slavatore, editor

RACISM, SEXISM, AND THE WORLD-SYSTEM

EDITED BY
Joan Smith, Jane Collins,
Terence K. Hopkins, and
Akbar Muhammad

STUDIES IN THE POLITICAL ECONOMY
OF THE WORLD-SYSTEM

Immanuel Wallerstein, ADVISORY EDITOR

CONTRIBUTIONS IN ECONOMICS AND
ECONOMIC HISTORY, NUMBER 84

GREENWOOD PRESS
New York • Westport, Connecticut • London

Library of Congress Cataloging-in-Publication Data

Racism, sexism, and the world-system / edited by Joan Smith . . . [et al.].

    p. cm.—(Studies in the political economy of the world-system) (Contributions in economics and economic history, ISSN 0084-9235 ; no. 84)

  Papers presented at the XIth Annual Political Economy of the World-System Conference held at SUNY-Binghamton, March 1987, sponsored by the Fernand Braudel Center for the Study of Economies, Historical Systems, and Civilizations, the Afro-American and African Studies Department, and the Women's Studies Program of SUNY-Binghamton, and the Political Economy of the World-System Section of the American Sociological Association.

    Bibliography: p.

    Includes index.

    ISBN 0-313-26331-0 (lib. bdg. : alk. paper)

    1. Capitalism—History. 2. Women—Employment—History. 3. Minorities—Employment—History. 4. Discrimination in employment—History. 5. Economic history. I. Smith, Joan, 1935- . II. Series. III. Series: Contributions in economics and economic history, no. 84.

HB501.R18   1988

331.13'3'09—dc19   88-10248

British Library Cataloguing in Publication Data is available.

Library of Congress Catalog Card Number: 88-10248

ISBN: 0-313-26331-0

ISSN: 0084-9235

First published in 1988

Greenwood Press, Inc.

88 Post Road West, Westport, Connecticut 06881

Printed in the United States of America

The paper used in this book complies with the Permanent Paper Standard issued by the National Information Standards Organization (Z39.48-1984).

10 9 8 7 6 5 4 3 2 1

Contents

v

SERIES FOREWORD

Immanuel Wallerstein

The Political Economy of the World-System section of the American Sociological Association was created in the 1970s to bring together a small but growing number of social scientists concerned with analyzing the processes of world-systems in general, and our modern one in particular.

Although organizationally located within the American Sociological Association, the PEWS Section bases its work on the relative insignificance of the traditional disciplinary boundaries. For that reason it has held an annual spring conference, open to and drawing participation from persons who work under multiple disciplinary labels.

For PEWS members, not only is our work unidisciplinary but the study of the world-system is not simply another "specialty" to be placed beside so many others. It is instead a different "perspective" with which to analyze all the traditional issues of the social sciences. Hence, the themes of successive PEWS conferences are quite varied and cover a wide gamut of topics. What they share is the sense that the isolation of political, economic, and socio-cultural "variables" is a dubious enterprise, that all analysis must be simultaneously historic and systemic, and that the conceptual bases of work in the historical social sciences must be rethought.

INTRODUCTION

Joan Smith

By all accounts, racism and sexism should no longer exist. Yet everywhere we look, skin color and features that mark one as a black or white, male or female, are crucial in organizing the social—not to mention the political—world. The very pervasiveness of racism and sexism has lent both the air of inevitability. If neither disappears when they theoretically should, then perhaps they are indeed inevitable. The authors of this volume who took part in the Eleventh Annual Political Economy of the World-System Conference disagree. Instead, they present accounts that either explain, in social, political, or historical terms, the pervasiveness of sexism and racism, or trace the relationship between the two and the organization of the contemporary political economy.

One of the criticisms most frequently launched against the attempts of social scientists to deal with the issues of sexism and racism is that formulations of the problems quite frequently appear separate and "tacked on." The chapters in this volume are distinct in their attempt to integrate an understanding of racial and sexual oppression with that of the other processes that constitute the world-economy.

The task, of course, is a difficult one. Its accomplishment may indeed require a fundamental rethinking of both the world-economy and how it works and the set of forces which racism and sexism give rise to and legitimate.

Although it may seem paradoxical, the concepts traditionally employed in the analysis of racial and sexual oppression have been both too monolithic and too fragmented—too large and too small—for the task at hand. Many authors in this volume find that racism and sexism are not specific enough, as concepts, to encompass the discriminatory phenomena that they are describing. Others find that concepts associated with the world-system have to be broadened in order to accommodate notions of race and sex. The chapters in this book argue strongly for both: that is to say, serious rethinking of racism and sexism as fundamental processes of the world-system, and a reconceptualization of the world-system in such a fashion that imperatives of race and sex as a way of organizing that world make conceptual as well as empirical sense.

Many of the authors emphasize the circumstances under which racism and sexism are created and recreated in various contexts. Immanuel Wallerstein comments on the historical flexibility of the boundaries that racism and sexism construct; June Nash discusses the need to distinguish the patriarchal forms of social organization that have emerged in various con- texts in the past from the male hegemony imposed by capitalism. All of the authors argue in one way or another that we need a new, more differen- tiated vocabulary to describe these forms of discrimination and oppression, and more analyses of the type presented here that will allow us to begin to discern how changes in the construction of racial and gender relations are related to particular processes that constitute the world-economy.

Many of the chapters take the form of theoretically informed case studies. These include the detailed historical work of Ann Forsythe, Roberto Korzeniewicz and Kathie Friedman Kasaba; the careful critical analysis of the construction of census categories by Martha Gimenez; and the "taking apart" of the myths of differential ethnic success (James Geschwender, Rita Carroll-Seguin, and Richard Williams). This type of research is essential in allowing us to populate our theories with real-life examples—in order to be able to think them through, raise new questions, and reveal contradictions.

Inevitably, given the current state of the field, many authors seem to run up against the problem of conceptual fragmentation that leads, at times, to mechanistic and functionalist renderings of complex problems. This dif- ficulty stems, in part, from a pervasive tendency in contemporary social science to separate out the categories *economy, culture,* and *ideology* for analysis, and then to attempt to put them back together again. This fragmentation takes the form of a tendency to see cultural practices that cannot be directly deduced from economic processes as "left-overs" from the past. This fragmentation is an illusory product of our disciplinary boundaries and our style of analysis. The world-economy is ideological and political. People do not insure their subsistence or their family wage and then go about behaving culturally and ideologically. The question is not what is a product of the market or the labor process and what is cultural, but how the market and the labor processes are cultural and shape the way we live our lives, the totality of which is the world-economy as a historical social system.

The attempt to grapple with problems of functionalism and mechanistic interpretation took many forms in the conference from which this book was drawn, such as Wallerstein's questions about the tensions between universalist ideologies and those that glorify the difference in its many forms—nationalism, ethnicity, and ultimately racial and sexual relations and thus boundaries. He asks, "What are we to make of cultural difference, of the resurgence of religious fundamentalism, or of French nationalism in Canada?" Many questions arose about how the expulsion of women from the work force in different historical periods affected power relationships in the home. What views of women emerge out of household relations where men have jobs and women have been cut off from them? There was a recurring concern with how the experience of unemployment affects class consciousness and political action and alliances. Though the discussions included in this volume present widely varying accounts, there is consensus among the authors that the effects of the world-economy are not only felt in the workplace; they may be mediated only indirectly through the labor process (as in the loss of employment), and they extend into relationships of family and community and into the socialization process.

Not surprisingly, and despite efforts to the contrary, the tendency toward functionalist explanations has not been completely overcome. Many of the chapters focus on the ways in which the drawing of ethnic boundaries "allows" capitalist enterprises to pay lower wages; or the designation of certain kinds of activities as "naturally" female allows women to be excluded from the workplace, and thus secures their production as a subsidy for workers who are receiving an insufficient wage. Obviously the struggle involved on the part of both capital and laboring classes and the class differences within racial and gender groupings require more than a mechanistic approach to the issues of gender and race. How did discriminatory practices get started? How are they "naturalized" and perpetuated? What are their implications for political action? How do we deal with cases where racist and sexist principles, once in existence, create contradictions that actually deepen crises? Forsythe and Korzeniewicz underscore the complexity of these processes when they argue that women are not consigned to unskilled jobs, but that jobs become classified as unskilled because they are performed by women. Kasaba provides an example of the interplay between economic necessity and cultural formulations in her discussion of Russian immigrant tailors who took jobs formerly classified as "women's work" and for whom this became a source of dominance in the family because they were the sole wage earners.

Many of the chapters focus on the implications of racial and sexual oppression for political struggle. Of particular interest have been the ways in which the current economic crisis is forcing realignment of popular movements, including women's movements and those representing racially and culturally oppressed groups. The quotations that Nash presents, from participants in the recent March for Life in Bolivia, exemplify a new sort of mobilization—not around workplace issues, but based on other forms of shared oppression felt in family, schools, the welfare system, and in the lack of jobs. Wallerstein sounds a note of caution with reference to these movements, referring to the conflicts that are bound to emerge as groups attempt to devise longer-range strategies for action. He suggests that much intellectual work is required to develop a common basis for action among such diverse interests. The chapters in this book, in many respects, turn their attention to just that task.

PART I

GENERAL ORIENTATION

1

THE IDEOLOGICAL TENSIONS OF CAPITALISM: UNIVERSALISM VERSUS RACISM AND SEXISM

Immanuel Wallerstein

The modern world, we have long been told, is the first to reach beyond the bounds of narrow, local loyalties and to proclaim the universal brotherhood of man. Or so we were told up to the 1970s. Since that time, we have been made conscious that the very terminology of universalist doctrine, as for example the phrase *the brotherhood of man*, belies itself, since this phrase is masculine in gender, thereby implicitly excluding or relegating to a secondary sphere all who are female. It would be easy to multiply linguistic examples, all of which reveal an underlying tension between the continuing ideological legitimation of universalism in the modern world and the continuing reality (both material and ideological) of racism and sexism in this same world. It is this tension, or more precisely this contradiction, that I wish to discuss. For contradictions not only provide the dynamic force of historical systems; they also reveal their essential features.

It is one thing to ask whence universalist doctrine, and how widely it is shared; or to ask why racism and sexism exist and persist. It is quite another to enquire into the origins of the pairing of the two ideologies, indeed what one might argue has been the symbiotic relationship of these presumed opposites. We start with a seeming paradox. The major challenge to racism and sexism has been universalist beliefs; and the major challenge to universalism has been racist and sexist beliefs. We assume that the proponents of each set of beliefs are persons in opposite camps. Only occasionally do we allow ourselves to notice that the enemy, as Pogo put it, is us; that most of us (perhaps all of us) find it perfectly possible to pursue both doctrines simultaneously. This is to be deplored no doubt; but it is also to be explained, and by more than the simple assertion of hypocrisy. For this paradox (or this hypocrisy) is enduring, widespread, and structural. It is no passing human failing.

In previous historical systems it was easier to be consistent. However much these previous systems varied in their structures and in their premises, they all had no hesitation in making some kind of moral and political distinction between the insider and the outsider, in which both the belief in the higher moral qualities of the insider and the sense of obligation by insiders to each other took precedence over any abstract concepts about the human species, if such abstractions were asserted at all. Even the three monotheistic world religions—Judaism, Christianity, and Islam—made such distinctions between insiders and outsiders despite their hypothetical commitment to a single God presiding over a singular human species.

This essay discusses first the origins of modern universalist doctrines, then the sources of modern racism and sexism, and finally the realities of the combination of the two ideologies, both in terms of what gave rise to it and what has been its consequences.

There are two main ways of explaining the origins of universalism as an ideology of our present historical system. One is to see universalism as the culmination of an older intellectual tradition. The other is to see it as an ideology particularly appropriate to a capitalist world-economy. The two modes of explanation do not necessarily contradict each other. The argument that it is the outcome or the culmination of a long tradition has to do precisely with the trio of monotheistic religions. The crucial moral leap, it has been argued, occurred when humans (or some humans) ceased to believe in a tribal god and recognized the unicity of God and therefore implicitly the unicity of humanity. To be sure, the argument continues, the three monotheistic religions pursued the logic of their position only partway. Judaism carved out a special position for the people chosen of God and was reluctant to encourage membership by adoption. Christianity and Islam both lifted the barriers to entry into the group of the chosen, and indeed went in the other direction with proselytization. But both Christianity and Islam normally required an affirmative act of allegiance (which one could make as a formerly nonbelieving adult by formal conversion) in order to gain full access to the kingdom of God. Modern Enlightenment thought, it is said, simply took this monotheistic logic one step further, deriving moral equality and human rights from human nature itself, a characteristic with which we are all born and as a result of which our rights become entitlements rather than earned privileges.

This is not an incorrect history of ideas. We have several important politicomoral documents of the late eighteenth century that reflect this Enlightenment ideology, documents that were given widespread credence and adherence as a result of major political upheavals (the French Revolution, the decolonization of the Americas, etc.). Furthermore, we can carry the ideological history forward. There were many de facto omissions in these ideological documents of the eighteenth century—and most notably those of nonwhites and women. But as time went on, these omissions and others have been rectified by explicitly including these groups under the rubric of universalist doctrine. Today even those social movements whose raison d'être is the implementation of racist or sexist policies tend to pay at least lip service to the ideology of universalism, thereby seeming to consider it somehow shameful to assert overtly what they very clearly believe and think should govern political priorities. It is not hard therefore to derive from the history of ideas a sort of secular upward curve of the acceptance of universalist ideology, and based on that curve, to make a claim about the existence of a sort of inevitable world-historical process at work.

The claim however that, since universalism has only been seriously pursued as a political doctrine in the modern world, its origins must be sought in the particular socioeconomic framework of this world also seems very strong. The capitalist world-economy is a system built on the endless accumulation of capital. One of the prime mechanisms that makes this possible is the commodification of everything. These commodities flow in a world market in the form of goods, of capital, and of labor power. Presumably, the freer the flow, the greater the degree of commodification. Consequently, anything that restrains the flow is hypothetically counterindicated.

Anything that prevents goods, capital, or labor power from being a marketable commodity serves to restrain such flows. Anything that uses criteria of evaluating goods, capital, or labor power other than their market value and then gives these other valuations priority makes the item to that extent nonmarketable, or at least less marketable. Hence, by a sort of impeccable logic, particularisms of any kind whatsoever are said to be incompatible with the logic of a capitalist system, or at least an obstacle to its optimal operation. It would follow then that, within a capitalist sytem, it is imperative to assert and carry out a universalist ideology as an essential element in the endless pursuit of the accumulation of capital. Thus it is that we talk of capitalist social relations as being a "universal solvent," working to reduce everything to a homogenous commodity form denoted by a single measure of money.

This is said to have two principal consequences. It is said to permit the greatest possible efficiency in the production of goods. Specifically, in terms of labor power, if we have a "career open to talents" (one of the slogans born out of the French Revolution), we are likely to place the most competent persons in the occupational roles most suitable for them in the world division of labor. And we have indeed developed whole institutional mechanisms—the public school system, the civil service, antinepotism rules—that are designed to establish what today we call a "meritocratic" system.

Furthermore, it is said, not only is meritocracy economically efficient but it is also politically stabilizing. To the extent that there are inequalities in the distribution of reward in historical capitalism (as in prior historical systems), resentment of those who receive greater rewards by those who receive fewer is less intense, it is argued, because its justification is offered on the basis of merit and not on the basis of tradition. That is, it is thought that privilege earned by merit is somehow more acceptable, morally and politically, to most people than privilege earned by inheritance.

This is dubious political sociology. The exact opposite is true in fact. While privilege earned by inheritance has long been at least marginally acceptable to the oppressed on the basis of mystical or fatalistic beliefs in an eternal order, which belief at least offers them the comfort of certainty, privilege earned because one is possibly smarter and certainly better educated than someone else is extremely difficult to swallow, except by the few who are basically scrambling up the ladder. Nobody who is not a yuppie loves or admires a yuppie. Princes at least may seem to be kindly father figures. A yuppie is nothing but an overprivileged sibling. The meritocratic system is politically one of the least stable systems. And it is precisely because of this political fragility that racism and sexism enter the picture.

The presumed upward curve of universalist ideology has long been thought theoretically to be matched by a downward curve of the degree of inequality generated by race or gender, both as ideology and as fact. This, however, has simply not been the case empirically. We could even perhaps make the inverse argument, that the curves of race and gender inequalities have actually been going up in the modern world, or at least have not been going down—certainly in fact, possibly even as ideology. To see why this might be so, we should look at what the ideologies of racism and sexism actually assert.

Racism is not simply a matter of having an attitude of disdain for or fear of someone of another group as defined by genetic criteria (such as skin color) or by social criteria (religious affiliation, cultural patterns, linguistic preference, etc.). Racism normally includes such disdain and fear, but it is far more than that. Disdain and fear are quite secondary to what defines the practice of racism in the capitalist world economy. Indeed, it could even be argued that disdain and fear of the other (xenophobia) is an aspect of racism that entails a contradiction.

Xenophobia in all prior historical systems had one primary behavioral consequence: the ejection of the "barbarian" from the physical locus of the community, the society, the in-group—death being the extreme version of ejection. Whenever we physically eject the other, we gain the "purity" of environment that we are presumably seeking, but we inevitably lose something at the same time. We lose the labor power of the person ejected and therefore that person's contribution to the creation of a surplus that we might be able to appropriate on a recurring basis. This represents a loss for any historical system, but it is a particularly serious one in the case of a system whose whole structure and logic is built around the endless accumulation of capital.

A capitalist system that is expanding (which is half the time) needs all the labor power it can find, since this labor is producing the goods through which more capital is produced, realized, and accumulated. Ejection out of the system is pointless. But if one wants to maximize the accumulation of capital, it is necessary simultaneously to minimize the costs of production (hence the costs of labor power) and minimize the costs of political disruption (hence minimize—not eliminate, because one cannot eliminate—the protests of the labor force). Racism is the magic formula that reconciles these objectives.

Let us look at one of the earliest and most famous discussions about racism as an ideology. When Europeans came to the New World, they encountered peoples whom they slaughtered in large numbers—either directly by the sword or indirectly by disease. A Spanish friar, Bartolomé de Las Casas, took up their cause, arguing that Indians had souls which needed to be saved. Let us pursue the implications of the Las Casas argument which won the formal assent of the church, and eventually of the states. Since Indians had souls, they were human beings, and the rules of natural law applied to them. Therefore, one was not morally permitted to slaughter them indiscriminately (eject them from the domain). One was obliged instead to seek to save their souls (convert them to the universalist value of Christianity). Since they would then be alive and presumably en route to conversion, they could be integrated into the work force—at the level of their skills, of course, which translated into meaning at the bottom level of the occupational and reward hierarchy.

Racism operationally has taken the form of what might be called the "ethnicization" of the work force, by which I mean that at all times there has existed an occupational-reward hierarchy that has tended to be correlated with some so-called social criteria. But while the pattern of ethnicization has been constant, the details have varied from place to place and time to time, according to what part of the human genetic and social pools were located in a particular time and place and what the hierarchical needs of the economy were at that time and place.

That is to say, racism has always combined claims based on continuity with the past (genetic and/or social) with a present-oriented flexibility in defining the exact boundaries of these reified entities we call races or ethno-national-religious groupings. The flexibility of claiming a link with the boundaries of the past combined with the constant redrawing of these boundaries in the present takes the form of the creation and constant re-creation of racial and/or ethno-national-religious groups or communities. They are always there, and always ranked hierarchically, but they are not always exactly the same. Some groups can be mobile in the ranking system; some groups can disappear or combine with others; while still others break apart and new ones are born. But there are always some who are "niggers." If there are no Blacks or too few to play the role, one can invent "white niggers."

This kind of system—racism constant in form and in venom, but somewhat flexible in boundary lines—does three things extremely well. It allows one to expand or contract the numbers available in any particular space-time zone for the lowest paid, least rewarding economic roles, according to current needs. It gives rise to and constantly recreates social communities that actually socialize children into playing the appropriate roles (although, of course, they also socialize them into forms of resistance). And it provides a nonmeritocratic basis to justify inequality. This last point is worth underlining. It is precisely because racism is anti-universalistic in doctrine that it helps to maintain capitalism as a system. It allows a far lower reward to a major segment of the work force than could ever be justified on the basis of merit.

But if capitalism as a system begets racism, does it need to beget sexism as well? Yes, because the two are in fact intimately linked. The ethnicization of the work force exists in order to permit very low wages for whole segments of the labor force. Such low wages are in fact only possible because the wage earners are located in household structures for which lifetime wage-income provides only a relatively small proportion of total household income. Such households require the extensive input of labor into so-called subsistence and petty market activities—in part by the adult male to be sure, but in much larger part by the adult female, plus the young and the aged of both sexes.

In such a system, this labor input in nonwage work "compensates" the lowness of the wage-income and therefore in fact represents an indirect subsidy to the employers of the wage laborers in those households. Sexism permits us not to think about it. Sexism is not just the enforcement of different, or even less appreciated, work roles for women, no more than racism is just xenophobia. As racism is meant to keep people inside the work system, not eject them from it, so sexism intends the same.

The way we induce women—and the young and the aged—to work to create surplus-value for the owners of capital, who do not even pay them a little bit, is by proclaiming that their work is really nonwork. We invent the "housewife" and assert she is not "working," merely "keeping house." Thus, when governments calculate the percentage of the so-called active labor force who are employed, "housewives" are neither in the numerator nor in the denominator of the calculation. And with sexism goes automatically ageism. As we pretend that the housewife's work is not creating surplus-value, so we pretend that the multiple work inputs of the nonwaged young and aged do not do so either.

None of this reflects working reality. But it does all add up to an ideology which is extremely powerful, and which all fits together. The combination of universalism-meritocracy serving as the basis by which the cadres or middle strata can legitimate the system and racism-sexism serving to structure the majority of the work force works very well. But only to a point, and that for a simple reason—the two ideological patterns of the capitalist world-economy stand in open contradiction to each other. The delicately poised combination threatens always to get out of hand, as various groups start to push the logic of universalism on the one hand and of racism-sexism on the other too far.

We know what happens when racism-sexism goes too far. Racists may try to eject the out-group totally—swiftly, as in the case of the Nazi slaughter of the Jews; less swiftly, as in the pursuit of total apartheid. Taken to this extreme, these doctrines are irrational and, because they are irrational, they are resisted. They are resisted, of course, by the victims, but they are also resisted by powerful economic forces who object not to the racism but to the fact that its primary objective—an ethnicized but productive work force—has been forgotten.

We can also imagine what happens when universalism goes too far. Some people may seek to implement a truly egalitarian allocation of work roles and work rewards in which race (or its equivalent) and gender genuinely play no part. Unlike taking racism too far, there is no swift way one can take universalism too far, for one has to eliminate not merely the legal and institutional barriers to universalism but the internalized patterns of ethnicization, and this inevitably requires at the very least a generation. So it is rather easy to resist universalism's going too far. In the name of universalism itself, one merely has to denounce the so-called reverse racism wherever step are taken to dismantle the institutionalized apparatus of racism and sexism.

What we see therefore is a system that operates by a tense link between the right dosage of universalism and racism-sexism. There are always efforts to push one side or the other of this equation "too far." The result is a sort of zigzag pattern. This could go on forever, except for one problem. Over time, the zigs and zags are getting bigger, not smaller. The thrust toward universalism is getting stronger. So is the thrust toward racism and sexism. The stakes go up. This is for two reasons.

One the one hand, there is the informational impact of the accumulation of historical experience, by all participants. On the other hand, there are the secular trends of the system itself. For the zigzag of universalism and racism-sexism is not the only zigzag in the system. There is also the zigzag of economic expansion and contraction, for example, with which the ideological zigzag of universalism and racism-sexism is partially correlated. The economic zigzag is also getting sharper. Why that is so is another story. Yet as the general contradictions of the modern world-system force the system into a long structural crisis, the most acute ideological-institutional locus of the search for a successor system is in fact located in the sharpening tension, the increased zigs and zags, between universalism and racism-sexism. It is not a question of which half of this antinomy will in some sense win out, since they are intimately and conceptually tied to each other. It is a question of whether and how we will invent new systems that will utilize neither the ideology of universalism nor the ideology of racism-sexism. That is our task, and it is not an easy one.

2

CULTURAL PARAMETERS OF SEXISM AND RACISM IN THE INTERNATIONAL DIVISION OF LABOR

June Nash

> Ms. Henrietta Holsman, a 1970 graduate and trustee of Wellesley College who runs a manufacturing concern in Los Angeles, raised a furor on campus when she remarked that Hispanics are lazy and blacks prefer pushing drugs to working in a factory, while Asians are likely to move on to managerial positions. Defending the position of the "successful entrepreneur . . . trying to share her experiences with other women," a Wellesley professor of economics stated that she was "describing her real life experiences on the factory floor." (*New York Times*, February 12, 1987)

> A Moroccan clothing factory manager explains that the female machinist who earns about 70 percent of the pay received by a male machinist doing the same work is just "working for lipstick" and does not have to support families. (Joekes 1985: 183)

The above incidents reveal attitudes, and the behaviors that underlie and reinforce them, that control the traffic into and out of jobs in both developed industrial centers and in Third World countries. In the growing integration of industrial and finance capital throughout the world, people are caught in the processes of industrialization and the cash economy in ways that challenge economic analyses. Ethnicity and race intersect with gender to enhance power relations in wage work and the domestic spheres. Understanding the ideologies of sexism and racism that structure the entry of these new populations into the world-economy requires a cultural analysis of the beliefs and behaviors that go beyond economic paradigms.

Ideological constraints are deeply embedded in material relations of production and reproduction that continually reinforce perceptions of what is
natural and therefore justified.

Development programs have been criticized for their failure to incorporate women and ethnic enclaves in ways that would overcome their subordination in political and economic spheres (Afshar 1985; Benería 1982;
Boserup 1970; Buvinic, Lycette & McGreevey 1983; Nash & Safa 1986;
Tinker & Bramsen 1976; Ward 1984; Wellesley Editorial Committee 1980;
Young et al. 1981; Youssef 1976); this critique is now being extended into a
critique of how they are being expelled from employment in the formal sectors in the growing crisis of world capitalism.

Ethnographic evidence points to a sharpening of the cleavages along
racial and gender lines during the expansive decades of capitalist penetration throughout the world. In order to clarify the particular historical circumstances in which these cleavages were forged, forms of male dominance
that rest on patriarchy and those that derive from the imposition of male
hegemony must be distinguished. The perpetuation of patriarchy in
capitalist enterprises within those countries with religious and moral commitments to elder male supremacy over women and young males is well
documented and provides us with insights into the working of cultural
premises in the restructuring of some economic systems. This process differs from the promotion of male dominance in Third World countries
where it was fostered in the introduction of capitalist enterprises. It should
also be distinguished from gender hierarchy in developed capitalist centers
where the reciprocal responsibilities of patriarchy for providing security and
protection for dependents are lacking. The tendency to universalize Judeo-
Christian categories such as patriarchy obscures the basis for exploitation,
as women and ethnic and racial minorities are drawn into capitalist wage
labor markets.

Ethnographic analysis of the cultural parameters of racism and sexism
also raises questions about trends assumed to be universal in the course of
capitalist expansion. Comparative research on the household and domestic
mode of production reveals that this has not only survived capitalist
penetration but, in fact, may be an increasing phenomenon. Women's subsistence production in ethnically distinct enclaves has contributed to the advance of capitalist enterprises at the same time that it serves as an alternative
form of survival. In the present crises of capitalism, with the stagnation of
whole economies burdened by debt in the Third World and with the decline
of production in developed countries, these enclaves that have resisted
capitalist encroachment may well become the basic nucleus for survival.

What is the relationship between the domestic reproductive sphere and
capitalist institutions? How are noncapitalist relations merged and built
upon in capitalist expansion? How are the ideologies regulating the labor
market shaped in culturally differentiated contexts? Where do they build on
preexisting patriarchal premises and where do they impose male hegemony

in societies where gender hierarchy is lacking? These questions will be examined in the context of domestic household production, import-substitution and export-processing industrialization, and in the informal economy of developed centers and developing periphery.

The framework of analysis in this chapter draws upon world-systems analysis tempered by a concern for culturally distinct social formations that co-exist with the capitalist mode of production (Nash 1981). In the international division of labor, the wage differentials between core and peripheral nations are growing (Chase-Dunn & Rubinson 1977; Hopkins & Wallerstein 1977) at the same time that disparities of income and opportunities of segments of the work force within nations are increasing. Rosa Luxemburg's thesis concerning the necessary coexistence of noncapitalist sectors with the advance of capitalist accumulation is also important. This process is increasingly recognized by analysts of Third World societies (Bennholdt-Thomsen 1981; Long 1984; Portes & Walton 1981). Subsistence production, whether in the family in advanced industrial countries or in peasant enclaves in the developing periphery, generates the producers and the consumers who are drawn into the market systems where supply and demand are structured in culturally defined ways.

In the process of transculturation, however, whereby both capitalist and noncapitalist institutions become transformed, the production and exchange of goods reproduce the society in ever-changing ways. Whereas neoclassical analyses take as given the structuring of supply and demand curves in accord with economic maximization, these are problematic, responding to the underlying cultural propositions conditioning them. The social relations that women and men enter into as they reproduce, exchange, and consume goods define as well as respond to the organization of production and reproduction. Contemporary Marxist-feminist analysis has gone beyond the definition of classes based on relations in production, to consider the dialectical relationship between these arenas. This chapter extends this analysis to show that the consciousness of both workers and manager/owners derives from culturally formed predispositions concerning gender, race, and ethnicity that control the entry of people into the labor force and effect the class relations that emerge in production.

Protest and resistance movements derive as much force from consciousness rising from these concerns as from the economic exploitation that governs their life conditions. Most of the liberation movements in developing countries throughout the twentieth century have sprung up from ethnic, racial, and gender roots. (In that same period, some sectors of the labor movement were transformed into economic interest groups that found accomodation within private capitalist expropriation.) Originating outside the workplace, the liberation movements flaunted the symbols that identified militants with the culturally constructed categories of gender and ethnicity, whether it was the women carrying symbols of female fertility in the Aba riots of Nigeria, the Cargo cults of Melanesia, the Kalala dance of

South African miners, the Huari ceremonies of Bolivian tin miners, or the freedom march led by Martin Luther King, Jr. A common theme in these manifestations in many different places throughout the world was a recognition of the threat to a way of life as people were drawn into the capitalist structures that denied their humanity. These movements enter into and inform labor struggles, particularly in the Third World and increasingly in the United States.

A useful framework for examining these transformations is that which Fernando Ortiz (1947) calls "transculturation"—the mutual, reinforcing changes in relations, behaviors, and beliefs with the advance of capitalism. We shall look at the structuring of gender, ethnicity, and race in the contexts of the household, the workplace, and the informal economy. As nations and enclave economies within them have moved from neocolonial exchanges of raw materials for manufactured goods, to import-substitution and export-processing zones, and finally to a shrinking of capitalist enterprises and resort to the informal economy, dramatic changes have occurred in all these arenas. The focus on the intersection of race and gender will be counterpointed in First and Third World countries as reciprocal and self-reinforcing changes transform both center and periphery.

CHANGES IN THE HOUSEHOLD ECONOMY

The household economy is the locus for the production of commodities, for sale as well as for use by its members, and for the transformation of exchanged goods into use values. Although the process of industrialization has paralleled the reduction of the household's involvement in the production of exchange values, it remains as a complementary site even in advanced capitalist economies. Marx and Engel's expectation of the demise of the family and the diminishing of household production activities has not been realized in the advancing industrialization that followed their prediction (Humphries 1977). This is a result of the cultural resistance mobilized both by household members to reject the cash nexus and by the wider polity that saw the threat to reproduction of the social order in the household's demise. An emic or inside view, of the operation of the household stresses the perception of members that they are rejecting the commoditization of personal relations in the exchanges that take place within kinship relations. The etic, or outside, view explains the noncash exchanges that take place as maintaining low costs of reproduction of the labor force.

Both emic and etic approaches are necessary to comprehend the reasons for the survival of the family and household organization of production. Norman Long's (1984) comparative analysis of the organization of production and reproduction in families and households throughout the world indicates the cultural priorities that condition the deployment of resources and the allocation of rewards. Contributors to his volume from a wide range of societies show that nonwage relationships based on kinship or neighborhood or community ties define the division of labor and the redistribution of social products in ways that defy monetary calculations. If there were a one-to-one relationship between the construction of roles in capitalist relations and those in households, then wage-earning women who contribute the major share of the family income would become household heads. It is clear that this is rarely the case. Similarly, if opportunity costs were the major basis for decisions about number of children to be born, then family size would be closely correlated with the economic contribution children make to the home. Occasionally there are correspondences in such equations (Rothstein 1986), but there are as many exceptions to the rule. High birth rates persist in many Third World countries whether or not there is development and despite the failure to absorb populations in the formal economy (Anker et al. 1982; Buvinic et al. 1983).

These priorities can be analyzed using a redistributional model that follows the culturally mediated terms of exchange within families and households. Karl Polanyi (1944) defined the political economy of redistribution as one based on the centralization of social surpluses and allocation of shares to individuals and groups in accord with culturally defined priorities. He illustrated its operation in noncapitalistic societies such as tribes and chiefdoms, where the power of governing individuals and groups was validated by their command over resources.[1]

But when we examine the operation of families and households cross-culturally, we find that power relations operate within these units in ways that defy the assumptions of communalistic exchange. Inequalities exist within families that affect the power, prestige, and share of the resources garnered by family members.

Patriarchal Roots of Oppression

Many feminist analysts (Eisenstein 1979; Hartmann 1979; Kuhn & Wolpe 1978; Mies 1986; Millett 1970; Mitchell 1973) attribute the persistent forms of inequality in household allocation and redistribution to patriarchy as a primary force usurping economic rationale in the material conditions governing women's lives as they enter into capitalist domains. Kate Millett (1971) was among the first feminists to extend the term *patriarchy* beyond its core meaning—dominance of the ascending male generation over women and youths—to the rule of men as a universal mode of power relationships. Roisin McDonough and Rachel Harrison (1978) have tried to reappropriate the term for a materialist-feminist approach that sees its operations within the context of historical class formation. This attempt fails, just as Millett's does, by robbing the term of its ethnographic meaning. "Patriarchy" refers to elder male authority in a gerontocracy. It provides reciprocal benefits to the subordinate females and youths in the society where it prevails, and it implies persistence from past institutions, principally those related to pastoral societies (Rubin 1975).

These conditions are rarely present in the contemporary societies where it is invoked to explain male hegemony. Colonial institutions often imposed what is called "patriarchy" on primordial bases where matrilineal kin groups or egalitarian societies may have prevailed (Etienne & Leacock 1980). The universalistic use of "patriarchy" distorts the evidence by suggesting that the existence of male dominance was prior and universal. The institutionalization of patriarchy in early states of the Middle East, Middle America, and Asia was a specific historical process in which women became subordinated to elder males within the household and domestic production of commodities was expropriated for the state. The rise of these institutions and their diffusion through military conquest and colonization can be traced historically and ethnographically (Nash & Rohrlich 1981; Silverblatt 1980). As the history of conquest and colonization shows, patriarchy had not arrived in all areas with the expansion of the world-system, and as ethnographies of contemporary societies reveal, female autonomy can be seen in many areas (cf. Schlegel 1977, especially the essays by Awe, Fluehr-Lobban, Lewis, Sutton, and Makiesky-Barrow).

If we limit "patriarchy" to those cases where it applies to intergenerational power relations monopolized by men and use "male hegemony" in those situations where it is imposed, we can appreciate the distinct processes of transculturation that occur in those countries that had developed patriarchal institutions in precolonial times and those that lacked gender hierarchy.

Cooptation of Patriarchy in the
Advance of Capitalism

In the modernizing nations of the Middle East and Asia, capitalist institutions have reinforced, and in turn been strengthened by, building on preexisting partriarchal relations. In the case of Iran, the Shah, and in particular his sister, challenged partriarchal control over women by advocating practices to overcome the signs of women's subordination, liberating them in the terms advocated by liberal, bourgeois feminist movements by removing the veil and purdah. Women were expected to add wage labor in the market to their home chores. In the expansion of trade with the West, women and young girls were employed full-time in the manufacture of carpets. With this additional burden they were even more intensively exploited by males in their households since they did not own the product or the means of production, and could not enter the market that remained a bastion of Islamic male leaders. Men disposed of their earnings in education for male children or in their own businesses, only summarily addressing the needs and interests of females in the household (Afshar 1985). In the backlash since Khomeini's revolution, the new regime appeals to patriarchal traditions in selective ways, with elite professional women the most stigmatized since they were expelled from highly paid professional and government jobs. Although labor force participation rates for women have declined along with those for men, the female share of the urban employed population has not changed (Moghadam n.d.). Village women continue to make carpets, but at a slower pace since the overseas market is cut off. The war with Iraq has created demand for their services in factories, offices, and other locales outside of their homes (Moghadam n.d.).

Another example of patriarchal oppression in which new capitalist production relations are "built on the backs of women," in Maria Mies's (1985) terms, comes from the lace makers in Narsapur, Andhra Pradesh. The expansion of the lace industry initiated by Christian missionaries to provide income for poor rural women integrated this enterprise in the world market. The fiction that these women were "just sitting at home" enabled their husbands to deny that they worked at the same time that they furthered their oppression. Marketing and profitable jobs related to the home industry were controlled by men who extracted the surpluses for their own ends. This perpetuated and deepened the asymmetric gender relations that prevailed in caste-constricted domestic enclaves.

The persistence of patriarchy is ensured in the control that men often exercised over marketing women's household-produced commodities in the Islamic-controlled markets where women dared not enter even as consumers. The power of males is also ensured by their prerogative in redistributing the wages of household members. Regardless of the contribution the patriarch makes to production, this prerogative guarantees and legitimates the power of male household heads over family resources: in the mediation of Gouru male elders of resources in granaries and livestock derived from the work of women and youths; in the disposal by Iranian fathers and husbands of the income of wives and daughters derived from carpet making; in the cooptations by Muslim fathers of daughters' wages from the electronics assembly plants in Malaysia; and in the redeployment by unemployed fathers and husbands in immigrant Italian households of the wages of wives and daughters in the garment trade in Greenwich Village at the turn of the century.

Ideologies of patriarchy contained in Islamic or Catholic religious orders are not in themselves sufficient to explain the persistence of forms that defy economic exchange theory. Although they give coherence to a variety of distinct social formations, they do not explain the cultural variation among societies that profess such religions. Penny Van Esterik (1982: 14ff.) summarizes the evidence from history and myth in southeast Asia that supports the notion of strong female political and legal figures despite the strictures of Muslim and Catholic religions. This derives from precolonial matrilineal structures allocating land and other resources to women as well as men. Although the entry of capitalized forms of agriculture has made more inroads into these privileged areas for the exercise of female initiatives (Stoler 1985), women continue to exert a more forceful control in trade and agricultural production than they do in the West.

The complexity of the articulation of cultural patterns in the household and family deriving from precolonial times with capitalist penetration is exemplified by Maila Stivens's (1985) analysis of peasantry in Rembau, Negeri Sembilan, Malaysia. Rejecting a simple polarization by sex, she argues that the colonial administration reconstituted matrilineal claims to land ownership as a means of social insurance for peasant families at the precise moment when they were losing land to the capitalist sector of large-scale rubber plantations. The importance of this lies in the way that cultural predispositions may inform policies that derive from economic problems. The particular form is not predictable from economic conditions, nor can it be derived from the culture of the dominant class in society. The resolution of the crisis of subsistence farmers in Malay was the product of government mediation drawing upon cultural predilection of the peasantry at a particular moment in time.

Patriarchy was a colonial overlay in Sri Lanka, where contradictory movements related to Buddhist and Muslim intrusions upset a preexisting pattern of gender relations that recognized matrilineal rights. British administration agents found the Muslim pattern of sexual subordination complementary to their imposition of cash cropping. They went beyond their Portuguese and Dutch predecessors in abolishing the last vestiges of communal property at the turn of the century. In this move, more than half the women paddy owners lost their land. As Jean Grossholtz (1984: 117) shows, this coincided with a time when large-scale plantations utilized male labor but bought destitute women for sexual service. In later developments, women played an essential role as a direct labor force working for extremely low wages in the tea harvest. The introduction of new capitalist enterprises in the modern period extended and deepened patriarchal patterns in a process of transculturation that masked direct wage exploitation in an ideology requiring female subordination.

Male Hegemony and the Imposition of Dominance

The tendency to assert the existence of patriarchy wherever male dominance is found distorts the evidence in those societies where gender is not a unitary category in the structuring of social relations. Niara Sudarkasa (1986) shows the ethnocentric bias in those analyses of societies where there are clusters of statuses for which gender is only one of the defining characteristics. The development of private property and the market created conditions in indigenous African societies where male and female gender relations approximated the hierarchical forms found in colonial white society. But for those populations that are less affected by capitalist intrusions, there is a lack of association between different measures of the role of women relative to men. To categorize as patriarchal those norms that arise in the modernizing sector would attribute to precolonial patterns a relationship imposed by the colonizer.

State intervention often subordinates women producers in household production, particularly in the case of land reforms to preserve the family farms. To designate as patriarchy the preferential position that men thereby attain eliminates from history the strength of women before the intervention and the political basis for their subordination through it. Susan Bourque and Kay Warren (1980) show how the selective appointment of men in government cooperatives controlling land received in the land reform program negates the power and autonomy of women that is often noted in Peruvian Indian villages (Isbell 1978). Another example of this is Mexico's *ejido* program of land reform that reinforced peasant subsistence farming at the same time that it established male-headed households as the basic unit of production. In cultural enclaves that proscribe women working in the fields, as in the case of the Maya, lands are allocated to male household heads who can work them; widows must rely on sons to gain access to land (Nash 1970). Despite this restriction in working in milpa land, women cultivate garden plots near their houses that provide corn and other vegetables for household consumption. When development programs are structured around cash-crop harvests, as in a Belize sugarcane production project described by Peta Henderson (1972), the designed absence of household plots for subsistence crops made impossible the whole range of garden farming women had carried out. Among the results, project women and their children suffered from dietary deficiencies. The project further ignored women's craft production that sustained families in times of crop failure or between harvests. A growing polarization in household income, derived from the loss of women's production, led to the impoverishment and landlessness of the majority of the farmers participating in the project while a few families prospered.

The subsistence base of the household is often eroded by commercialized agricultural production even without government intervention. This threat is particularly aggravated in the case of "green revolution" practices that increase the cash needs of farmers for hybrid seeds, fertilizers, pump sets, and pesticides. While these innovations benefit richer farmers and provide higher-paid jobs for men, poor farmers and particularly the women of marginal farms and landless households are losers in a game that polarizes economic class groups and the gender hierarchy (Kabeer 1985; Mencher 1974; 1978). Anna Rubbo (1975) shows the antagonistic relationship that arises when men in poor rural farms in coastal Colombia turn from subsistence farming to producing cash crops that have a fluctuating return on the market. Women try to hold on to the truck crops that, while yielding less profit, ensure survival in bad years. Their responsibilities for the survival of their children take precedence over the more profitable but risky ventures in the new green revolution. Gita Sen (1982) shows a parallel gender opposition in the green revolution in India, where women have lost many subsistence-based activities on family farms that are no longer viable in commercialized crop areas. Many are forced into low-wage work as casual laborers.

Even as proletarianized farm workers, women are often employed as family adjuncts with the wage paid to men and housing and other benefits obtainable only when there is a male household head. Neuma Aguiar (1983) has explored this paternalistic relationship in Brazilian agro-industrial enterprises where women, once divorced from men, lose any claim to a paycheck or to housing. This extension of the family structure into the workplace reduces opportunities for the development of class consciousness and autonomous political action, reinforcing the assumption that women are by nature docile and malleable at the same time that it provides a material basis for male dominance.

These are clearly not the products of partriarchal relationships predicated on traditional kinship relations. Recognition of the variation in gender relationships and their restructuring in contemporary capitalist contexts would assist policy planning that takes the interests of women into account. This can have unexpected consequences, however. When a women's cooperative for the production and marketing of traditional pottery produced in the home was created with the intervention of the Mexican National Institute of Indians in the Maya village of Chiapas, orders for the tourist market were placed directly with the cooperative's president and were picked up by government trucks. This circumvented men's control over marketing and the proceeds from pottery sales at the same time that the cooperative provided an independent power base for women. When the president of the cooperative ran for mayor, she received threats on her life, and eventually was killed. Although the stories vary as to who the killer was, and what his motive was, men in the civil authority openly objected to the cooperative president's tactics of organizing the production of pottery, giving orders, they told us, only to women who did not have men in their households. Although women continued to produce pottery for the tourist market, they abandoned the cooperative and returned to their homes. This case illustrates the cultural embeddedness of economic production in the household and how changes in the relations in production threaten gender hierarchy.[2]

The undervalued work of women in the household is characteristic of commodity production in many parts of the world. Carried on sometimes under very primitive conditions and with little or no technological innovation, such production survives in many parts of the world precisely because the undervalued or nonvalued work of women in their households allows their products to be sold at prices that can compete with machine-made goods. This kind of production defies market analysis since supply curves follow the needs of the household members rather than the prices offered (Nash 1970). Response to cultural norms—whether they involve expenses for a life-cycle ritual, village fiestas, or meeting everyday needs for food, shelter, or sickness—conditions the supply of labor and the production levels sustained by the family.

Economic market analysis cannot possibly fathom the complexity of household calculations in meeting its goals. There are, however, certain trends that Carmen Diana Deere and Magdalena Léon de Leal (1982) illustrate in the Andean countries where peasant women have always worked in agriculture. To the degree that women can participate in work free of the restrictions imposed on them by men in their families or households, then slavery is the most liberating institution from patriarchy, as W.E.B. Dubois said (cited in Davis 1971).

The greater prosperity of families in advanced industrial countries apparently lessens the influence of economic strictures, yet women's decisions to enter wage work or to have a reduced number of children are more likely to take opportunity costs into consideration. This is related to the greater imperative to consume as well as the higher costs for the reproduction of the family unit. The higher costs for household help, which sometimes equal the net income of women entering the wage-labor force, have a limited effect on enhancing the value of women's work in the household. These costs have, however, contributed to the diminished number of children women are willing to bear.

Redistributive patterns that obtain in households provide the basis for culturally ascribed roles that are not reducible to the direct contribution made to family income. The low valorization of women's work comes in part from the fact that they are not as likely to perform wage labor that would set a price on their production, and in turn, when they do enter into market labor, their wages reflect assumptions based on their household role. Reinforcing the material conditions of their subordination are ideologies regarding their contribution to production that have little to do with economic performance.

CHANGES IN THE WORKPLACE

The way in which women enter the workplace differs with the level of integration of the enterprise in the nation and in the world system. The consolidation of monopoly capital at the turn of the century in the United States and other developed nations laid the basis for a distinction between primary and secondary workers. As the large industries became organized in the 1930s the gender hierarchy was crystallized in bureaucratic rules that narrowed the range of jobs filled by women. Women and ethnic and racial minorities occupied the lowest rungs of these occupational ladders in corporations covered by union contracts, or they were channeled into secondary jobs that were available in the remaining competitive capitalist firms.

Holistic studies of industrial communities show the way in which the differential intregration in the world capitalist system influences the labor-control system (Nash 1985). Uneven development is as characteristic of older industrial centers in the United States as it is in newly developing areas. In my study of Pittsfield, Massachusetts, I found a segmented work force with women concentrated in the lower rungs of the production force in General Electric Company and in competitive paper, plastics, and textile companies.[3] Ethnic divisions that used to divide the work force were less significant after World War II (there are very few black or Hispanic migrants in this city).

Women were the principal reserve labor force for the major corporations throughout the first half of the century. They were hired in large numbers during World War I, and the remarkable growth of the electrical industry in the interwar years meant a constantly expanding female labor force. Women were the preferred workers in this new industry, both in the United States and abroad. Miriam Glucksman (1986) claims that their entry in large numbers into semiskilled assembly-line work created a new class relationship with a different structural relation to capital from that occupied by men. In fact, the employment of women in these relatively debased jobs used the same labor control systems as those operating with the male labor force, particularly the introduction of recent immigrants to intensify the exploitation of labor.

During the Depression General Electric exercised an affirmative firing policy, laying off married women first and then men without dependents. Many were rehired during World War II when the women were permitted to enter jobs such as welding and machining—jobs that had been the exclusive terrain of men. Following the unionization of workers in northern plants and after World War II, when the unions were able to raise wages, the corporation diverted many of the production lines in which women were concentrated to southern states. This dispersion of labor-intensive processes continued their relocation overseas after the mid-1960s as large corporations looked for reserve labor abroad. The increased employment of women in the service sector did not offset a rising unemployment rate relative to that of men after World War II. In 1950, women's unemployment rate (as officially measured) was 5.8% compared to 5.1% for men, and in 1973 it was 7.0% compared to 4.1% for men (Milkman 1976). The few remaining competitive capitalist industries in the city employ principally a female labor force at half the wage paid in the large corporation.

The consistently lower value placed on women's labor is justified on the basis that it is unskilled or semiskilled. A Pittsfield General Electric employee who worked the control panels for fighter planes was so skilled that the U.S. Air Force used to send planes to Pittsfield for her to analyze when they were out of order. She was paid at the level of an R14, the entry level for most men. Clearly the calculation of wages is based on the sex of those who do the work, rather than its content, as Anne Phillips and Barbara Taylor (1980: 85) contend. What enters that calculation is a combination of cultural and structural conditions of female labor, both in the labor market and at home, that renders their real contribution invisible or undervalued.

Bracketing all these dimensions of male dominance as patriarchy distorts the historically constructed systems of biological reproduction and the social reproduction of capitalism. The struggle of U.S. trade unions to establish the family wage limited women's entry into the paid labor force.

The unpaid labor of women in the home subsidized the costs of reproducing the paid wage force and ultimately deepened the gap in the bargaining power of women that persisted in the labor force (Mackintosh 1981). This was not a product of earlier subordination in patriarchal extended farm families but a newly created division of labor within urban industrial contexts that confirmed male hegemony in the home and at work. Affective relations within family units obscure the real exploitation that exists within these units and hinder the formation of consciousness regarding their subordination when women enter the labor market (Bennholdt-Thomsen 1981).

When the exchange value is made explicit, as when the Chase Manhattan Bank calculated women's unpaid labor to be equivalent to $10,000—the salary of an associate professor in the 1960s (Mitchell 1973)—few people were prepared to accept the dimensions of it or to respond in policy proposals for an infrastructure that would adequately respond to the growing need as women entered the labor force in increasing numbers in the 1970s. Gender relations are, as Ann Whitehead points out (1981), an important battleground where male dominance is continuously challenged in the sphere of marital and family relations. These relations reflect capitalist relations of expropriation, not a primordial loyalty forged in kinship. The development of shelters for battered wives and the women's centers that reach out to the guerrilla fighters in these formerly privatized spheres are cracks in the armory of a pseudopatriarchal dominance.

Current labor-market segmentation theory ignores the diverse interests of men and women and of white, black, and Hispanic workers in the labor force and in the domestic sphere. David Gordon, Michael Reich, and Richard Edwards (1982) equate the consciousness of all members of families of primary independent workers, primary dependent workers, and secondary workers in unitary categories that deny emergent family forms. With more than one-third of families headed by women, this new underclass of workers enjoys none of the securities and few of the benefits of unionized male workers as they enter in increasing numbers into low-paid service jobs. These women, freed of the dependency implied in patriarchal relations, are most committed to working full-time. But as yet their independent status has not won recognition. Their wages continue to be calculated in terms of secondary-earner status as they earn 60 percent of male wages. As the last hired and first fired, they had unemployment rates of 30 to 40 percent higher than those of men. Government policies continue to discriminate against women in the labor force, since they are taxed at a higher rate determined by their husbands' income brackets rather than as individual earners. And they do not receive the same benefits from Social Security that nonemployed wives receive (Lloyd & Memi 1979).

The core of the productive work force in competitive firms in the United States and other industrial countries is made up of immigrant workers (Tracy 1983; Fernandez-Kelly & Garcia 1985). Women migrants often find jobs in domestic or factory work more quickly than male members of their households. Colombian women, for example, often migrated to the United States before their husbands or parents to take advantage of openings in firms employing young guest workers (Castro 1986). Mexicans are part of the ebb and flow of workers hired in southwestern electronics and food processing plants where they are preferred workers *because* they have no political guarantees to back their claims for workers' rights (Fernandez-Kelly & Garcia 1985). Trace (1983: 125) concludes that the contradiction of capitalism in striving to maximize profits on the basis of a vulnerable reserve work force now incorporates the contradictions of immigrant relationships, placing women as "core troops in the front line" of production rather than in the "reserve army."

The transect of racist and sexist discrimination is revealed in the convergence of incomes of white and black women in segregated labor markets where they are increasingly cast in competitive relations. Abelda (1985) traces this occupational convergence as pay rates of white and black women move in a parallel direction while diverging from the wages of white men. In the period from 1948 to 1981, the mean income ratios of white women and white men declined from .472 to .437. In that same period, there was a narrowing of the gap in the mean income ratios of black women and black men, of black men and white women, of black men and white men, and a virtual equivalence of incomes of black and white women that rose from a ratio of .538 to .919. The convergence of the latter categories is due to the movement of black women into occupations once reserved only for white women as they left behind domestic work. White women lost both in terms of the depressed wages of household help to replace their labor in the domestic sphere in the competitive position vis-à-vis rising demand for black women in sex-segregated jobs.

The Move Overseas

The racist and sexist calculus for deploying and compensating labor is transferred overseas with the industries that seek even cheaper female labor. The unequal exchange predicated on low-cost raw materials produced in the periphery in exchange for manufactured goods from core industrial countries was supplanted by import-substitution policies that tried to replicate in developing nations competitive capitalist industrialization. Lacking the backward linkages of core-area industries, however, these new enterprises failed to generate the employment needed to absorb rising populations. A major shift in investment policies then took place as developing countries moved from industries that produce goods for internal consumption to industries producing components for export.

Each of these stages promoted labor policies that replicated some of the sexist policies of core industrial countries. Added to these were the racist policies that characterized colonization and neocolonial exchange relations. In the export-processing industrialization, transculturation processes began to replicate some of the features of underdevelopment hitherto characteristic of the periphery in the core industrial countries. Dislocation of industries, high unemployment rates caused by the loss of jobs overseas, imbalance of exports, and disintegration of the back linkages that promoted growth were increasingly seen in core industrial centers as well as the periphery. Women and blacks experienced the highest impact of these changes (Nash & Fernandez-Kelly 1983).

The first industries to be promoted by nationalist governments trying to forge a power base in their countries with import-substitution schemes were relatively low-capitalized consumer industries characteristic of competitive enterprises in core industrial countries. Most of the employment was in low-paying female segregated jobs that failed to alleviate the high unemployment rates for men. Helen Safa (1981) shows that more than half of the jobs in the new industries introduced into Puerto Rico in the 1960s and 1970s went to women, and even after the 1973 recession, their unemployment rate was lower than that of men. She found that Brazilian families try to send as many members as possible into the wage-labor force, while in the United States, women who work in these industries tend to have fewer children and by their own wages capitalize the mobility of offspring through education. This patterns was already beginning to affect Mexican households with wage earners in the import-substitution industries fostered by the government (Rothstein 1986). The more nationalistic industrial policy followed by Mexico in the central plateau (Rothstein 1986) and Queretero (Keren 1987) fostered a higher proportion of male employment than the export-processing industries at the border (Fernandez-Kelly 1983). This policy, possibly a response to trade union demands, contrasts with the more dependent industrialization of Puerto Rico.

Import-substitution industries fostered some of the backward linkages that improved the lot of workers in the developing nations in the 1960s and 1970s. The entry of multinational corporations in these earlier decades expanded economic opportunities that offered better-than-average pay and working conditions. The real problems seem to center in the export-processing or "free trade" zones, where more than a million people are employed (Fuentes & Ehrenreich 1984).

While large-scale import-substitution industries increased the dependency of developing nations on the industrial centers, many small-scale industries provided employment in labor-intensive operations that were not so dependent on raw materials and technology from outside the country. Judith-Maria Buechler (1986) shows that many of the industries that women create are extensions of domestic activities and often rely on family labor to survive in an uncertain economy.

The expansion of export-processing zones with tax holidays, subsidies of credit, and freedom of duty on raw materials creates a sheltered area for a new kind of industrialization involving high percentages of women workers. At the same time that low wages, guaranteed by the prohibition of unions, prevent demand from increasing, the lack of tax returns from corporations to the government prohibits redistribution policies of the state from becoming activated. These two curbs built into contracts made by the transnational companies with the host countries hinder the development of autonomous productive capacity in the periphery.

The discriminatory practices of corporations in the core industrial countries are deepened as these are transferred abroad where the general wage rates for all workers are one-tenth that of workers in the core economies. Humphrey (1985) notes the pervasive discriminatory wage policies in an electrical factory that was a subsidiary of a multinational corporation in Brazil. Eighty-seven percent of the women were employed in the three lowest grades where they earned far less than men who were found in the upper levels of the ten-tiered job hierarchy.

Export-processing zones are even more restrictive than import-substitution industries in their labor practices. Multinational corporations are given guarantees by the host nation that labor organization will be prohibited with the use of state police forces. Institutions of male dominance, often introduced during the colonial period when they were shrouded as patriarchal overlays, are complementary to the development of a temporary superexploited female labor force. The assumption that these young women will get married after a brief period in the labor market defeats their own aspirations to find a career niche in the industry. The nature of the work performed, which fails to develop basic skills and could be applied outside the factory, and the health hazards that debilitate their eyesight in a short period, confirm the ideological prescription of short tenure in the wage-labor market. The very mobility of the firms that allowed their movement into the country in the first place makes it possible for them to relocate as soon as they lose their comparative cost advantage (Lim 1983). The conjuncture of gender exploitation—the differential between wages paid to First World and Third World workers—enhances the competitive positions of corporations that engage in these operations (Lim 1983).

As one of the earliest sites along with Hong Kong for the development of off-shore production, Singapore represents one of the more mature economies for testing some of the questions raised by Linda Lim (1983). What are the prospects for developing sustained economic growth with off-shore operations? What are the possibilities for women's escaping imperialist and gender domination? Aline K. Wong (1981) provides some interesting insights. The Singapore government has developed some highly successful social planning projects that rival anything now available in the United States, including public housing estates, family planning, and social development. These programs have stifled political dissent and controlled labor movements and mass organizations, she says, but the overall status of women is adversely affected. Women are predominantly employed in foreign investment enterprises where they were first to feel the impact of the recession in 1974. Of the 16,900 workers retrenched, 19 percent were women. A constant stream of young Malaysian women keep wages low, and they have little recourse to expressing their dissatisfaction other than through the mass hysteria that breaks out in the factories. This is far from the liberating effects that employment might be expected to bring to a work force.

The socialization of girls into female roles of submissiveness and self-abnegation found in many noncapitalist societies abets the exploitation of women when they enter factory work. Celia Mather (1985) shows how the chemical, plastic, food processing, and other industries that moved into Indonesia in the 1970s were able to take advantage of this socialization to employ women at very low wages. Local male dignitaries recruited both women and young men in such a way as to avoid threat of immorality and permit conformity to Islamic traditions. She relates this form of patriarchal control to the submissive behavior whereby dissatisfied youths prefer to leave rather than make trouble within the factory: "By recruiting young people, especially young girls, from hamlets of Kelompok into the factories, the industrial capitalists are able to make use of the traditional forms of subordination of women to men, and youth to age, to create a labor force which is cheap and relatively easy to dominate" (1985: 168-69).

The migration of young women from Malaysian Kampangs to Singapore's industrial workshops is a result of rural unemployment as well as the pull of the new industries (Heyzer 1982). The employment policies of the foreign subsidiaries are designed to discourage this female-segregated labor force from becoming a permanent part of the work force. Noeleen Heyzer (1982) shows how employers control the work force by requiring workers to report the results of pregnancy tests, dismissing those who are pregnant or get married. This emphasis on a mobile, docile, and temporary work force is abetted by the socialization of females in the household that emphasizes these same characteristics. M. Patricia Fernandez-Kelly (1983) has seen the same exercise of control over women employees' biological reproduction in border industries of Mexico, where birth control pills are purveyed at the check-out clock.

In these ethnographic studies of the workplace we can see the projection of socialization patterns in household settings. The increasing imperative in the capitalistic mode of accumulation is intensifying the appropriation of surplus and accelerating the pace of capital accumulation—but in such a way as to destroy the reproduction of society. This is evident in the industrial policies of transnational corporations in Third World countries, and it is becoming increasingly apparent in First World countries.

THE INFORMAL ECONOMY

Just as the gap between rich and poor nations is increasing in the world economy, so is the one between rich and poor people and particulary that between men's and women's share of a dwindling portion of the resources within nations and regions. Myra Buvinic, Margaret A. Lycette, and William Paul McGreevey (1983) have assessed the position of women relative to men as follows: Women are less educated than men, earn less when they work, and work longer hours. Poverty is, hence, a woman's issue in both First and Third World countries and capitalist intervention increases their subordination throughout the world (Benería 1982; Boserup 1970; Nash & Fernandez-Kelly 1983). Their disprivileged position, undermined with the loss of subsistence production throughout the 1960s and exacerbated by the recession of the mid-1970s, is becoming increasingly intolerable with the debt crisis of the 1980s. Always the predominant population in the "informal economy," women are found in increasing numbers in the poorly remunerated ranks of the self-employed. When there are no adult males in the household, women are even more likely to have recourse to the informal economy (Bolles 1986).

Once considered a transitional phenomenon in the development process, the informal economy is increasingly recognized as a structural feature of peripheral accumulation (Portes & Walton 1981). The kinds of activities carried out by women and men in the informal economy include petty vending, production of foodstuffs, transfer of products from villages, garbage recycling, and building houses for personal occupancy (Portes and Walton 1981). Such activities allow women to carry out child tending more effectively than would formal employment (Arizpe 1977; Bunster & Chaney 1985). Occasionally they have developed into collective activities that stimulate a political consciousness of class relations. This can be seen in the *comedores populares* of Peru, where women's sale of cooked foods has become centralized in locales supported by church and political parties.

More often the informal sector goes underground as entrepreneurs try to escape regulation by industry or unions. In these clandestine operations, often found in the garment industries of New York and Mexico, or in almost any competitive enterprises of the developed or developing world, women operatives bear the risk of entrepreneurship at the same time that they are subject to legal penalties for operating without licenses. This anomaly rises in the underground work sites because women own sewing machines, and they and other female members of the household sew orders that are parceled out to them by jobbers. They earn very little in these operations, maintaining low costs of production in a very competitive industry (Alonso 1987).

The debt crisis looming in Third World as well as First World countries is sharpening the contradictions in the world capitalist system. In Latin America, there was a negative flow of capital into the periphery after 1982 as the major industrial powers of the southern hemisphere paid more than a quarter and in some cases more than half of their export earnings on servicing the debt. This marked the end of capital extraction through investment in productive enterprises and a move toward nonproductive extraction of surpluses through financial manipulation. Brazil's announcement of the moratorium on payment of finance charges in March 1987 presages a greater swell in the future.

In the indebted nations of Latin America and Africa, nationalist enterprises in import substitution are being sacrificed to the policies of the International Monetary Fund (IMF). Taxes that lower internal demand, debt servicing using more than 50 percent of income from exports, relieving tariffs that protect such industries, cancelling nationalized industries where redistribution programs are concentrated—all of these are destroying the infant industries spawned by import-substitution programs. In the emerging economic structure there is an even greater participation of women in the growing service and informal economy. Diversification of activities by various members of a family permits survival in the growing uncertainties of economic life. Where economic stagnation has brought production to a standstill, women have engaged in independent protest actions confronting military force, as in Chile and Bolivia. In their role as housewives, women are more alert to the threat to life imposed by those countries that have conformed to the conditions for the payment of the debt.

The threat to survival, which is becoming increasingly evident in the penetration of capitalism into the remaining enclaves of peasant and household subsistence production, is beginning to mobilize people throughout the world. In the new movement for peace, for environmental security against pollution, for jobs and the right to live, the vanguard is made up of the nonproletarianized sectors of the population—housewives, the unemployed, and de-classed environmentalists and humanists. The boundaries between these movements and working-class struggles are breaking down as the unemployed and marginalized populations become incorporated in a broadened base for demanding change.

I will illustrate this growing alliance of the disinherited people of the world capitalist system with an account of my experience with one such movement in Bolivia in the summer of 1986 when the crisis in the mining sectors reached a peak. Like most primary raw materials-producing countries, Bolivia has been hard hit by the decline of commodity prices on the international market. Added to this was the decline in productivity in the major nationalized mines due in part to the failure to invest in technology and exploration for new veins during the decade of military rule from 1971 to 1982. Shortly after coming into office in July 1985, President Paz Estenssoro decreed the New Economic Policy, setting forth the conditions of the IMF for paying the debt. Following the advice of the IMF advisor Jeffrey Sachs, this called for taxes on all households and the closing of nationalized mines. People of the mining communities in the departments of Potosi and Oruro mobilized with civic committees, religious organizations, peasant unions, and university and school professors and students in a "March for Life" that challenged Paz Estenssoro's policies.

Over 8000 marchers set out on August 22 to walk the 140 miles to La Paz to bring their demands for revitalization of the mines and a veto of the taxes to the president and parliament. After six days on the road, the marchers were intercepted by thousands of national troops, using armored tanks to disperse the marchers. Frustrated in their attempt to change the government's move to shut down the mines, miners and women in the housewives' association started a hunger strike that involved hundreds during the month of September. A young man who was in his fifth day of the hunger strike explained the reason for their move:

The government has not established the minimal conditions for worthwhile survival. For this reason, for us the survival of the mining centers is more than a love for the mines. We are posing the question: How are we going to live? What will be the basis for our survival? The government leaves it up to us to seek forms of survival. And because there are few alternatives, the unemployed have in desperation sought employment in the drug traffic or in the illegal mining of gold or in contraband merchandise. The government has not undertaken its role, as they should, of guaranteeing work or legal means of making a living. They have left it up to the unemployed to seek jobs that are illegal and corrupt. (June Nash, field notes, August 1986).

A woman who particpated in a hunger strike undertaken by the Association of Housewives of Siglo XX analyzed what this crisis meant to people of the mines:

We have joined the fight to preserve the mines as property of the state and to deepen the nationalization process. Our parliament is composed of people linked to the great international oligarchy of the IMF. They are not carrying out the aims of the people. We live in constant dependency on the great firms of South American Placer, Shell and others that set the prices of our national resources. They are trying to dismantle the nationalized sectors of the economy and thrust us into the informal sector. We will not have any of the rights we have gained from years of struggle. (June Nash, field notes, August 1986).

These unemployed workers and housewives were more acutely aware of the destructive nature of capitalist accumulation than the managers and employed who work within these structures or the workers laid off in deindustrializing areas of the core. They lost their fight, and the mines were closed, but as others find themselves in the same condition, a movement of the outcasts may become the core of resistance in the future.

CONCLUSION

What is the relationship between the domestic reproductive sphere and capitalist institutions? How are noncapitalist relations merged and built into capitalist expansion? And how are the ideologies regulating labor markets shaped in culturally distinct contexts?

Productive and Reproductive Spheres. The entry of women into the paid labor force is related to and defined in terms of domestic responsibilities.

Even in those societies where women's productive activities are complementary to those of men and highly valued in noncapitalist institutions, their role in wage-paying work in capitalist enterprises is prejudiced by assumptions regarding the priority of their domestic responsibilities and the devaluation of their labor in the home.

The Merging of Capitalist with Noncapitalist Institutions. Patriarchal relations preexisting colonialism and capitalist penetration account for only some of the cases where male dominance is found. Capitalist overlays promote the subordination of women in countries of the Middle East and Asia where patriarchy preceded the advent of colonial administration; but in the process of transculturation occurring in the evolving institutions, male hegemony of both colonizing agents and colonized is invented and reproduced in areas where gender hierarchy was not characteristic of noncapitalist societies. It is important to recognize these gender egalitarian societies (Leacock 1980) since they defy tendencies to universalize the gender hierarchy that is often the export product of developed capitalist economies. When they are ignored or forgotten, it is easy for sociobiologists or other pseudoscientific analysts to conclude that gender hierarchy is biologically based.

Ideologies of Racism and Sexism. Gender exploitation found in both core and periphery is compounded with racial exploitation in peripheral countries integrated in the world capitalist system. This conjuncture in turn depresses the position of women and minorities in the labor markets of core industrial countries as they come into direct competition in the export-processing zones.

These ideologies, and the real social relations that underlie and reinforce them, have penetrated the institutions of capitalist society to such an extent that they have not been formulated in class struggle issues. As a result, the trade unions that would liberate the working class perpetuate male hegemony and racial subordination in the struggles they wage. For these reasons, the liberation movements throughout the world are forming outside working-class institutions.

The entry of the Third World people into direct competition has transformed the class struggle in core industrial countries. The boundaries between "lumpen" and "vanguard" proletariat, domestic household production and the factory, are lowered as impoverishment threatens the survival of increasing numbers of people. In a process of transculturation both core and periphery are beginning to experience the global transformations brought about by integration of production on a world scale.

NOTES

1. In a later work with Arensberg and Pearson (1957) he included welfare policies in modern states as another example of redistribution.

2. Berber women of Morocco are similarly exploited by male members of their households who sell the carpets and knitted items they make in their homes (Maher, 1981).

3. Field work was carried out in 1982 with a grant from the National Science Foundation and the National Endowment for the Humanities, for which I am grateful.

REFERENCES

Abelda, Randy (1985). "'Nice Work If You Can Get It,' Segmentation of White and Black Women Workers in the Postwar Period." *Review of Radical Political Economics*, 17, 3, 72–85.

Afshar, Haleh (1985). "The Position of Women in an Iranian Village." In Haleh Afshar, ed., *Women, Work and Ideology in the Third World*. London: Tavistock, 66–82.

Aguiar, Neuma (1983). "Household, Community, National, and Multinational Industrial Development." In June Nash and M. Patricia Fernandez-Kelly, eds., *Women, Men and the International Division of Labor*. Albany: SUNY Press, 117–37.

Alonso, Jose A. (1987). "Clandestinidad Industrial y Marginalidad Urbana en la Metropoli Mexicana," unpublished paper.

Anker, R., M. Buvinic, and N. Youssef, eds. (1982). *Women's Roles and Population Trends in the Third World*. London: Croom Helm.

Arizpe, Lourdes (1977). "Women in the Informal Sector: The Case of Mexico City." In Wellesley Editorial Committee, ed., *Women and National Development: The Complexities of Change*. Chicago: University of Chicago Press, 25–38.

Beechey, V. (1977). "Some Notes on Female Wage Labour in Capitalist Production." *Capital and Class*, 3, 45–65.

Benería, Lourdes, ed. (1982). *Women and Development: The Sexual Division of Labor in Rural Societies*. New York: Praeger.

Bennholdt-Thomsen, Veronika (1981). "Subsistence Production and Extended Reproduction." In K. Young et al., eds. *Of Marriage and the Market*. London: Routledge & Kegan Paul, 41–90.

Bolles, A. Lynn (1986). "Economic Crisis and Female-Headed Households in Urban Jamaica." In June Nash and Helen Safa, eds., *Women and Change in Latin America*. South Hadley, Mass.: Bergin & Garvey Press, 65–82.

Boserup, Ester (1970). *Woman's Role in Economic Development*. London: Allen & Unwin.

Bourque, Susan, and Kay Warren (1980). *Women of the Andes*. Ann Arbor: University of Michigan Press.

Buechler, Judith-Maria (1986). "Women in Petty Commodity Production in Bolivia." In June Nash and Helen Safa, eds., *Women and Change in Latin America*. South Hadley, Mass.: Bergin & Garvey Press, 165–88.

Bunster, Ximena, and Elsa M. Chaney (1985). *Sellers and Servants: Working Women in Lima, Peru*. New York: Praeger.

Buvinic, Myra, Margaret A. Lycette, and William Paul McGreevey (1983). *Women and Poverty in the Third World*. Baltimore: Johns Hopkins University Press.

Castro, Mary Garcia (1986). "Work Versus Life: Colombian Women in New York." In June Nash and Helen Safa, eds. *Women and Change in Latin America*. South Hadley, Mass.: Bergin & Garvey Press, 231–59.

Chase-Dunn, Christopher, and Richard Rubinson (1977). "Toward a Structural Perspective on the World System." *Politics and Society*, 7, 4, 453–76.

Davis, Angela (1971). "Reflections of the Black Woman's Role in the Community of Slaves." *The Black Scholar, Journal of Black Studies and Research*, 3, 4, 2–16.

Deere, Carmen Diana, and Magdalena Léon de Leal (1982). "Peasant Production, Proletarianization, and the Sexual Division of Labor in the Andes." In L. Benería, ed. *Women and Development: The Sexual Division of Labor in Rural Societies*. New York: Praeger, 65–93.

Eisenstein, Zillah R. (1979). *Capitalist Patriarchy and the Case for Socialist Feminism*. New York: Monthly Review Press.

Elson, Diane, and Ruth Pearson (1981). "The Subordination of Women in the Internationalization of Factory Production." In K. Young et al., ed., *Of Marriage and the Market*. London: Routledge & Kegan Paul, 18–40.

Etienne, Mona, and Eleanor Leacock, eds. (1980). *Women and Colonization: Anthropological Perspectives*. South Hadley, Mass.: Bergin & Garvey Press.

Fernandez-Kelly, M. Patricia (1983). *For We Are Sold, I and My People: Women and Industry in Mexico's Frontier*. Albany: SUNY Press.

Fernandez-Kelly, M. Patricia, and Anna M. Garcia (1985). "The Making of an Underground Economy: Hispanic Women, Home Work, and the Advanced Capitalist State." *Urban Anthropology*, 14, 1–3, Spring–Summer, Fall, 59–90.

Fuentes, Annette, and Barbara Ehrenreich (1984). *Women in the Global Factory*. Boston: South End.

Glenn, Evelyn Nakano (1985). "Racial Ethnic Women's Labor: The Intersection of Race Gender and Class Oppression." *Review of Radical Political Economy*, 17, 3, 86–108.

Glucksman, Miriam (1986). "In a Class of Their Own? Women Workers in the New Industries in Interwar Britain." *Feminist Review*, No. 24, October, 625–55.

Gordon, David, Michael Reich, and Richard Edwards (1982). *Segmented Labor, Divided Workers*. New York: Basic Books.

Grossholtz, Jean (1984). *Forging Capitalist Patriarchy: The Economic and Social Transformation of Feudal Sri Lanka and Its Impact on Women*. Durham, N.C.: Duke University Press.

Hartmann, Heidi (1979). "Capitalism, Patriarchy, and Job Segregation by Sex." In Zillah R. Eisenstein, eds., *Capitalist Patriarchy and the Case for Socialist Feminism*. New York: Monthly Review Press, 206–47.

————— (1981). "The Unhappy Marriage of Marxism and Feminism: Towards a More Progressive Union." In Lydia Sargent, ed., *Women and Revolution: A Discussion of the Unhappy Marriage of Marxism and Feminism*. Boston: South End, 1–41.

Henderson, Peta M. (1972). "A Sugar Usina In British Honduras." In H. R. Bernard and P. J. Pelto, eds. *Technology and Social Change*. New York: Macmillan, 136–63.

Heyzer, Noeleen (1982). "From Rural Subsistence to an Industrial Peripheral Work Force: An Examination of Female Malaysian Migrants and Capital Accumulation in Singapore." In L. Benería, ed., *Women and Development: The Sexual Division of Labor in Rural Societies*. New York: Praeger, 179–202.

Hopkins, Terence K., and Immanuel Wallerstein (1977). "Patterns of Development in the Modern World-System." *Review*, 1, 2, Fall, 111–45.

Humphrey, John (1985). "Gender, Pay and Skill: Manual Workers in Brazilian Industry." In Haleh Afshar, ed., *Women, Work and Ideology in the Third World*. London: Tavistock, 211–31.

Humphries, Jane (1977). "Class Struggle and the Persistence of the Working-Class Family." *Cambridge Journal of Economics*, 1, 3, 241–58.

Isbell, Billie Jean (1978). *To Defend Ourselves: Ecology and Ritual in an Andean Village*. Austin: Institute of Latin American Studies, University of Texas Press.

Joekes, Susan (1985). "Working for Lipstick? Male and Female Labour in the Clothing Industry in Morocco." In Haleh Afshar, ed., *Women, Work and Ideology in the Third World*. London: Tavistock, 183–210.

Kabeer, Naila (1985). "Do Women Gain from High Fertility?" In Haleh Afshar, ed., *Women, Work and Ideology in the Third World*. London: Tavistock, 3–36.

Keren, Donna (1987). "Miracle to Crisis; Creating the Industrial Labor Force in Mexico." Ph.D. Diss., Graduate Center, City University of New York.

Kuhn, Annette, and Ann Marie Wolpe (1978). *Feminism and Materialism: Women and Modes of Production*. London: Routledge & Kegan Paul.

Leacock, Eleanor (1980). "Montagnais Women and the Jesuit Program for Colonization." In M. Etienne and E. Leacock, eds., *Women and Colonization: Anthropological Perspectives*. New York: Praeger, 25–43.

Lim, Linda Y. C. (1983). "Capitalism, Imperialism and Patriarchy: The Dilemma of Third-World Women Workers in Multinational Factories." In June Nash and M. Patricia Fernandez-Kelly, eds., *Women, Men and the International Division of Labor*. Albany: SUNY Press, 70–91.

Lloyd, Cynthia B., and Beth T. Memi (1979). *The Economics of Sex Differentials*. New York: Columbia University Press.

Long, Norman, ed. (1984). *Family and Work in Rural Societies: Perspectives on Non-Wage Labour*. London: Tavistock.

Luxemburg, Rosa (1951). *The Accumulation of Capital*. London: Routledge & Kegan Paul.

McDonough, Roisin, and Rachel Harrison (1978). "Patriarchy and Relations of Production." In Annette Kuhn and Ann Marie Wolpe, eds., *Feminism and Materialism: Women and Modes of Production*. London: Routledge & Kegan Paul, 11–41.

Mackintosh, Maureen (1981). "Gender and Economics: The Sexual Division of Labour and the Subordination of Women." In K. Young et al., eds., *Of Marriage and the Market*. London: Routledge & Kegan Paul, 3–17.

Maher, Vanessa (1981). "Work, Consumption and Authority Within the Household: A Moroccan Case." In K. Young et al., eds., *Of Marriage and the Market*. London: Routledge & Kegan Paul, 117–35.

Mather, Celia (1985). "'Rather Than Make Trouble, It's Better Just to Leave': Behind the Lack of Industrial Strife in the Tangerang Region of West Java." In Haleh Afshar, ed., *Women, Work and Ideology in the Third World*. London: Tavistock, 153–80.

Mencher, Joan (1974). "Conflicts and Contradictions in the 'Green Revolution': The Case of Tamilnadu." *Economic and Political Weekly of Bombay*, 9, 69, 309–43.

———— (1978). *Agriculture and Social Structure in Taminadu*. Chapel Hill: Carolina Academic Press.

Mies, Maria (1982). "The Dynamics of the Sexual Division of Labor and Integration of Rural Women into the World Market." In L. Benería, ed., *Women and Development: The Sexual Division of Labor in Rural Societies*. New York: Praeger, 1–28.

———— (1986). *Patriarchy and Accumulation on a World Scale: Women in the International Division of Labour*. New York: Zed.

Milkman, Ruth (1976). "Women's Work and Economic Crisis; Some Lessons of the Great Depression." *Review of Radical Political Economy*, 8, 1, 73–97.

Millett, Kate (1970). *Sexual Revolution*. New York: Doubleday.

Mitchell, Juliet (1973). *Woman's Estate*. New York: Vintage.

Moghadam, Val (n.d.). "Women, Work and Ideology in the Islamic Republic," unpublished manuscript.

Nash, June (1970). *In the Eyes of the Ancestors: Belief and Behavior in a Maya Community*. New Haven: Yale University Press.

———— (1980). "Aztec Women: The Transition from Status to Class in Empire and Colony." In M. Etienne and E. Leacock, eds., *Women and Colonization: Anthropological Perspectives*. South Hadley, Mass.: Bergin & Garvey Press, 134–48.

———— (1981). "Ethnographic Aspects of the World Capitalist System." *Annual Review of Anthropology*, 10, 393–423.

———— (1985). "Deindustrialization and the Impact on Labor Control Systems." *Urban Anthropology*, 14, 1–3, Spring–Summer–Fall, 151–82.

Nash, June, and M. Patricia Fernandez-Kelly (1983). *Women, Men, and the International Division of Labor*. Albany: SUNY Press.

Nash, June, and Ruby Rohrlich (1981). "The Patriarchal Puzzle: State Formation in Mesopotamia and Mesoamerica." *Heresies*, 13, 30–65.

Nash, June, and Helen Safa (1986). *Women and Change in Latin America*. South Hadley, Mass.: Bergin & Garvey Press.

Ortiz, Fernando (1947). *Cuban Counterpoint: Tobacco and Sugar*. New York: Knopf.

Phillips, Anne, and Barbara Taylor (1980). "Sex and Skill: Notes Towards a Feminist Economics." *Feminist Review*, No. 6, 79–88.

Polanyi, Karl (1944). *The Great Transformation*. Boston: Beacon Press.

Polanyi, Karl, M. Arensberg, and Harry W. Pearson (1957). *Trade and Market in the Early Empires*. New York: Free Press.

Portes, Alejandro, and John Walton (1981). *Labor, Class and the International System*. New York: Academic Press.

Rohrlich, Ruby, and June Nash (1981). "The Patriarchal Puzzle: State Formation in Mesopotamia and Mesoamerica." *Heresies*, 13, 30–65.

Rothstein, Frances (1986). "Capitalist Industrialization and the Increasing Cost of Children." In June Nash and Helen Safa, eds., *Women and Change in Latin America*. South Hadley, Mass.: Bergin & Garvey Press, 37–52.

Rubbo, Anna (1975). "The Spread of Capitalism in Rural Colombia: Effects on Poor Women." In Rayna R. Reiter, ed., *Toward an Anthropology of Women*. New York: Monthly Review Press, 333–58.

Rubin, Gayle (1975). "The Traffic in Women." In Rayna Reiter, ed., *Toward an Anthropology of Women*. New York: Monthly Review Press, 157–210.

Safa, Helen (1981). "Runaway Shops and Female Employment: The Search for Cheap Labor." *Signs*, 7, 2, Winter, 418–53.

Sen, Gita (1982). "Women Workers and the Green Revolution." In L. Benería, ed., *Women and Development: The Sexual Division of Labor in Rural Societies*. New York: Praeger, 29–64.

Schlegel, Alice, ed. (1977). *Sexual Stratification*. New York: Columbia University Press.

Silverblatt, Irene (1980). "'The World Has Turned Inside Out . . . There Is No Justice for Us Here': Andean Women Under Spanish Rule." In M. Etienne and E. Leacock, eds., *Women and Colonization: Anthropological Perspectives*. South Hadley, Mass.: Bergin & Garvey Press, 149–85.

Stivens, Maila (1985). "The Fate of Women's Land Rights: Gender, Matriliny, and Capitalism in Rembau, Negeri Sembilan, Malaysia." In Haleh Afshar, ed., *Women, Work and Ideology in the Third World*. London: Tavistock, 66–82.

Stoler, Ann (1985). *Capitalism and Confrontation in Sumatra's Plantation Belt, 1870–1979*. New Haven: Yale University Press.

Sudarkasa, Niara (1986). "'The Status of Women' in Indigenous African Societies." *Feminist Studies*, 12, 1, 91–104.

Tinker, Irene, and Michele Bo Bramsen (1976). *Women and World Development*. Washington, D.C.: Overseas Development Council.

Tracy, Constance Lever (1983). "Immigrant Workers and Postwar Capitalism: In Reserve or Core Troops in the Front Line?" *Politics and Society*, 12, 2, 125–58.

Van Esterik, Penny (1982). "*Women of South East Asia*." Northern Illinois University Center for South East Asian Studies. Monograph Series on Women, Occasional Paper No. 9.

Ward, Kathryn B. (1984). *Women in the World-System: Its Impact on Status and Fertility*. New York: Praeger.

Wellesley Editorial Committee (1980). *Development and the Sexual Division of Labor*. Chicago: University of Chicago Press.

Whitehead, Ann (1981). "'I'm Hungry, Mum': The Politics of Domestic Budgeting." In K. Young et al., eds., *Of Marriage and the Market*. London: Routledge & Kegan Paul, 93–116.

Wong, Aline K. (1981). "Planned Development, Social Stratification and the Social Divison of Labor in Singapore." *Signs*, No. 7, 434–53.

Young, Kate, Carol Wolkowitz, and Roslyn McCullagh (1981). *Of Marriage and the Market*. London: Routledge & Kegan Paul.

Youssef, Nadia (1976). "Women in Development: Urban Life and Labor." In I. Tinker and M. Bo Bramsen, eds., *Women and World Development*. Washington, D.C.: Overseas Development Corporation, 70–77.

PART II

THE WORLD–SYSTEM AND THE CREATION OF RACE AND GENDER

3

Minorities and the World–System: Theoretical and Political Implications of the Internationalization of Minorities

Martha E. Gimenez

My location in the class structure and the division of labor (at the state and world-system levels of analysis) and my structurally determined outlook and choice of theoretical perspectives unavoidably shape the content of this chapter: "[T]here are no detached observers in world-system studies. All observers without exception are participants as well" (Hopkins & Wallerstein 1982: 33). This does not denote an admission of the "subjective" (i.e., arbitrary) nature of the analysis; on the contrary, it is a recognition of its objective character, as an intellectual product grounded in concrete historical conditions.

This chapter is the result of reflections about the relationship between people historically oppressed in the United States, commonly identified as "minority groups," and immigrants. Having found out that the affirmative action office of the university where I work was including me in the list of "minority" faculty, as I am an Argentine citizen with permanent resident status, I sent an explanatory note, thinking they might have made a mistake. I was told I was a member of the "Hispanic ethnic group," as defined by the federal government. I wrote back stating that, while my inclusion within this "ethnic group" might satisfy the letter of the law, it went against the spirit of affirmative action and against the objective interests of U.S. minorities to count as minority faculty relatively privileged immigrants like myself. The university, I argued, if serious about compliance with affirmative action, should acknowledge in practice the qualitative differences between foreign-born and minority faculty, hiring foreign-born scholars if considered the most qualified, but refraining from counting them—for internal accounting purposes—as "minority faculty," to avoid creating a misleading sense of success in minority recruitment. Also, minority students' needs should be considered; those needs are not fully served if the "minority faculty" includes foreign-born scholars who, for obvious reasons, may have less in common with minority students than U.S. "majority faculty." Needless to say, my protest was unsuccessful and my suggestions have not been taken into account.

Awareness of this situation, on the other hand, led me to examine, from the standpoint of world-systems theory (Wallerstein 1979; 1983; Hopkins & Wallerstein 1982), the theoretical and political implications of the definitions currently used to identify minority groups, and to implement civil rights legislation and affirmative action. The fact that foreign workers from peripheral countries become minority workers in the United States clearly shows that the development of capitalism as a world-system entails not only the existence of a world-scale labor force and reserve army of labor, but also the hierarchical ranking of the world's population according to racial and ethnic categories (Wallerstein 1983: 75–79; 1985; also Blauner 1972: 51–81). In the context of the United States and its periphery, this phenomenon takes a historically specific form that can best be described as the internationalization of minorities. Most countries are multiethnic societies in which racism acquires forms peculiar to their historical development and location in the world-system (see, e.g., Castles & Kosack 1973 for an excellent analysis of the links between immigration and racism in western Europe). However, none has gone as far as the United States in giving race and ethnicity such a salient role in the ideological explanations of social inequality.

In the typical political, media, and commonsense discourse, class inequalities would seem to be nonexistent; on the other hand, racial and ethnic (and sexual) discrimination is viewed as *the* major kinds of inequality, the only ones legitimately open to recognition and some form of amelioration. An elaborate system of civil rights legislation has been developed to that effect, and it is there, in the definitions used to identify racial and ethnic minorities to implement this legislation, that the internationalization of minorities (i.e., the automatic incorporation of immigrants from the periphery into already existing minority groups) has been formally institutionalized:

Black: all persons having origins in any of the African racial groups not of Hispanic origin.

Hispanic: all persons of Mexican, Puerto Rican, Cuban, Central or South American, or other Spanish culture or origin, regardless of race.

Asian and Pacific Islander: all persons having origins in any of the original peoples of the Far East, Southeast Asia, the Indian subcontinent, or the Pacific islands.[1]

From the standpoint of the world-system, these definitions capture the real location of these workers in the world working class. At the state level, on the other hand, these definitions are statistical categories that obliterate the differences between ethnic and racial groups that have been historically oppressed in the United States: groups whose original entry was colonial or semicolonial (Blauner 1972: 53–57) and immigrants who, in the eyes of those who lobbied for and constructed those definitions, share similar racial, ethnic, or cultural characteristics. Black Americans have been replaced by "blacks"; Japanese and Chinese Americans by "Asians"; and Puerto Ricans, Chicanos, and Mexican Americans have been transformed into "Hispanics." Consequently, immigrants who fall under those definitions are considered members of U.S. minority groups and are counted as such by employers complying with affirmative action.

In the light of the important political and socioeconomic effects of this practice, and considering the staggering heterogeneity of the populations thus classified, it should be obvious that these are not simply neutral statistical categories used to classify the population of the United States and to identify members of "protected classes" of people; they are inherently racist categories because they strip people of their historical identity and reduce them to imputed common traits. The dialectic between the transnational and the national nature of minorities is of great importance for the analysis of working-class formation and consciousness. It acquires unique features in the United States because of legal practices designed to overcome the effects of past and present racial and ethnic discrimination.

In this chapter, I intend to examine the theoretical and political significance of the internationalization of minorities in the United States. This examination can shed light on the structural and ideological determinants of this phenomenon and its relevance for understanding future racial/ethnic alignments and conflicts, as well as future changes in working-class organization and political activity. The form and direction of those processes will be contingent on the manner in which this important but overlooked political fact is recognized and incorporated in the political consciousness and organization of U.S. racial and ethnic minorities, and the working class as a whole.

THE INTERNATIONALIZATION OF MINORITIES

The internationalization of minorities reflects the operation of capitalism on a world scale. The laws of capital accumulation affect the location of investments and the quantity and quality of labor demanded at a given time which, in turn, affect the composition of national working classes in terms of national origin, culture, race, ethnicity, language, and so forth. These processes shape the linkages between the fates of the U.S. working classes and of workers from all over the globe. Affecting as they do both the economies of core and peripheral countries, they trigger processes of changes in the spatial distribution of the workers, pushing the unemployed and the underemployed to seek employment within and across state boundaries. International and national migrations are thus the empirically observable effects of economic, social, and political changes affecting core and peripheral states. In time, these processes led to the development of a "labor aristocracy" in the core countries; as immigrant workers took on the worse jobs, native workers in core countries experienced considerable "upward mobility" and improvements in their standard of living.

Racism on a world scale has always been an important tool for the control of the working classes both in core and peripheral countries. In the United States, racism and the development of a heightened mass consciousness of racial and ethnic differences are tightly intertwined. This succeeded so well that in the 1980 U.S. census only 6 percent of the population identified itself as "American" (Collins 1985: 16). Everyone else chose a racial or ethnic group as primary identification. The Census Bureau was constrained, in the way questions were constructed, by the racial and ethnic categories (listed above) promulgated by the Office of Management and Budget in 1978, designed for use in all federal statistics and program administrative reporting (Lowry 1982: 50). The use of those categories for implementing civil rights legislation has the effect of granting minority status, within the United States, to immigrant workers whose "minority" status was grounded at the level of the world system.

Such definitions depict in clear terms the division of the world between two classes of people: the white "majority" and the rest, who have both a world-system level minority status as inhabitants of the periphery, and a latent minority status from the standpoint of core states, thus becoming minorities de facto when they enter a core state. Essentially, this entails the racialization and ethnicization of nationality, and reflects the hegemony of the core over the periphery (see Hayes-Bautista & Chapa 1987 for an excellent analysis of these processes in the context of U.S.-Latin American relations). In the course of the development of the world-system, racial categories expressed the core-periphery opposition, whereas national categorizations emerged as expressions of the competition between nation-states (Wallerstein 1985: 17).

The denial of identity based on national origin to foreign workers from the periphery reflects the powerlessness of their countries of origin in the hierarchy of states. The case of Japan, a peripheral country which has become core, challenging U.S. economic hegemony in the world-system, raises an interesting question: How long will Japanese-Americans' "minority" status continue? In a real sense, the locus where "minority" groups (i.e., "ethnic" groups which have less social, economic, and political power than the "majority") are to be found has been expanded from states to the world-system: in the world work force, workers from the periphery are, at the level of production, a major sector of the world working class and reserve army of labor, while at the level of world social stratification they are minority workers. The power of core countries over the periphery is asserted as white power; within core states, racism is strengthened by the transformation of all peripheral immigrants into minority workers by administrative fiat.

THEORETICAL AND POLITICAL ISSUES

Within core countries there are political and economic limits to the ability of capital to pull into the labor force most members of the "native" reserve army of labor. To the resistance of unionized workers, the effect of welfare policies, the reluctance of unemployed skilled workers to accept jobs below their skills and earning capacity, and the relative high cost of U.S. labor (even at the lowest wages) when compared with foreign labor must be added the political and economic costs inherent in the enormous expansion of day care that the full incorporation of women into the labor force would require. In this context, the use of immigrant workers willing to work as domestic servants or for minimum wages (which seem ample in the light of their meager possibilities in their country of origin) becomes a crucial mechanism for capital accumulation and political control. Because immigrant workers from the periphery become de facto minority workers in the United States, their presence is not only economically important but acquires extraordinary ideological and political significance.

As the "middle-class" status of the "labor aristrocracy" crumbles, a sense of privilege and superiority can be maintained, even by the most downtrodden members of the white working class, through the "minoritization" (i.e., the reduction to inferior status) of immigrants. Current official definitions used by employers, uncritically accepted by social scientists and the mass media, will eventually make it possible and "natural"—in the eyes of the average U.S. citizen—to think foreigners falling under those categories partake of whatever traits are imputed to those "ethnic" groups. The minoritization of some sectors of the labor force influences commonsense perceptions of the U.S. population: its basic class divisions are masked by the "majority/minority" split. The "majority," itself economically and ethnically stratified, gains a false sense of homogeneity and commonality of interests when opposed to the "minorities" (likewise stratified on the basis of occupation, income, and education). Immigrant status and national origin would seem to be reserved primarily for Europeans; foreign workers from the periphery are likely to be perceived—by the average American—as "minority" workers, just more of the same kind the country already had. Conversely, minority U.S. citizens might be perceived as foreigners: for example, Mexican-Americans have complained of harassment by immigration authorities at the time of heightened searches for undocumented workers, and a Chinese-American young man, taken for Japanese by unemployed auto workers, was beaten and killed on June 19, 1982 (U.S. Commission on Civil Rights 1986: 43–44).

Racism: Its Changing Content, Scope, and Structural Supports

An important ideological unintended structural effect of the internationalization of minorities—at the level of commonsense understanding and even social science perception of "minority" groups—is the devaluation and denial of the unique historical experiences, struggles, culture, and identity of U.S. racial and ethnic minorities who are reduced to an abstract statistical category capable of indefinite expansion through legal and illegal immigration. The historically specific roots of the oppression of U.S. minorities is mystified by inherently racist definitions that reduce people to imputed common traits which are, presumably, the source of common bonds, interests and—what is even more debatable—problems. People are deprived of their historical identity and reified into interchangeable, equivalent units that can be counted for political and administrative purposes. Needless to say, this situation also entails the negation and devaluation of the unique experience, culture, nationality, and identity of immigrants who are now labeled, counted, and treated as members of a minority group and, as such, attributed a variety of "ethnic" traits, attitudes, dispositions, culture, and so forth.

At the level of analysis of the world-system, foreigners and members of U.S. minorities are equivalent; the minoritization of the periphery reflects the relations of political and economic domination that link core states with their colonial and neocolonial peripheries. From this vantage point, immigrants are, indeed, colonized minorities (Blauner 1972), and these definitions do capture—in ways unanticipated by their authors—the consequences of capitalist expansion on a world scale. On the other hand, at the level of analysis of the core country (the United States in this instance) immigrants cannot possibly be considered equivalent to and interchangeable with members of U.S. minority groups. The racism inherent in this notion should be obvious. The fact that it goes unnoticed in the media, in social science usage, and the practices of the government and other employers that use these definitions in routine compliance with affirmative action guidelines shows, better than any carefully designed research could, the pervasive and invisible strength of racism in the consciousness of the average U.S. citizen.

These considerations are not intended to argue that one form of "primordial" identity (nationality) is "better" than another (ethnicity) in the case of immigrants, nor to reify the "ethnicity" imposed on U.S. minorities through enslavement and colonial conquest; they are intended to call attention to the ideological and structural pervasiveness of racism which obfuscates an important social process: the transition from a state-based to a world-system-based concept of minority group, which intensifies (because of the minoritization of middle, upper-middle, and petty bourgeois foreigners) class contradictions within state-level minority groups masked by racial-ethnic definitions of oppression.

This is a very difficult task because the old forms of objectivity (i.e., the historically evolved minority groups)—themselves the product of previous world-system economic processes and U.S. colonial expansion which brought to the United States African slaves, Chinese and Japanese workers, and placed under U.S. state jurisdiction Puerto Rico and part of Mexico—confront and coexist with the new forms (current statistical categories defining race and ethnic "majority" and "minority" groups), which reflect more recent changes in the capitalist world-economy. Both "old" and "new" concepts of "minority group" reflect patterns of labor force allocation; racism is a set of practices and corresponding ideologies that develop in the course of restricting the labor force participation of certain groups of people to inferior places in the occupational structure. Ideologically, racism is "always post hoc," a legitimation of economic and political oppression on the grounds of the racial or cultural inferiority of the oppressed (Wallerstein 1983: 78–79).

Racial, ethnic, and minority groups are, therefore, historically developed clusters whose boundaries, sense of past, identity, culture, and political and economic power alter in response to changes in the material conditions upon which they rest. Each one of these "old" forms (i.e., national origin and minority status historically defined) is a unity of opposites: it is both the result of processes of political, cultural, and economic domination, and a source of political identity around which political struggles and antisystemic movements have been and could be organized. In opposition to the statistical categories, the old categories have a rich historical heritage which includes civil rights struggles in the United States, and anti-imperialist struggles in the periphery.

On the other hand, the statistical definitions reflect an emergent historical reality: the success of minority leaders who lobbied for these categories seeking larger numbers to strengthen their groups' claims (for an excellent critique of the politics of ethnic enumeration, see Lowry 1982: 42–61), the influx of large numbers of immigrant workers from the periphery, and, consequently, the makings of a new historical past rooted in world-scale boundaries which, at this point in time, are largely unrecognized by most of the people whom census officials, employers, social scientists, the mass media, and the average U.S. citizen categorize as members of such "ethnic" groups. The issue is not whether the established identities are "real" and, therefore, not racist, while the emergent ones are "false" and racist. Both are "real" and racist; they are the historical results of past practices of economic exploitation and racial-ethnic discrimination. The established identities have a longer history and are actually, albeit unevenly, embedded in the consciousness and practices of people who have used them, politically, to organize and fight back.

On the other hand, the statistical categories are in a real sense like the characters in Luigi Pirandello's (1957) famous play: they are still in search of an author, waiting for their past to be created (e.g., not the history and struggles of black Americans or of Puerto Ricans, but the history of blacks and the history of "Hispanics"). Depending on the outcome of future economic and political changes at the world-system level, and of future class, racial, and ethnic struggles in the United States, it is possible that future generations will see themselves solely or primarily as "Asians," "blacks," or "Hispanic." At this point in time, however, state-level minority groups are, albeit in a fragmented, disorganized way, *für sich*, while the aggregates constituted by both state-level and world-system-level minority workers are still *an sich*.

As long as statistical categories remain primarily "imaginary concrete terms" (Marx 1970: 205)—purely quantitative, descriptive, ahistorical categories, used for the purposes of ethnic enumeration and identification—they will continue to have racist ideological effects; and as long as they are not seized as banners for political grass-roots struggles, they will have the effect of depoliticizing the concept of minority group by reducing it to a statistical, taxonomic category of analysis.

Of course, these categories are useful to establish claims under present federal regulations; they can also be used to identify/create potential voting blocs (to the advantage of politicians) and markets; while their usefulness for the state, political, and business elites, and upwardly mobile individuals is clear, their usefulness for the working classes and the poor is less evident. The politicization of those categories could take the form of international working-class solidarity seeking better working conditions and economic opportunities, or the emergence of a "middleman minority" elite (Bonacich 1980: 14–15) composed of U.S. and foreign petty bourgeois businessmen and politicians, concerned with delivering votes and personal gain, stressing intra-ethnic solidarity and the politics of civil rights while minimizing differences in social class and economic interests within minority groups. Whatever directions these processes take in the future, the minoritization of middle-class and petty bourgeois foreigners cannot but have important social and political effects upon state-level minority groups.

The Minoritization of the "Brain Drain:" Structural and Political Effects

The exploitation of human and natural resources imposed by core states on peripheral states creates profound distortions in their economies and the inability to generate employment for most of their professional and skilled workers, and for vast numbers of unskilled workers as well. The material conditions in which the rural and vast sectors of the urban populations reproduce themselves add a demographic component to the source of potential migrants. While skilled and unskilled workers migrate across international boundaries, the common notion that most immigrants are poor and uneducated is false. In fact, when compared to the native population, immigrants have a bimodal occupational distribution; they are to be found in slightly larger proportions in the lowest and the highest level occupations with relatively few in middle level, white-collar occupations (Bouvier & Gardner, 1986: 25). The proportion of immigrants in professional and technical occupations is higher than in the native population; for example, in 1980, 16.1% of the U.S. native population age 25 and over was employed in technical and professional occupations while the proportion of such workers among immigrants who entered the United States legally between 1971 and 1979 was 26% (Simon 1986: 26–27). A comparison between the educational attainment of immigrants and that of the total U.S. population age 25 and over in 1980 indicates higher proportions having completed high school and college among African and Asian immigrants. In 1980, 66.5% of the total U.S. population age 25 and over had completed high school; 16% had completed college. The proportions for African immigrants were 81.9% and 38.7%, and for Asians 73.0 and 35.0%, respectively (Bouvier & Gardner 1986: 22).[2]

It is also important to examine the differences among the populations included in the politically created "Hispanic" ethnic group, which attributes a spurious "ethnicity" and commonality of values and culture to groups historically oppressed in the United States (Mexican Americans, Chicanos, and Puerto Ricans), and to Latin American and Spanish people. "Hispanic" is not a neutral term with an objective empirical referent but a political code word to identify a minority group historically subject to racial discrimination for reasons other than Spanish ancestry (Hayes-Bautista 1980: 355).

In the 1980 census, Latin American immigrants and people of Latin American descent were forced to identify themselves as "Hispanic": accurate alternatives (Central and South American), included in the 1970 "Spanish origin question," were excluded in 1980.[3] Those who refused to do so and indicated their Central or South American origin elsewhere, were classified as "inconsistent respondents" in an analysis of the consistency of responses to the "Spanish/Hispanic origin or descent" question (Tienda & Ortiz 1986: 3–20). They also had higher levels of education and income than the "consistent" respondents, who were primarily of Mexican and Puerto Rican origin.

In a striking example of the mystifying power of "ethnic" categories, rejection of "Spanish/Hispanic origin" is interpreted as follows:

The extent of reporting nationality-specific items suggested to us that these individuals were likely to be Hispanics with *ambivalent ethnic identities who misreported their origin either because they objected to the lack of response choices on the full enumeration item* (e.g., no Venezuelan, Argentine, etc. choices) or who *deliberately denied their Hispanic origins.* . . . [The status inconsistency perspective] . . . suggests that Hispanics with ambivalent social identities will be of higher socioeconomic status. . . . Presumably the ambiguity in their social identity derives from their desire to be recognized by the majority group (non-Hispanics) based on their socioeconomic credentials. (Tienda & Ortiz 1986: 11, 15; emphasis added).

This is a remarkable feat of sociological interpretation. The authors recognize that even consistency in responses does not entail the structural or cultural validity of an ethnic "Hispanicity" (Tienda & Ortiz 1986: 18). Nevertheless, they assume its objective reality by treating it as a constraining "social fact" that can be used patronizingly to explain and dismiss the accurate reporting of national origin as evidence of "ambivalent ethnic identity" and "status inconsistency."[4]

The census documents the existence of socioeconomic differences between U.S. Mexican and Puerto Rican origin populations and Latin Americans, thus supporting the case for excluding the latter from affirmative action, if not on the grounds of the racist nature of the ethnicization of national origin, then on the basis of their greater market resources. Educational differences among these heterogeneous groups are considerable. According to a report of the U.S. Bureau of the Census, from all persons 25 years and over of Mexican origin, only 5.5% have 4 years of college or more; the percentage for persons of Puerto Rican origin is 7%; for Cubans, 13.7%; for persons of Central or South American origin, 15.5%; and for other Spanish, 15.3% (U.S. Bureau of the Census, 1985: 4); among persons not of Spanish origin, 20.1% have 4 years of college or more. Had information for the foreign-born been available, it would have shown higher levels of education.

The data clearly indicate that, given current practices of ethnic identification and accounting for affirmative action purposes, an old and familiar process—the "brain drain"—is rendered invisible by the internationalization of minorities: foreign professionals and technical workers disappear into the statistics designed to show progress in "minority recruitment." Institutions of higher education and other employers can thus show increases in their hiring of blacks, Asians, and Hispanics, although the figures released to the mass media are never broken down to indicate what percentage of those "minority" workers are middle- or upper-middle-class immigrants or persons of Spanish, Latin American, African, Indian, or other descent.

Obviously, such figures overstate the extent to which individual members of U.S. minorities experience "upward mobility," as well as the extent to which employers have stopped discriminating against U.S. racial and ethnic minorities. The results of an investigation about the compliance with affirmative action of a California bank showed that 45 percent of the sample of executive-level employees were Basque, Spanish, or South American, while most of the other workers (janitors, secretaries, tellers) were Chicano or Mexican (Hayes-Bautista 1980: 355). If comparable investigations were undertaken in institutions of higher education and organizations hiring large numbers of professional and technical workers, they would very likely produce similar results. Therefore, figures showing higher rates of minority recruitment (e.g., Takaki 1987: 232) offer the media, politicians, policy makers, and minority groups a somewhat misleading record of civil rights success that has the potential to be used, in the future, to lessen the urgency in the implementation of such legislation on the grounds that a great deal has already been accomplished.

Even if immigrants from the periphery and their descendants were not legally defined and counted as minorities, their presence would still have important effects upon the boundaries, stratification, and structure of opportunities of U.S. minority groups, because of the prevalence of racist stereotypes and labor allocation practices that "assimilate" them into local minority groups structurally and ideologically. But the fact they are also counted as such for affirmative action intensifies the effects of their presence upon U.S. minorities. Given that U.S. minorities are "over-represented" in the lower-paid jobs, affirmative action functions primarily to ensure minority recruitment to the upper echelons of the occupational structure. It is evident that its intent is thwarted when foreign-born, often middle- and upper-middle-class, workers are considered equivalent U.S. minority workers. Given the economic structural barriers that restrict the possibilities for advancement of most minority individuals, which limit the usefulness of affirmative action to the privileged few (see also Wilson 1987: 233–40; Bonacich 1987: 99–116), the counting of foreigners satisfies, ultimately, the interests of those doing the counting rather than the interests of the minority groups in question.

From the standpoint of U.S. oppressed minorities, whether the influx of immigrants has positive or negative consequences depends on objective conditions (e.g., competition for jobs, the counting of foreigners as minorities for affirmative action) and on the characteristics of the immigrants themselves (their social class, nationality, and political allegiances). But nationality is not as important in determining patterns of association and participation in the "host" society as social class. Working-class immigrants, particularly those coming from intensely politicized countries, might be more politically aware of class issues. Their political consciousness may lead them to feel solidarity with U.S. minority workers based on a common heritage of domination by capital, instead of (from their standpoint) an artificially constructed ethnicity.

On the other hand, middle- and upper-middle-class immigrants might welcome being ethnically coded; that gives advantages in the labor market which increase in direct relation to their professional credentials, skills, and social class. Middle- and upper-middle-class immigrants are more likely to share the values of the dominant classes, including class, racial, and ethnic prejudices. They can also be perceived as more desirable employees than members of state-level minorities, who might be too political and might make too many demands on behalf of their communities. As a critic has pointed out, the government has created incentives to belong to the "protected classes". For example, Indians from the subcontinent have successfully lobbied to be included in the Asian category (Glazer 1983: 193). What started as legislation aimed at redressing the effects of past racial/ethnic discrimination has led to a system that singles out for special treatment ethnic groups and nationalities who have never been historically discriminated against in this country.

Most foreign workers are likely to be unaware of their administratively imposed minority status. "Typically, an ethnic identity is assigned to each employee by his employer. . . . Employees rarely know how they have been classified" (Lowry 1982: 60–61). Those who learn about it may or may not take advantage of it, depending on their class consciousness, political awareness, and the extent to which they may or may not feel solidarity with the minority to which they have been assigned membership. Those who are working-class will add to the vast number of U.S. minority workers who are already working-class. Working-class and poor workers, particularly those who are undocumented, are more likely to experience negative effects from minoritization; they and their children are more likely to suffer from discrimination. Among the more privileged workers, knowledge of minoritization could lead to three possible kinds of general responses: (1) indifference, as long as they and their families are not discriminated against. Middle- and upper-middle-class people have more social and economic coping resources, and can intervene actively in schools and other settings to protect their children from the racism of teachers and peers; (2) acceptance, taking economic and, perhaps, political advantage of the structurally produced scarcity of state-level minority professional, technical, and skilled workers. Depending on their class and political views, they could become "middleman" minorities, or get involved in conservative or liberal minority politics; (3) rejection, which can take two forms: an ideological, purely nationalist form or a political form. Furthermore, rejection of minority status need not entail solidarity with the cause of minority rights, while acceptance need not be primarily instrumental. These are profoundly divisive issues, of great and explosive political significance which have not yet been empirically investigated from the standpoint of those directly affected by them. It cannot be taken for granted that ethnicity and race, no matter how obvious they may appear in the eye of the white American beholder, mean the same or override the significance of social class and national origin for foreign-born "minority" workers.

It may be argued, by government officials and minority representatives, that counting immigrants as minorities does have a positive effect because the greater the size of an ethnic minority, the greater are its claims and the advantages its members will have in affirmative action programs. On the other hand, while counting foreigners does increase the pool of people who can benefit from such programs, it also ensures—given the relatively low level of education of U.S. minorities—that a substantial number of professional and managerial jobs will be filled by immigrants. Once the word gets out in the rest of the world (maybe it already has) that professionals and skilled workers coming to the United States become eligible for preferential treatment under federal legislation, access to managerial and professional jobs for U.S. minorities might become more difficult than it already is to the extent they cannot match the credentials of foreign workers, especially those trained in elite European and U.S. universities.

How would most members of U.S. minority groups feel, particularly those who are poor and working-class, if they knew that petty bourgeois, middle- and upper-middle-class professionals count as minorities for affirmative action? Do they know what is going on? If so, is their silence a sign of powerlessness or acquiescence? The artificial expansion of the middle and upper strata of minority groups is an obvious and immediate effect of the minoritization of foreigners. Are minority leaders aware of this? What would working-class and poor white Americans feel about the fact that affirmative action makes no class or nationality distinctions? We do not know, because the questions, to my knowledge, have not been asked; even to formulate them in writing seems somehow illegitimate, because they seem to challenge the desirability of affirmative action and the efforts of the state to eradicate racial and ethnic discrimination. These questions are important, however, because they illustrate how class conflicts and contradictions are masked by conflicts of interest between state- and world-system-level minorities, and between minorities and the "majority." Specifically, they illustrate the contradiction between the effects of the "economic and the political organization principles of the world-system" (Hopkins & Wallerstein 1982: 87).

Economic and political changes at the world-system level produce migration flows toward the core countries which always affected their social and ethnic stratification, and state-level class and racial-ethnic struggles. These struggles, given that political activity is, so far, never world- but state-oriented (because people are politically organized as subjects of a state), are designed to improve *their* economic and political gains within the state. The outcome of such struggles, on the other hand, is undermined by the restructuring of state-level minority groups brought about by the minoritization of foreign workers. Affirmative action, a civil rights' victory for state-level minority groups, cannot entirely fulfill its limited promise to them as long as it also applies to world-system-level minority workers. If it applied exclusively to state-level minority groups, the presence of relatively large numbers of professional and managerial workers from the periphery would not affect the opportunity structure and socioeconomic stratification of state-level minorities, creating the appearance of greater upward mobility and lesser discrimination toward them. All workers, whatever their race, ethnicity, or national origin, are protected against racial discrimination in employment by civil rights legislation; to exclude foreign-born workers from affirmative action would not leave them unprotected, and it would compel employers to contemplate the needs of U.S. historically oppressed minority groups.

The Class Contradictions of Affirmative Action

The internationalization of minorities is an outcome of world-scale economic processes. It is also the predictable result of political thinking and political struggles at the state level which ignore the determinant role of social class in the life chances of individuals, regardless of race and ethnicity. As long as the effects of capital accumulation at the world-system level, and its impact upon capital-labor relations at the state level, are experienced only or mainly in terms of conflicts at the level of social, racial, ethnic, and sexual stratification (which pit different strata of the working class against each other), it can appear self-evident that the reason why minority persons are disproportionately unemployed and poor is to be found in racism and racial-ethnic discrimination.

However, minority groups are themselves stratified on the basis of class and socioeconomic status; while civil rights legislation protects everyone, regardless of class, affirmative action tends to benefit the more privileged, and even this can be open to question to the extent that immigration brings in thousands of foreign skilled workers and professionals who are administratively counted as minorities. Under these conditions, it is obvious that the politics of civil rights ought to be linked to the politics of class. Civil rights struggles, in themselves, tend to be self-defeating, similar to earlier political struggles for membership, on the basis of equality, in the "heavenly life" of the state (Marx 1975: 146–74).

The problem is that political struggles for racial-ethnic equality and against discrimination are, in fact, the political expression of class struggles for greater economic participation and economic gain. The attainment of political goals, however, is not necessarily linked to the attainment of economic goals. While the state may abolish criteria that stand in the way of people's full participation in the political and economic spheres (e.g., religion, ownership of private property, sex, race, or ethnicity), it abolishes them ideally, not materially, leaving them unchanged as components and determinants of people's lives (Marx 1978: 153). The state, in fact, rests upon the preservation of those distinctions; the ideal abolition of race and ethnicity as a condition for full political and economic participation does not affect everyone equally; it benefits primarily those whom social class has given economic or "human" capital, so that the only factor that stands in their way to full participation is their race or ethnicity. For the rest, race and ethnicity are not the primary obstacles in their admission to the "heavenly life"; only public and open recognition of "the declining significance of race" (Wilson 1978) will open the way for new and more and effective political struggles designed to change the structural conditions that affect not only state-level minority individuals, but aggregate opportunity structures, thus undermining the persistent correlations between race/ethnicity, low-paid occupations, poverty, and unemployment.

The impact of the internationalization of minorities upon the consciousness of U.S. minorities is not yet clear. A transition from the politics of civil rights to class politics that incorporate civil rights as a central demand will require greater public awareness of these issues, as well as social scientists and minority leaders willing to confront the structural economic determinants of minority problems, and of the minoritization process itself (for a discussion of these issues, see Young 1986: 67–75).

CONCLUSION

Examining the determinants of the internationalization of minorities in the context of world-systems theory led me to realize that this concept is an "imaginary concrete": an empiricist grasp of a complex set of world-scale processes and relationships. As a "concrete concept," a "totality comprising many determinations and relations" (Marx 1970: 205–6), the internationalization of minorities is the empirically observable form of the effects, at the core state-level of analysis, of world-scale ideological, political, and economic processes.[5] Patterns of labor force allocation in the capitalist world-economy resulted in the ethnicization of the work force both at the world-system and state levels of analysis; the ongoing transformation of the world-system's organization of production and division of labor periodically changes the forms of "ethnic" differentiation in core states. State-level minority groups are an integral part of the world-system-level minority work force while members of the latter, by immigrating from one state to another, may or may not become integrated in state-level minority groups depending not only on their national origin and social class, but on the ideological, economic, and political conditions dominant in the "host" state. These conditions, in the United States, are conducive to the racialization/ethnicization of national origin, thus assimilating, ideologically and administratively, workers from the periphery into established minority groups.

The analysis of the determinants and structural effects of the internationalization of minorities raises questions about the theoretical and methodological adequacy of the categories used to identify minority groups in the United States; it sheds light on the politically and ideologically constructed nature of "ethnicity" and "minority group," and directs theoretical and empirical inquiry toward the ideological and political effects of changes in their boundaries and location in the class and socioeconomic structures within the United States due to the minoritization of foreigners. This chapter has focused on three important dimensions of this phenomenon: its racist implications, its effects upon the life chances of U.S. minorities and workers from the periphery, and its impact upon affirmative action. In the process of doing so, a theoretical distinction has been made between state-level and world-system-level minorities, important to understanding their shared characteristics as members of the world work force, and the origins of their qualitatively different state-based social identities, culture, and political outlook. An examination of the historical unfolding of "ethnic" groupings from the standpoint of world-systems theory undermines the reification of their experience into cultural traits useful for legitimating their location in the state work force, and exposes the class relations that underlie ethnic struggles and limit the impact of civil rights gains. In this respect, the internationalization of minorities simply uncovers already present class-based limits to the ameliorating goals of affirmative action. This analysis, however, does not suggest that affirmative action should be abolished; it urges, instead, that it should try to overcome those limitations by focusing upon those who, for economic and historical reasons, need it most.

Finally, this line of thinking calls for the development of theoretical analyses of race-ethnic relations that go beyond the perspectives of the dominant classes, or of state-level minority groups, to incorporate the perspectives of minoritized workers from the periphery as well. Only from the standpoint of the world system can such a theory overcome the subtle forms of social science racism and ethnocentrism, the limits of nationalism, and the dangers of romanticizing inherently contradictory racial-ethnic cultures and identities; these are, after all, both sources of people's autonomy and integrity and tools of ideological legitimation and control (Blauner 1972: 67; Wallerstein 1985: 21).

This chapter is, essentially, a preliminary examination of very complex issues. Besides its potential value as a source of theoretical debate and future empirical research, it illustrates the relationship between theory and practice, between existence and consciousness. It remains, as such, open-ended, because the issues it raises will be ultimately settled politically, not by the accumulation of isolated research findings. Had I been indifferent to the fate and struggles of U.S. minority groups, this chapter would not have been written, or would have been quite different. But, for better or worse, "we are of our times, so is our consciousness, and so is all our work" (Hopkins & Wallerstein 1982: 140).

The author would like to thank Russell Endo, Benjamin Hadis, John Horton, Tom Mayer, Michael Neuschatz, Sean Sayers, and Immanuel Wallerstein for their helpful suggestions.

NOTES

1. There are two other categories: "*American Indian or Alaskan Native.* A person having origins in any of the original peoples of North America, and who maintains cultural identification through tribal affiliation or community recognition. *White.* A person having origins in any of the original peoples of Europe, North Africa or the Middle East" (Lowry 1982: 51).

2. The differences are more pronounced if specific nationalities are considered. The proportions for Indians were 88.95% and 66.2%; for Koreans, 77.8% and 34.1%; and for Philippinos 74% and 41%, respectively. The lowest levels of education are found among Mexican (21.3% and 3%) and Latin American immigrants (41% and 8.9%, respectively). The level of education of immigrants from Europe and the Soviet Union is lower than that of immigrants from Asia and Africa, and of the U.S. population (Bouvier & Gardner 1986: 22).

3. Those options were deleted because "they had picked up many non-Hispanics who interpreted them to mean 'Central or Southern United States' and Brazilians who are technically not Hispanic" (Davis et al. 1983: 6-7).

4. For a timely debate about the political and methodological adequacy of the label *Hispanic* see Yankauer 1987; Hayes-Bautista & Chapa 1987; and Treviño 1987.

5. Although the unintended consequences of affirmative action policies have been pointed out by some authors (see, e.g., Hayes-Bautista 1980: 353–56; Glazer 1983: 183–208), neither the theoretical nor political significance of the internationalization of minorities has been systematically analyzed.

REFERENCES

Blauner, Robert (1972). *Racial Oppression in America*. New York: Harper & Row.

Bonacich, Edna (1980). "Class Approaches to Ethnicity and Race." *The Insurgent Sociologist*, 10, 2, Fall, 9–23.

_____ (1987). "The Limited Social Philosophy of Affirmative Action." *The Insurgent Sociologist*, 14, 1, Winter, 99–116.

Bouvier, Leon F., and Robert W. Gardner (1986). "Immigration to the U.S. The Unfinished Story." *Population Bulletin*, Vol. 41, No. 4. Washington, D.C.: Population Reference Bureau.

Castles, Stephen, and Godula Kosack (1973). "The Function of Labor Immigration in Western European Capitalism." *New Left Review*, No. 73, May–June, 3–21.

Collins, Glenn (1985). "A New Look at Intermarriage in the U.S." *The New York Times*. February, 11, p. 16.

Davis, Cary, C. Haub, and J. Willette (1983). "U.S. Hispanics: Changing the Face of America." *Population Bulletin*, Vol. 38, No. 3, Washington, D.C.: Population Reference Bureau.

Glazer, Nathan (1983). *Ethnic Dilemmas 1964–1982*. Cambridge, Mass.: Harvard University Press.

Hayes-Bautista, David E. (1980). "Identifying 'Hispanic' Populations: The Influence of Research Methodology on Public Policy." *American Journal of Public Health*, 70, 4, April, 353–56.

Hayes-Bautista, David E., and J. Chapa (1987). "Latino Terminology: Conceptual Bases for Standardized Terminology." *American Journal of Public Health*, 77, 1, January, 61–68.

Hopkins, Terence K., and Immanuel Wallerstein (1982). *World-Systems Analysis*. Beverly Hills, CA: Sage.

Lowry, Ira S. (1982). "The Science and Politics of Ethnic Enumeration." In Winston A. Van Horne, ed., *Ethnicity and Public Policy*. Madison, Wis.: University of Wisconsin System, 42–61.

Marx, Karl (1970). *A Contribution to the Critique of Political Economy*. New York: International Publishers.

_____ (1975). "On the Jewish Question." In Karl Marx and Frederick Engels, *Collected Works*, vol. 3, 1843–1844. New York: International Publishers, 146–74.

Pirandello, Luigi (1957). "Six Characters in Search of an Author." In *Naked Masks: Five Plays*. New York: Dutton.

Simon, Julian L. (1986). "Basic Data Concerning Immigration into the United States." In R. J. Simon, ed., *Immigration and American Public Policy. The Annals of the American Academy of Political and Social Science*, vol. 487, September, 12–56.

Takaki, Ronald (1987). "To Count or Not to Count by Race and Gender?" In R. Takaki, ed., *From Different Shores. Perspectives on Race and Ethnicity in America*. New York: Oxford University Press, 231–32.

Tienda, Marta, and V. Ortiz (1986). "'Hispanicity' and the 1980 Census." *Social Science Quarterly*, 67, 1, March, 2–20.

Treviño, Fernando M. (1987). "Standardized Terminology for Hispanic Populations." *American Journal of Public Health*, 77, 1, January, 69–71.

U.S. Bureau of the Census (1985). "Persons of Spanish Origin in the United States: March 1985." *Current Population Reports*, Series P-20, No. 403, December.

U.S. Commission on Civil Rights (1986). *Recent Activities Against Citizens and Residents of Asian Descent*. Washington, D.C.: U.S. Government Printing Office.

Wallerstein, Immanuel (1979). *The Capitalist World-Economy*. New York: Cambridge University Press.

_____ (1983). *Historical Capitalism*. London: Verso.

_____ (1985). "The Construction of Peoplehood: Racism, Nationalism, Ethnicity." Keynote address for Conference on "Ethnic Labels, Signs of Class: The Construction and Implications of Collective Identity," Center for the Study of Industrial Societies, Chicago, October.

Wilson, William J. (1978). *The Declining Significance of Race*. Chicago: University of Chicago Press.

_____ (1987). "The Black Community in the 1980s: Questions of Race, Class, and Public Policy." In Ronald Takaki, ed., *From Different Shores. Perspectives on Race and Ethnicity in America*. New York: Oxford University Press, 233–40.

Yankauer, Alfred (1987). "Hispanic/Latino—What's in a Name?" *American Journal of Public Health*, 77, 1, January, 15–17.

Young, Richard P. (1986). "History and the Politics of Race." *Socialist Review*, 16, 3/4 (87/88), May–August, 67–75.

4

IMAGES OF DOCILITY: ASIAN WOMEN AND THE WORLD–ECONOMY

Nancy Melissa Lutz

In 1976, the Republic of China (Taiwan) ran an ad in the *New York Times* that described the attractions of Taiwan's labor force as follows:

One of the most attractive features of the Taiwan investment climate is its inexpensive, hard-working, and well-educated labor force. . . . Taiwan's labor force is generally considered the best bargain in Asia, if not the world, when efficiency as well as cost is taken into account. And the island workers are well-disciplined; there is practically none of the costly labor strife that characterizes the industries in many parts of the world. There are no strikes. (Republic of China advertisement in the *New York Times*, January 25, 1976; quoted in Kung 1983: 39).

The ad's depiction of Taiwanese labor as "hard-working," "well-disciplined," and lacking in "costly labor strife" is characteristic of other depictions of Asian labor, particularly of those advocating the advantages of Asian women for industrial manufacturing.

"We hire [Malaysian] girls," said a personnel officer for Intel Corporation in Penang, Malaysia, "because they have less energy, are more disciplined, and are easier to control" (Grossman 1979: 1). A Malaysian government brochure, entitled *Malaysia: The Solid State for Electronics*, goes even further in its description:

The manual dexterity of the oriental female is famous the world over. Her hands are small and she works fast with extreme care. Who, therefore, could be better qualified by nature and inheritance to contribute to the efficiency of a bench-assembly production line than the oriental girl? (Lim 1978: 7)

These industrial attractions, moreover, are often contrasted to the unfavorable labor conditions prevailing in other parts of the world. A 1981 World Bank Research publication, entitled *Why the Emperor's New Clothes Are Not Made in Colombia*, for example, describes the so-called "cultural differences" between East Asian and Latin American workers:

Because of a long Confucian tradition of respect for authority, the degree to which the work force is susceptible to organization and discipline tends to be high in Korea. For similar reasons, it is also quite high in Taiwan and Hong Kong—but it is considerably lower in Colombia. Several interviewees in Colombia and New York described instances in which Colombian workers successfully resisted attempts to change production flows, seating arrangements, or the way in which items were sewn. As [a United States garment industry production engineer] pointed out, "This could not have happened in the United States or East Asia. There you just say, 'this is how it will be done', and it is done." (Morawetz 1981: 134–35)

Even in the United States, the characteristics of Asian laborers are used as a threat against agitation by American workers. As Cynthia Enloe describes, "today women textile workers in the industrialized countries are being encouraged by businessmen, labor leaders, and government officials to see Third World women as their enemies, as threats to their jobs, as low paid and exploitative as those jobs may be" (Enloe 1983: 410). These sentiments are expressed, for example, by textile workers in the American South:

Mill women . . . are familiar with the union-busting tactics of the textile industry. They know it is a runaway shop that came south after unionization of northern mills, and that East Asian textiles currently represent a formidable competitor to the southern mill owner. In Kannapolis [home of Cannon Mills, now owned by Fieldcrest Mills], mill workers who had been laid off were recently rehired at a lower wage to work solely at sewing local labels over Taiwanese labels. The risk of organized protest is that the American textile industry will leave the South for the Asian Third World, where another hardworking, eager, and cheap labor force of women and children awaits it. (Byerly 1986: 7)

Likewise, in California, says Rachel Grossman, "when [electronics] workers try to organize themselves, their employers threaten to move the plant to Asia—even when technical considerations make this unlikely" (1979: 1).

What is behind these depictions of Asian labor (and particularly of Asian female labor) as "docile," "controllable," and "hard-working"? The Malaysian government brochure cited above looks to "nature and inheritance," as does David Morawetz, the author of *Why the Emperor's New Clothes Are Not Made in Colombia*. As he argues:

Evidence from physical anthropology suggests that East Asians may indeed have smaller hands and more slender fingers than Europeans and, probably, than South

Americans. [And] all East Asians receive considerably more generalized societal training in manual dexterity than do Colombians. The use of chopsticks rather than fork and spoon as food conveyors, the widespread use of the abacus, and the precision required in calligraphy all condition East Asians' fingers to be particularly nimble. (Morawetz 1981: 134–35)

Nevertheless, Morawetz's next sentence suggests a more powerful explanation. "It is considerably less difficult and less costly," he notes, "to fire an employee in East Asia than it is in Colombia." Depictions of Asian workers as "docile" labor have their roots, not only in the racism of a misapplied anthropology, but also in the structure and ideology of the capitalist world-economy. Contemporary industrial production, particularly in those industries that predominantly employ women such as textiles and electronics, is supported by ideologies stressing the docility of female labor. These ideologies, moreover, are most explicit where the female labor is also Asian. This suggests that as world industrial production has expanded to incorporate Asia, ideologies of "docile" labor are also increasingly Asia-focused.

This suggestion can be examined by considering the case of the textile industry. An analysis of labor-force structure in the cotton mills, and of the rhetoric and stereotypes that are used to depict mill workers—by industrialists, by labor recruiters, and by the mill workers themselves—can provide insight into the ideological aspects of industrial textile production. Such insight is crucial for an understanding of the subtleties of racism and sexism in industrial labor-force structures, and for the relation of labor-force structures to racism and sexism in the capitalist world-economy.

Textile Production and Capitalist World Economy

World-systemic analyses have rarely focused on ideological aspects of the capitalist world economy. Immanuel Wallerstein suggests the value of ideological analysis in his discussion of systemic crises, noting the need to look at the "basic metaphysical paradigms that have been the consequence and bulwark of the emergence of capitalism as a world-system" (Wallerstein 1983: 29). Such metaphysical paradigms, he notes, include a universalist ideology from the European Enlightenment which seeks to interpret physical, biological, and social conditions in terms of universal laws (Wallerstein 1983: 32). Wallerstein's discussion, though, is highly abstract, and while he sketches an encompassing ideological framework, he does not outline a method for further analysis. To develop a more socially and historically grounded analysis of capitalist ideology, we must turn instead to specific sectors of the capitalist world-economy. In examining the ideologies of industrial textile production, for example, we must look at specific case studies of textile production. From these case studies, we can then develop the basis for a world-systemic discussion of industrial ideologies.

Textile production provides especially interesting material with which to examine ideological aspects of labor-force structures in the capitalist world-economy. Textile production and trade have long been at the heart of the capitalist world-system. Easily portable and in demand worldwide, textiles were the dominant industrial product even before the nineteenth century. As Fernand Braudel has noted, the capricious and ever-changing whims of fashion and the luxury trade "increasingly dictated demand for textiles in the most advanced and commercialized sectors" (Braudel 1979: 178). "Long live textiles, then, was the motto of trade" (1979: 312), as first silk, then English woolens, and finally Indian cottons swept across Europe as the symbols of social prestige. Indian calicoes, especially, "which were printed and dyed by techniques unknown in Europe . . . quickly became all the rage, [and] cotton was soon the leading textile" (Braudel 1979: 313). In the face of an onslaught of Indian imports, Europe began to weave and print cotton herself, and the late eighteenth century saw a virtual "cotton revolution" (Braudel 1978).

As European cotton textile production expanded in both scale and mechanization, moreover, cloth goods could be produced both in large quantities and at low cost. As a result, "the clientele for textiles acquired a popular character" (Braudel 1979: 313), and cotton goods shifted from being a luxury item to being a necessary and accessible commodity. In European markets and societies, then, the industrialization of cotton production came to symbolize not only a revolution in commerce and production, but also a revolution in consumption.

As Jules Michelet described for France:

This is what we saw in 1842. . . . Prices fell . . . until cotton cloth stood at six *sous*. Then something completely unexpected occurred. The words *six sous* aroused the people. Millions of purchasers—poor people who never bought anything—began to stir. Then we saw what an immense and powerful consumer the people is when it is engaged. . . . That was a revolution in France, little noted but a great revolution nonetheless. It was a revolution in cleanliness and embellishment of the homes of the poor; underwear, bedding, table linen, and window curtains were now used by whole classes who had not used them since the beginning of time. (Michelet 1973: 43–44)

Even more importantly, industrial cotton production engendered, and came to symbolize, a social revolution. As E. P. Thompson has noted, "the cotton mill is seen as the agent not only of industrial but also of social revolution, producing not only more goods but also the 'Labor Movement' itself" (Thompson 1963: 192). The cotton mill became equated with the new industrial society, and contemporary observers in the late eighteenth and early nineteenth centuries exclaimed at the "correspondence between new forms of production and of social relationship" (Thompson 1963: 189). Even in the 1830s and 1840s, observers were still commenting on the novelty of the "factory system." "It was not only the mill owner but also the working population brought into being within and around the mills," notes

Thompson, "which seemed to contemporaries to be 'new'" (1963: 190). As a British rural magistrate wrote in 1808, "the instant we get near the borders of the manufacturing parts of Lancashire, we meet a fresh race of being, both in point of manners, employments, and subordination" (quoted in Thompson 1963: 190).

The characterization of these "manners, employments, and subordination," in fact, can give us important insights into the images of industrial labor that developed concurrently with Europe's industrial textile production. Since the industrialization of cotton textiles was seen an engendering a social as well as a technological revolution, much of the commentary on the growth of the cotton mills took the form of social commentary on conditions in the mills and on the characteristics of the mill workers. Descriptions of the mill workers—this "fresh race of being"—were both laudatory and highly critical. Attitudes toward the new industrial labor force were often ambivalent, as contradictory as the conditions of work in the mills themselves. Yet out of these social commentaries grew a rhetorical idiom for industrial labor that has characterized the cotton textile industry ever since.

As a journeyman cotton spinner described in 1818 in a public address in Manchester:

I know it to be a fact that the greater part of the master spinners are anxious to keep wages low for the purpose of keeping the spinners indigent and spiritless . . . and for the purpose of taking the surplus to their own pockets. . . . What then must be the men or rather beings who are the instruments of such masters? Why, they have been for a series of years, with their wives and their families, patience itself—bondmen and bondwomen to their cruel taskmasters. . . . The workmen in general are an inoffensive, unassuming, set of well-informed men, though how they acquire their information is almost a mystery to me. They are docile and tractable, if not goaded too much; but this is not to be wondered at, when we consider that they are trained to work from six years old, from five in the morning to eight and nine at night. . . . There they are, (and if late a few minutes, a quarter of a day is stopped in wages) locked up until night in rooms heated above the hottest days we have had this summer, and allowed no time, except three-quarters of an hour at dinner in the whole day: whatever they eat at any other time must be as they are at work. . . . The English spinner slave has no enjoyment of the open atmosphere and breezes of heaven. Locked up in factories eight stories high, he has no relaxation till the ponderous engine stops, and then he goes home to get refreshed for the next day; no time for sweet association with his family; they are all alike fatigued and exhausted. This is no over-drawn picture: it is literally true. (Thompson 1963: 200–201).

The view of textile workers as "patient," "spiritless," "inoffensive," "unassuming," "docile," and "tractable" has been consistently applied to mill workers (often in the face of considerable labor unrest) throughout the history of European textile production. Even more interesting, this image has been transferred—along with the industrial technology for cotton textile production—to mill workers in the United States and in East and Southeast

Asia. It is of particular interest for an analysis of ideological aspects of the capitalist world-system, therefore, to examine the extent to which this image of cotton mill workers (with the substitution of women for men as the typical mill operatives) has characterized the social and ideological relations of textile production, not only in nineteenth-century England, but also in nineteenth-century United States, in nineteenth- and twentieth-century China and Japan, and contemporarily in the smaller industrializing countries of East, South, and Southeast Asia.

The Cotton Textile Industry in Europe and Asia

From its very inception, the cotton textile industry in Europe was linked to the textile-producing countries of Asia. The first introduction of cotton cloth on a major scale to Europe had been through Indian calicoes, and even after the advent of British industrialization, Indian cottons remained of superior quality. British colonialists in India, therefore, undertook to crush the Indian textile industry, transforming India from a center of indigenous textile production to a market for British textile consumption. In Great Britain, notes E. J. Hobsbawm, "cotton was and remained essentially an export industry . . . [and] after the middle of the nineteenth century it found its staple outlet in India and the Far East" (Hobsbawm 1969: 58). The United States followed suit, producing cotton textiles for export as well as for domestic consumption. Their overseas markets, though, especially in Asia, turned the British pattern on itself, and began to develop—or, in the case of India, to re-develop—their own textile industries. Initially producing cotton goods for domestic use in order to decrease their reliance on British and American imports, the Asian industries increasingly began to produce textiles for export, as their products gained a competitive edge on the world market.

Ironically, therefore, the British cotton textile industry, which had begun by trying to destroy the production of Indian cottons, itself was destroyed by the rapidly expanding textile industries of its own imperial markets. As Hobsbawm describes:

The British cotton industry was certainly in its time the best in the world, but it ended as it had begun by relying not on its competitive superiority but on a monopoly of the colonial and underdeveloped markets which the British Empire, the British Navy and British commercial supremacy gave it. Its days were numbered after the First World War, when the Indians, Chinese, and Japanese manufactured or even exported their own cotton goods and could no longer be prevented from doing so by British political interference. . . . When the last great receptacles of cotton goods developed their own textile industries—India, Japan, and China—the hour of Lancashire tolled. (Hobsbawm 1969: 58, 151)

By the early 1900s, both China and Japan were major cotton textile producers. The first cotton mill in China, the Shanghai Machine Weaving

Bureau, was established in 1888, and by 1890 it employed 4000 workers (Honig 1986: 15). After the outbreak of World War I in 1914, the Shanghai cotton textile industry flourished, as imports of cotton goods were sharply curtailed. Following World War I, British and Japanese industrialists also established cotton mills in Shanghai. The number of Japanese mills in Shanghai tripled between 1919 and 1925 (from eleven to thirty-two), and by 1930 the Japanese community was the largest foreign community in Shanghai's international settlement (Honig 1986: 28).

Japanese industrial expansion in Shangahi was matched by a similar expansion of the cotton textile industry at home in Japan. "As early as 1894," Mark Selden notes, "Japan had broken the grip of . . . unequal treaties, initiated military industries and a flourishing textile industry, and launched an expansionist path" (1983: 61). Even though as late as 1880 Japan's cotton yarn imports had exceeded domestic production, "by the First World War and continuing in subsequent decades, Japan dominated world cotton textile markets. At its peak in 1937, 37% of all cotton fabrics traded internationally were made in Japan" (Selden 1983: 63).

More recently, the smaller countries of East and Southeast Asia have followed a similar path. As Enloe notes, in the years between 1920 and 1940, "textile jobs in Europe fell by 290,000, while Japan and India doubled their textile employment" (1983: 411). Between 1960 and 1969, Hong Kong quadrupled its employment in textiles, and in South Korea and Taiwan one out of every three new jobs created was in textiles (Enloe 1983). Expanding yet further in the 1970s, as "a total one million jobs in the textile industry disappeared in Western Europe . . . in the late 1970s, the governments of Indonesia, Sri Lanka, Bangladesh and Egypt stepped up their industrializing textile efforts" (Enloe 1983: 411).

With this background in mind, then, it is useful to trace the structure and rhetorical descriptions of the labor force that developed with the internationalizing cotton textile industry. Although in both England and China the cotton mill workers were initially male, as the industries expanded it became cheaper and "more efficient" to hire women. In a pattern that has striking parallels across nations and historical periods, from nineteenth-century England to the United States, and then to China, Japan, and Southeast Asia, the cotton textile industry has relied upon, and has encouraged, the development of a highly mobile, transient labor force of young unmarried women, especially those from rural and immigrant backgrounds.

The Labor of Dutiful Daughters

Many authors have chronicled the development of the textile mills in Great Britain and New England. Often patterned on the model of the Lowell mills in Massachusetts, the early American cotton mills reached their greatest expansion in the Amoskeag Mill in Manchester, New Hampshire. At its peak in the early twentieth century, the Amoskeag Mill was "the world's largest textile plant, employing up to 17,000 workers'' (Hareven & Langenbach 1978: 10). The Amoskeag was also an all-encompassing social and industrial world. "To the people who lived and worked there, the Amoskeag was a total institution, a closed and almost self-contained world" (Hareven & Langenbach 1978: 11).

Like Lowell, Manchester founded a community of young women working together in the mills and living together in boarding houses, within the social system of corporate paternalism—a philosophy of benevolent control—which treated workers as the "corporation's children" and which permeated all aspects of life; the organization of work, the strict management of the boarding houses, the founding of charities, and the endowment of charities. In the mid-nineteenth century, when the majority of the labor force consisted of young, unmarried women from rural New England, the company also regulated their behavior after working hours in order to reassure their parents. The boarding houses were closed and locked at 10:00 p.m., church attendance was compulsory, and alcoholic consumption was prohibited. However, Manchester never achieved the fame of Lowell as a city of mill girls. (Hareven & Langenbach 1978: 14)

Less well-known, perhaps, is the extent to which Lowell's Waltham system (the factory system developed by Francis C. Lowell, which involved highly capitalized mills that integrated both spinning and weaving under one roof, and whose labor force consisted primarily of young farm women) was also a model for the industrializing cotton mills of East and Southeast Asia. Like Lowell, a number of Japanese cotton mills instituted a dormitory system for their young female employees that

provided management a cheap and effective mechanism for labor control, including forced overtime, by isolating women workers within a policed environment subject to virtually unlimited company scrutiny. This system also provided parents appropriate assurances of the moral environment to which they dispatched their soon-to-be-married daughters. (Selden 1983: 67)

As John Orchard, an observer who visited a number of Japanese factories in 1927, described:

The girls were not permitted to leave the factory grounds except on holidays and with permission. In a fourth large spinning mill it was stated that the girls and women were permitted to go beyond the factory gates only if the local labor union assumed the responsibility. In this particular mill, the dormitories and the factories are surrounded by a high board fence, the gates are locked at night, and the only exit to the outer world is through a turnstile by the office. (1930: 3)

The self-enclosed world of the cotton mill was also a world from which it was often difficult to escape. As Sharon Sievers has described for these same early Japanese textile mills:

In most cases, there was considerable risk involved, and often very harsh punishment for those who were caught. The typical mill dormitory was designed for security—that is, to keep workers in. Doors were locked at night; barbed wire was strung around walled factory compounds; supervisors patrolled the dormitories and watchmen patrolled the grounds. The workers themselves clearly knew the dormitory for what it was: "The dormitory windows had heavy metal screens to prevent [escape], but if a woman did escape, the watchmen would jump on their horses and ride in all directions, closing the passes and the roads. Eventually the railway station would be closed. Usually the woman was brought right back. It was literally a prison." (1983: 66)

The high frequency of escapes that did occur, moreover, was used by the mill owners to justify low wages and poor working conditions. As Sievers describes:

The runaway or "escaped" worker became a symbol of the industry's preference for recruiting new labor and using it up, rather than investing in improved working conditions and higher wages. An annual turnover rate of fifty percent was typical of Meiji textile mills, and some owners seem to have gotten into the habit of replacing virtually their entire female work force each year. (1983: 65)

Furthermore, even where the workers were free to leave the mills, the poverty of their families at home forced many of the young girls to stay. Across nations and historical periods, the predominant cotton mill workers have been daughters—young, unmarried girls from rural backgrounds who were "excess" labor at home, and whose wages in the mills provided their families with critically needed additional income.

Nevertheless, given the extremely low rate of pay in the cotton mills, the workers could barely support themselves, and even if they were living at home, they could only rarely support dependents. The girls' parents knew this as well, and so did the mill owners. As Celia Mather describes for a contemporary textile factory in Indonesia:

Most adults with dependents to support regarded such wages as impossibly low, and insecure too. . . . Instead, they sent their young daughters and sons, or sisters and brothers, into the factories. The wages of these young workers were then regarded by both parents and employers as "supplementary" rather than the central source of income, even though they were the only *regular* cash income coming into many households, and were vital to buy the necessary commodities such as kerosene for lamps and cooking, matches, and soap. . . . Low wages meant that workers could not support dependents, but also caused the young workers themselves to be dependent upon others, their parents or older brothers and sisters, for a good proportion of their subsistence needs. . . . There was, then, a tacit agreement between parents and factory managers that these young workers, especially daughters, were dependent, and this allowed the investors in the area to pay wages which did not cover the daily subsistence cost of their workforce. (1985: 158, emphasis in original)

In an increasingly vicious circle, therefore, low wages were used to justify high employee turnover, frequent layoffs, and "temporary" rather than permanent labor contracts. This pattern, though, was already in place in nineteenth-century New England. As the nineteenth-century industrialist, Samuel Batchelder, described, "the great part of those at work in our mills are only a succession of learners, who leave the business as soon as they begin to acquire some skill and experience" (Batchelder 1972: 89). This situation was also highly adaptive for an industry with frequent downturns. Whenever there was a need to decrease the size of the labor force, it was useful to have hired "daughters," as they could then always "return home." As Batchelder notes, "such usually having a home to which they could return in case of any interruption of the business, they were not subject to be left dependent or exposed to suffering" (1972: 75).

Industrial recruitment policies which focused predominantly on rural areas also reinforced the mills' employment of "dutiful" and dependent daughters. Peasant and farm women were especially desired, as they usually had little education (and thus were more "tractable") and were used to hard work and to physical labor. Especially for the "dirtier" jobs in the mills, farm girls were often the mill owners'—or their recruiters'—first choice. As Emily Honig notes, for example, the Shanghai cotton mills often had to recruit women from the countryside to work in the roving department, as local women were unwilling to do this job (1986: 51).

Recruiting peasant and farm women from rural areas, moreover, ensured that in times of industrial layoffs the workers would be reabsorbed into the countryside. They would not, in other words, swell the ranks of an urban or industrial proletariat. Many mill workers, in fact, went back and forth between agricultural and industrial employment, as was the case in Shanghai following World War I. As Honig describes, women moved in and out of the mills, from the countryside to the city. "Even in the city the line between peasant and proletarian was blurred, because a woman who worked in a cotton mill one year might spend the next year eking out a living by picking vegetables in the suburbs near the mills" (1986: 166).

Not all women, though, had such options. For many girls, especially those from landless or land-poor families, work in the cotton mills was virtually their only opportunity for employment. Industrial labor recruiters, therefore, scoured the countryside for young workers, appearing especially in villages that were hit by famines or poor harvests. As a 1926 Y.W.C.A. report on Japan describes:

It is said that . . . a district is "worked out" for recruiting purposes in seven years. Probably this is somewhat exaggerated. Nevertheless, it is true that the recruiting areas are moving further and further from the industrial areas. There is no perennial source from which a new supply of workers can constantly be drawn. Year after year the recruiting territory shifts to a remoter distance. It is said that if a man has a daughter, no matter if he lives in the remotest inland village, he will have five or six recruiting men visiting him every day. They call on him not only at home but in the fields if he is working there. Some people have been driven to put notices at their doors with the statement: "No daughter for factory work in this house!" to keep off the importunate recruiters. (Y.W.C.A. 1926: 179)

The recruitment of young farm girls was most extreme in the case of their recruitment by labor contractors—men (who, in the case of China, were often connected with the underworld) who would "buy" young girls for mill work. Labor contracting was a standard practice in both China and Japan. As Selden notes for Japan at the turn of the twentieth century, "the typical industrial worker at this time was the woman silk weaver or cotton spinner of tenant or poor peasant origin, employed through labor contractors on two-to-three-year contracts signed by peasant fathers with little or no consultation or consent" (1983: 63).

Likewise in China, says Honig, Shanghai labor contractors in the 1930s referred to the business of buying and selling young girls as "plucking mulberry leaves" (Honig 1986: 96). As Honig describes:

The first step in the process was for a contractor to pay a visit to his or her home village. There the contractor looked for teenage girls, usually from fourteen to eighteen years old, who could be lured to Shanghai. In some cases the contractor posted an announcement in the village and then signed contracts with those who responded. . . . More frequently, however, the contractor would talk to friends and relatives, determine which families were in particularly dire circumstances, and then pay them a visit. . . . The prospective recruit's family was promised that she would have meat and fish for dinner every day, a house to live in with other girls, a job, a chance to learn a skill, and a day off every week to see the skyscrapers, double-deck buses and other "strange, amusing, foreign sights of Shanghai." (1986: 98–99)

Even in the United States, as labor recruitment for the cotton mills shifted increasingly toward immigrant women (and toward immigrant families, in the case of those mills that hired entire families), mill recruiters began to go "straight to the source." As Meredith Tax described for the Lawrence mill in Massachusetts:

By 1912 there were twenty-five different ethnic groups in the Lawrence mills, although most of the workers were Italians, Poles, Russians, Syrians, or Lithuanians. . . . Immigrants were drawn to Lawrence by posters placed in towns throughout the Balkans and the Mediterranean showing happy workers carrying bags full of money from the factory gate to the bank. (1980: 242–43)

"Docile" or Militant Labor?

Were the workers so recruited in fact the "docile" labor force that mill owners desired? Or is the image of textile workers as docile labor contrary to fact? Abundant evidence exists that the image is, in fact, contrary to fact. In each of the cases examined—Great Britain, the United States, China, Japan, and Southeast Asia—textile workers (even young female textile workers) participated actively in acts of both individual and collective resistance. Acts of resistance ranged from suicide or escape from the early Japanese cotton mills to the massive and organized strikes of the May 30th

Movement in China. As Enloe has noted, "women textile workers have been in the forefront of political activism in every industrializing country" (1983: 420). Each of the authors cited above gives examples as well of mill workers' acts of resistance.

The "docility" of their acts of resistance can be seen in the commentaries of actual participants and by the reports of contemporary observers. The textile workers' strike of 1912 in Lawrence, Massachusetts, for example, provides an interesting and illustrative example. "The Lawrence strike," notes Tax, "was a great, militant, even (it was thought at the time) revolutionary uprising of the United States working class" (1980: 203). As she describes:

The Lawrence strike was fought over a pay cut of thirty cents a week, the cost of five loaves of bread. Massachusetts textile workers lived so close to the bone that thirty cents was the difference between bare survival and starvation for them and their children. "Better to starve fighting than to starve working," they cried, and 20,000 of them struck in the second week of January 1912. (1980: 241)

"About half of the Lawrence strikers," notes Tax, "were women and, along with the wives and children of male strikers, their role in street actions was noticeable from the beginning" (1980: 254). As she describes:

In the course of the strike women became increasingly active; from February on clashes between the women and the police and militia grew more frequent. The police, mill owners, and press raised loud objections to the role women played in the street. The Lawrence district attorney said in court that the strike committee was made up of cowards who sent their women onto the picket line; he thought they should put men there instead, since "one policeman can handle ten men, while it takes ten policemen to handle one woman." (1980: 254).

Nevertheless, despite the high participation of textile workers in strikes and in other acts of resistance, analysts of the textile industry have also noted the difficulties that unions and labor movements have had in trying to organize textile workers. These difficulties—and the factors that divide textile workers from themselves as well as encourage their "docility"—provide a key to understanding the structure and ideological dynamics of the textile industry in the capitalist world economy.

From the very beginning, workers in the textile industry have been divided: initially by sex and by age, and then increasingly by sex, age, ethnicity, and geographical origin. As early as the 1840s and 1850s in New England, for example, the influx of Irish immigrants changed the nature of industrial labor. As Louise Lamphere has noted, "it created a more permanent working class but one that was divided between Yankee and immigrant" (1987: 64). "In Rhode Island, as in Lowell," she continues, "the presence of the Irish added ethnicity to the age and sex hierarchy in the mills. This created conflict among wage-earning daughters" (1987: 65). The

Irish immigrants to New England were followed by French Canadians, British, Scots, Poles, Portuguese, Syrians, and most recently, Colombians, all of whom took up work in the New England textile mills. In the Lawrence mill in Massachusetts, notes Tax, where workers came from up to twenty-five different ethnic groups, "the employers made an effort to get workers from as many different language groups as possible in order to prevent them from uniting to make trouble; if they competed rather than combined, wages would be kept down" (1980: 242).

Likewise in the Asian textile mills, job hierarchies were created between workers of different ethnic, linguistic, and regional backgrounds. As Honig has described:

In Shanghai, natives of a particular region congregated in certain departments of the mills and lived in the same neighborhoods. . . . Most weavers, for example, were from Wuxi, most spinners from Shanghai, and most rovers from Subei. . . . Localism—expressed in dress styles, eating habits, marriage customs, and dialects—was the basis of the most important divisions and antagonisms among workers. . . . The perdurance of these regional prejudices underlines the fact that the pre-Liberation female work force was in no sense a homogeneous one. Women were more likely to perceive their fellow worker from a different region as their foe than they were to see the capitalist as the enemy. (1986: 4–5)

Even where workers were from the same regional, linguistic, and ethnic backgrounds, minute differentiations in their job classifications and wage categories isolated and divided them. "The net result," notes Lamphere, "was that each worker was divided from his or her coworker, even in the same room where many workers were doing the same job" (1987: 87).

This complex of factors segmenting the labor force is reinforced by employment policies that keep many mill workers in temporary or "probationary" positions, sometimes for several years. A 1980 labor dispute in the P. T. Textra textile mill in Indonesia, for example, "found its origins in the bad working conditions and in the workers' continuing status as trainees, even though a number of them had been in [the mill's] employ for more than eight years. Instead of a wage they received 'pocket money' [*uang saku*] (Borkent et al. 1981: 2). Mather found a similar situation in the Indonesian textile factory that she studied in West Java, noting that workers could be employed 'on probation' or laid off on short notice (1985: 158).

These structural factors of labor force segmentation are then further reinforced by cultural and industrial ideologies stressing the "docility" and compliance of women workers. As Mather describes for Indonesian textile workers in the Islamic regency of Tangerang in West Java:

The public attitude deemed most appropriate for women . . . especially of poor families, is *malu*. This refers to both mental and physical attitudes, encouraging them to appear shy, embarrassed, and retiring, deferring to superiors and remaining at a distance from them, averting their eyes, and so on. They are also encouraged to feel afraid (*takut*) of new experiences and new people. . . . Once inside the factories the young girls consistently . . . say that they feel too *malu* and *takut*, so deferential to their bosses (usually older men) that direct confrontation, individually or in groups, is almost unthinkable. They say that they are too *malu* to be straightforward about any grievances, too *takut* to complain about low pay or unfair treatment, and would rather leave the factory than "make trouble." (1985: 168–69)

Similar examples can be cited for China, Japan, and the other countries of East and Southeast Asia—the very countries, we might note, that stress the "docility" of their female labor force. As the above example suggests, moreover, the ideologies of docility may be internalized by the workers themselves as well as be espoused by mill owners and recruiters. These ideologies of docility are also underscored by prevailing values in the surrounding communities. Whether "Christian," "Islamic," "Confucian," "paternal," or "patrimonial," these local societal values often reinforce the industrial ideals of docility. Young female mill workers, then, as Mather suggests, "are trebly subordinate—as client-employees, as young people, and as women" (1985: 167)

Mill workers are, in fact, quadrupally subordinate, as they are also subject to the repressive measures of their encompassing nation-states. Both historically and contemporarily, industrial labor control has been tied to the agencies for state repression. In the Amoskeag Mill in New Hampshire, for example, "management retained close ties with the police force, which proved a most useful connection during the ensuing strikes" (Hareven and Langenbach 1978: 16). In China and Japan as well, as Selden has documented historically, labor militancy has been closely tied to periods of political freedom or repression. It is not coincidental that in China, "the formation of the short-lived Republic in 1911 stimulated a wave of labor organizing. The 1912 provisional constitution provided the right of association for the first time, and in that year, 5,000 female silk workers struck factories at Shunde near Canton in a landmark protest" (1983: 85).

In times of repression, by contrast, labor agitation is sharply curtailed, and workers' resistance turns inwards, to individual acts of sabotage or (where feasible) to flight and withdrawal from the labor force. It is particularly striking that many of the same Asian countries that today advertise the docility of their labor force and the lack of industrial unrest also have the largest military and police forces in their regions and the most repressive political systems. As Enloe has noted, governments in East and Southeast Asia increasingly rely on coercive force in order to compete in the international political economy (1983: 408). "In the newly industrializing countries of Asia," she notes, "it has been extremely difficult for women textile workers to protest. Unions, when allowed at all, are coopted by the companies and the government" (Enloe 1983: 421).

In these countries, moreover, where strikes or other forms of labor protest do occur, the military and police are often called in, and the strikers are often arrested. The contemporary case of Indonesia, for example, provides apt illustration. Large numbers of labor organizers were arrested following the attempted coup in 1965, and many were held in detention until 1979. Since that time

political judgements are also used as a basis for selection, and discrimination. Accusation of involvement or sympathy with communist or leftist groups prior to the 1965 military coup has been enough to refuse anyone a job. Ever since 1965, anyone so implicated (or even accused without evidence) has been denied proper employment. All state employees must hold a Certificate of Non-Involvement (*Surat Bebas G.30/S.*), and under government encouragement private companies have also made this a *de facto* requirement for applicants. Even now job advertisements in newspapers sometimes still specify that ownership of the Certificate is required as well as other more usual qualifications of education and age. By the late 1970's such advertisements reading "Age Range 20–25 years" meant that suitable recruits would have been only 6–11 years old at the time of the 1965 coup. (Borkent et al. 1981: 118–19)

Strikes are also illegal in Indonesia, where they are considered "unnecessary" and contrary to [the state government's ideology of] "*Pancasila* labor relations." In the event that labor protests do occur, moreover, the Indonesian army acts as the employers' "right arm" in "solving" the labor disputes (cf. the examples cited in Borkent et al. 1981). Under such conditions, and under the similar labor conditions prevailing elsewhere in East and Southeast Asia, is it really any surprise that young women workers are "docile"? It is perhaps more of a surprise that they prove their image contrary to fact.

Labor relations that exist under conditions of political repression are vivid reminders of the need to include the state in world-systemic analyses. "The study of the working class," Selden notes, "is inseparable from the study of the nature of the state, its legal structure, its power and penetration, and its relationship to social classes" (1983: 111). As we monitor racism and sexism in the capitalist world-economy, therefore, we must pay close attention to the state as well as to the structures of labor-force organization and the ideologies of industrial labor.

A prevailing ideology of industrial labor has been the image of female textile workers—especially Asian female textile workers—as "docile" labor. Structurally and ideologically, as well as across different countries and historical periods, female textile workers have shared strikingly similar experiences. The labor image that has grown up around them, moreover, is now being applied to Asian women in other branches of industrial production. As Enloe has noted, "South Korean women textile workers had lessons to tell Philippine and Singapore women, and they all could pass along caveats to Sri Lankan women now being hired in the newest of Asia's . . . factories" (1983: 411).

There are also indications that Asian women factory workers are becoming aware of—and are subverting—their image as "docile" labor. Electronics workers in California's Silicon Valley, for example, as Karen Hossfeld has discovered, are starting to use their "shyness" and "timidity" as resources to improve their working conditions (personal communication). Efforts to change the racist and sexist image of Asian women as "docile" labor should by no means be limited to such struggles—to the resistance strategies of the Asian women workers themselves. Nevertheless, given their historical and contemporary role in the world-economy, women workers' consciousness of their image as "docile" labor, and their development of strategies to combat the ideologies in which such images are embedded (as well as the social and industrial conditions in which such ideologies are produced), will also be steps toward combatting the broader issues of racism and sexism in the capitalist world-economy.

NOTE

I would like to thank the participants in the Eleventh Annual PEWS Conference and the following individuals for their helpful comments and suggestions on an earlier draft of this chapter: Gregory Acciaioli, Susan Bell, Micaela di Leonardo, Daniel Levine, and David Vail. While I have tried to incorporate some of their comments, I have not incorporated all of them. The flaws of this work, therefore, remain incontestably my own.

REFERENCES

Batchelder, Samuel (1972). *Introduction and Early Progress of the Cotton Manufacture in the United States*. Clifton, N.J.: Augustus M. Kelley.
Borkent, Hans, et al. (1981). *Indonesian Workers and Their Right to Organise*. Leiden: Indonesian Documentation and Information Centre.
Braudel, Fernand (1979). *The Wheels of Commerce*. New York: Harper & Row.
Byerly, Victoria (1986). *Hard Times Cotton Mill Girls: Personal Histories of Womanhood and Poverty in the South*. Ithaca: Cornell University Press.
Enloe, Cynthia H. (1983). "Women Textile Workers in the Militarization of Southeast Asia." In J. Nash and M. P. Fernandez-Kelly, eds., *Women, Men, and the International Division of Labor*. Albany: SUNY Press, 407–25.
Grossman, Rachel (1979). "Women's Place in the Integrated Circuit." *Southeast Asia Chronicle*, 66, 2–17.
Hareven, Tamara K., and Randolph Langenbach (1978). *Amoskeag: Life and Work in an American Factory-City*. New York: Pantheon.
Hobsbawm, E. J. (1969). *Industry and Empire*. Harmondsworth: Penguin.
Honig, Emily (1986). *Sisters and Strangers: Women in the Shanghai Cotton Mills, 1919–1949*. Stanford: Stanford University Press.
Kung, Lydia (1983). *Factory Women in Taiwan*. Ann Arbor: UMI Research Press.
Lamphere, Louise (1987). *From Working Daughters to Working Mothers: Immigrant Women in a New England Industrial Community*. Ithaca: Cornell University Press.

Lim, Linda Y. C. (1978). "Women Workers in Multinational Corporations: The Case of the Electronics Industry in Malaysia and Singapore." *Michigan Occasional Papers*, 9, Fall.

Mather, Celia (1985). "'Rather Than Make Trouble, It's Better Just to Leave': Behind the Lack of Industrial Strife in the Tangerang Region of West Java." In H. Afshar, ed., *Women, Work and Ideology in the Third World*. London: Tavistock, 153–80.

Michelet, Jules (1973). *The People*. Urbana: University of Illinois Press.

Morawetz, David (1981). *Why the Emperor's New Clothes Are Not Made in Colombia*. New York: Oxford University Press.

Orchard, John (1930). *Japan's Economic Position*. New York: McGraw-Hill.

Selden, Mark (1983). "The Proletariat, Revolutionary Change, and the State in China and Japan, 1850–1950." In I. Wallerstein, ed., *Labor in the World Social Structure*. Beverly Hills: Sage, 58–120.

Sievers, Sharon L. (1983). *Flowers in Salt: The Beginnings of Feminist Consciousness in Modern Japan*. Stanford: Stanford University Press.

Tax, Meredith (1980). *The Rising of the Women: Feminist Solidarity and Class Conflict, 1880–1917*. New York: Monthly Review Press.

Thompson, E. P. (1963). *The Making of the English Working Class*. New York: Random House.

Wallerstein, Immanuel (1983). "Crises: The World-Economy, the Movements, and the Ideologies." In A. Bergesen, ed., *Crises in the World-System*. Beverly Hills: Sage, 21–36.

Y.W.C.A. (1926). *Women in Industry in the Orient*. New York: Woman's Press.

5

CAPITAL AND GENDER IN THE THIRD WORLD: THEORETICAL ANALYSIS OF THE CURRENT CRISIS

Peter F. Bell

While the intense level of exploitation of women in the Third World has been well documented, the problem has not be sufficiently theorized. The aim of this chapter is to assist in the struggle against capitalism and its attendant forms of oppression through the development of a feminist-Marxist theoretical framework. This will permit us to analyze the changing forms of global development and their impact on women, and thus reveal the possibilities for the augmentation and circulation of struggle against these conditions and the global system that sustains them.

Several fundamental propositions underlie this political-economy framework:

1. It is presupposed that women's oppression is interwoven within the structure of capitalism. Maria Mies argues that capitalism is by nature "a patriarchal, predatory mode of appropriation of producers, products and means of production" (1986: 66). The sexual division of labor that accompanied the development of capitalism was, as Mies argues, not simply functional (to the development of greater efficiency), but was always violent in nature and asymmetrical in structure, with women the recipients of both its violence and oppression. At every stage in the development of capitalism, accumulation changes the social and technical basis of production and reproduction on a world scale, and thus also the structure of gender relations.

2. "The accumulation of capital" refers to a process involving both the widening and deepening (or intensification) of capitalist social relations, and includes the oppression of women as well as the exploitation of labor generally. Capital accumulation, furthermore, arises not from some mysterious "laws of motion" (or "capital-logic") but out of the struggles within the social (class) relations.[1]

Accumulation is the articulation of the various moments of class struggle at the level of the system as a whole (Cleaver 1978).

3. It follows from this that crises, such as the period of the 1970s and 1980s, are interruptions in the process of accumulation which emanate from class and gender struggles.[2]

4. Gender struggles in capitalist society are class struggles in that the reproduction of labor power is the fundamental condition for the production of commodities, and is itself value- and commodity-producing. Thus "housework" creates the commodity of labor power (Cleaver 1978; Dalla Costa & James 1972).

5. Capital accumulation is a global process; all parts of the world form a single system. This has been true since the era of "primitive accumulation" (which Marx describes in *Capital*, vol. 1, 1973); it was equally true in the maturation period of the nineteenth century, and remains true in the current period of "socialist accumulation."[3] This means that gender oppression in the periphery cannot be analyzed without reference to the process of accumulation at the center (i.e., the industrial core of the West and Japan). This chapter attempts to show how capitalist accumulation in the West has dramatically transformed gender relations in the Third World, and thus transformed the material basis for struggle.

A MODEL OF CAPITALIST ACCUMULATION AND GENDER ON A WORLD SCALE

Figure 5.1 provides a schema for analyzing the impact of capital on gender showing the interrelationships between the core and periphery. It is derived from Marx's reproduction schemes in the second volume of *Capital*, and developed by Harry M. Cleaver (1978). Whereas Marx uses this to discuss the nature of crises arising from disproportional development between sectors of production, the model reveals the interconnections

Figure 5.1
Circuits of Production and Social Reproduction in Core and Periphery

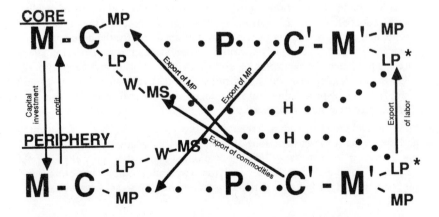

between capital and gender in the core and periphery. It develops the circuits of capital to reveal the reproduction of labor power and thus the fundamental role of gender within capitalist production.

The circuit of industrial capital in the core and periphery can be represented by the following expression:

$$M -- C \ldots P \ldots C' -- M' \qquad (M < M')$$

In the circuit of industrial capital, M (money) is advanced to buy necessary inputs for production MP and LP (means of production and labor power). The production process (P) leads to an outflow of commodities (C') whose value exceeds value of the inputs and which is then sold for M (money). The circuit is then repeated as long as $M' > M$ by a satisfactory amount (the rate of profit).

The circuit of social reproduction in core and periphery can be represented as follows:

$$LP -- W -- MS \ldots H \ldots LP*$$

The reproduction of labor power (a fundamental condition for the circuit above) takes place in a parallel way: wages (W) are exchanged for means of subsistence (MS), which are transformed by households (H) into new labor power, available to be sold for wages (W) in the next round. Unpaid housework lowers the value of labor power and hence lowers the cost to the capitalist in the next round.

Interconnections of circuits in the core and periphery, including social reproduction, can be seen in Figure 5.1 The interrelationship between the circuits in core and periphery takes a number of important forms.

Flows of Capital from Core to Periphery (and Return Flow of Profit). Foreign investment (and, more recently, finance capital from banks and international agencies such as the IMF) have provided a tremendous stimulus to the growth of capital in the Third World. This occurred first through the import-substitution policies of the 1960s, which gave considerable stimulus to the rise of a new capitalist class and a new manufacturing sector. The capital flows are indicated by the line joining M in the core to M in the periphery (for data, see Fröbel et al. 1980).

Flows of Commodities. The export-oriented economies of the periphery export consumer goods and raw materials to the core, which enter into the means of subsistence and production of workers and capitalists in that sector, lowering the value of labor power, and also cheapening the production of commodities in the core. Their continued reliance on the industrialized West for the import of the capital goods required for manufacturing makes the peripheral economies extremely dependent upon manufactured exports as a source of revenue. The highly competitive environment of export economies intensifies the need for cheap labor. These flows are indicated by the line adjoining C' in the periphery to MS and MP in the core, and C' in the core joining MP in the periphery.

Flows of Labor. The relative surplus population of the peripheral countries leads to the export of (male) labor to work in, for example, the Middle East and the export of (female) labor to the bars and brothels of Western Europe. The influx of tourist dollars in the periphery leads to a boom in the service sector, especially sex-related industries. These flows are indicated by the line joining LP^* in the periphery to LP^* in the core.

The crisis of capital that began in the late 1960s has manifested itself in declining profitability, declining productivity, the end of the accumulation boom of the post-1945 period, and the radical transformation of the "social structure of accumulation" (the relationship of capital to labor, labor to labor, capital to capital, and government to economy) (Bowles & Edwards 1985). This crisis resulted from a breakdown in capital's ability to impose work in the factory, household, and school and to suppress social revolt in the center as well as in the periphery (e.g., Vietnam). The social structures of accumulation that underlay the twenty-five years of expansion after 1945 were eroded and the system entered into a new period of crisis (Cleaver 1978).

Conditions of profitable accumulation include: *Attempts to restore control over the rate of surplus value in the core through both absolute and relative forms of surplus value extraction* (increased work, lower wages, and increased productivity). Recession/depression has been used as a weapon to restore control over the wage and reimpose divisions within the working class (e.g., renewed racism against blacks and many Asian and nonwhite immigrants in the United States and an antifeminist backlash).

A new international division of production and labor. The impact of the shifting of production out of the high-wage core to the low-wage periphery has been a proliferation of manufacturing for export, free production zones, and increased flows of capital. Cheap commodities (exported to workers in the core) and high rates of return on investment capital both help offset the tendency toward a falling rate of profit in the core.[4] This means a further level of global integration of class and gender relations, and thus of class struggle. Capital, labor, and commodity flows enter into global calculations of the rate of profit. Global recession has further concentrated the locus of economic decision making in the hands of few huge multinational firms which direct those flows. Furthermore, the IMF and World Bank directly control many national economies through these flows.

An increase in the number of women in the wage-labor force. Estimates are that between 70 to 90 percent of new jobs in manufacturing are occupied by women, with a preponderance of these in the 14 to 24-year age group. Wages are typically 25 to 50 percent lower than those received by men for the same jobs, and turnover rates range from 40 to 100 percent per year. Also, an increase in the use of child labor has been noted (one estimate puts the number at fifty-four million in 1977) (Fröbel et al. 1980).

The superexploitation of women engaged in the newly generated employment through: (1) increased intensity of work; (2) the lengthening of the work day; and (3) the establishment of wages below the value of labor power (i.e., the worker is not guaranteed all of the conditions that ensure the reproduction of his/her labor power).[5] This creates the need for subsistence activity (scavenging, petty trading, prostitution, migration back to the countryside, theft, etc.). This mechanism means that the cost of reproducing workers is externalized by capital, and either passed on to noncapitalist or traditional sectors, or thrown back to the larger family unit which ekes out a bare minimum subsistence.

IMPACT OF THE CRISIS ON GENDER RELATIONS

Marx's analysis of the process by which changes in the technical division of labor transform the social (and sexual) division of labor offers important insights into processes currently operating in the periphery. In *Capital*, volume 1, chapter 15, he reveals how the introduction of machinery (since it lightened the physical exertion required) permitted the use of women and children in factories for the first time. This in turn led to important changes in both the family and in the process of social reproduction.

Parallel processes are operating in the periphery as women and children get drawn into capitalist production in both traditional forms and in the newer electronics and computer-based industries. As Marx foresaw, an international divison of labor has emerged in which exploitation in the center rests on the "veiled slavery" and child labor of the periphery. This process has been intensified by the crisis of the 1970s and 1980s as capital seeks lower costs of production globally, and seeks to move manufacturing increasingly out of the high-waged sectors of the center into the low-wage periphery.

The surplus labor economies ensure low wages, and the preexisting sexism (in many forms) provides a suitable basis for the exploitation of women workers.[6] In addition, foreign exchange constraints imposed on the periphery by the shrinking trade of the 1980s and growing protectionism have encouraged the promotion of tourism (and thus the sexual services industry) as a source of foreign exchange. The particular form of exploitation and sexual oppression that arises depends on both the degree of exposure to the world economy and the preexisting patterns of patriarchy and cultural forms of oppression. Nash has distinguished forms of sexual oppression that are laid over existing patriarchal patterns from those that are newly created. Male dominance and patriarchy, she argues, are distinct and require separate analyses (Nash, this volume).

Exposure to the world market includes the pattern of colonial history, forms of capitalist penetration, and state policies toward, for example, foreign investment, export zones, labor unions, and the rural areas. The degree to which sexual oppression becomes a significant element in the pattern of development, and the particular forms of oppression that arise reflect the changing relation of a particular society to the world-economy, the particular patterns of development followed, and the preexisting patriarchal divisions.

Three tendencies can be distinguished: (1) the intensification of existing forms of gender subordination; (2) decomposition of existing forms; and (3) recomposition of new forms of gender subordination. Factory work in export-oriented factories exhibits in some cases all of these three tendencies: for example, the fathers' authority over their daughters may be strengthened in spite of the wages earned by the women. On the other hand, early marriages may be circumvented, but at the expense of commodifying women in the open market so that they may compete for husbands. Women are also subject to the new authority of men as supervisors and bosses in the factory (Elson & Pearson 1981: 157–59).

Since women's role remains defined primarily by their role in reproduction, entry into the export-production market, whether in agriculture or industry, while changing the traditional division of labor, often serves only to reinforce existing gender oppression.[7] Mies's study of the lace makers of Narsupur revealed a growing feminization of production, but the wage-work done by women was considered simply an extension of their role as housewives as they continued to bear all of the burden of domestic labor, while the men retreated from active wage earning into nonproduction jobs. Exposure to the world market in this case did not challenge existing patriarchal concepts or provide social power for women, but reinforced the earlier ideology of female seclusion. The result was a polarization of both gender and class (Mies 1982). On the other hand, rural migration from agricultural areas as a result of increased productivity brought about by capitalist growth (Bell 1986) has often left women as heads of households in rural areas, and increased (at least temporarily) their social power and also their social burdens and responsibilities.

In Malaysia, over 80 percent of all jobs in the electronics industry were occupied by women in 1980, and over 70 percent of all unskilled textile workers were women. These two industries together accounted for about two-thirds of total manufacturing exports in 1980 (Yun 1984). Again the role of women in production was defined by their role in the domestic sphere, and their weak position in the labor market reinforced their subordination in the domestic sphere; their wages were seen as secondary to their role in the family.

Several factors specific to young women in Malaysia reinforce both their subordination and lower wages in the factory: (1) their double work (both waged and unwaged) leaves them little time for political involvement; (2) cultural patterns reinforce docility and mitigate any predisposition toward aggressive labor struggles; and (3) since young women are not the only breadwinners in their families, they feel less pressure to struggle for wages and are more easily pressured into overtime (Halim 1983).

Cultural factors everywhere reinforce sexual oppression. For example, the principle of "reciprocity" in Malaysia reinforces control over women within multinational factories in Malaysia (McLellan 1985). Buddhism in Thailand provides an important justification for sexual oppression and eases the transformation of traditional sexual patterns into the modern sexual services industry (Karnjanauksorn 1987).

The interconnections between the circuits of production and reproduction in the core and periphery have had a dramatic effect on all aspects of gender relations. A few of these changes can be briefly summarized.

The cheapening of the commodities that enter into the subsistence of workers in the core permits a lowering of the value of labor power. Declining wages have led to the increase of the two-wage family as more women are required to enter the wage-labor force to maintain family income. This relative surplus value strategy tends to augment profits at the center and to restore control over labor in that sector of the world-economy. The shift toward services, in addition, entails a general shift from traditional high- to low-wage activities. The demise of the blue-collar worker in the United States is complemented by the rise of the same, although without the protection of unions and labor legislation, in the periphery.

Mies argues that the working class has become divided into free (male) proletarians and marginalized, unfree (female) labor. This draws a dramatic, if not entirely accurate picture of the impact of the changes of the last ten years or so on gender. Mies also believes that the world is now divided into dichotomous areas of consumption in the core and production in the periphery (Mies 1986). This is clearly not factually correct, but it serves heuristically to remind us of the dramatically lower standards of living of over 80 percent of the people living in the periphery.

Women have become increasingly integrated in the international circuits of capital, not only by their entry into low-wage manufacturing, but also as a result of sex tourism (particularly in Asia) and by the export of women to the core as prostitutes, mail brides, bar girls, and so on. One estimate is that 200,000 Thai women are working as prostitutes in Europe (Karnjanauksorn 1987). A burgeoning capitalist class in the periphery is able to exploit women in new and more elaborate ways, drawing on the unlimited supply of labor into the sexual services industry.[7]

Increased linkages with international capital through foreign investment and finance capital flows (resulting from the increased levels of debt) have resulted in a greater degree of exposure and vulnerability of the periphery to the world-economy.

The patterns of consumption in the periphery increasingly encourage women to adopt Western notions of beauty and sexuality (as seen in the growth of cosmetics industries, diet consciousness, etc.).

FORMS OF RESISTANCE

While a complete analysis of gender struggles requires a detailed examination of the content and circulation of existing movements, a few theoretical implications will be suggested here. Many autonomous struggles have risen in response to the intensified gender exploitation, including campaigns against violence, rape, dowry murders, prostitution, and labor conditions, as well as campaigns against industrial accidents and harmful consumer products (Mies 1986: 230). There is a newly emerging feminist movement in much of the periphery. A persistent problem is the linking of feminist struggles with the concerns of the traditional (Marxist) left who have long ignored this issue in both theory and practice (Bell 1982). Women's struggles have tended to remain isolated. While this isolation has allowed the struggles to develop their own autonomous content and form, they have not yet broken male-defined conceptions of struggle, revolution, and socialism.

Maria Mies ("Towards a Feminist Perspective of a New Society") suggests important new directions for struggle. First, there is a need to develop a feminist concept of labor, based on biological and social reproduction, not simply on the fetishized notion of production of *things*. Secondly, the struggles must reject what she calls the "colonizing" dualisms based on class, gender, and the separation of people from nature. Thirdly, there exists a basis for unity of struggles by all women centered around their collective participation in the spheres of production, consumption, and reproduction (including fertility) (Mies 1986).

The relationship between women in the core and periphery is a contradictory one in that struggles in one sector may intensify the exploitation of women in the other (and vice versa). But this by no means denies the importance of maintaining and building linkages. Indeed, the strength of these struggles will depend on both the degree to which autonomous struggles are linked together into a movement against capitalist exploitation as well as patriarchy, and the degree to which these struggles circulate.

NOTES

1. For a fuller discussion of this understanding of the central categories in Marx's analysis, and for a critique of the orthodox (reified) view of these categories, see Bell 1977; and Cleaver 1978.

2. Marx's crisis theory distinguishes between the possibility and necessity of crises (see Bell & Cleaver 1982 for an elaboration). It is important to note that gender struggles in the center, in the 1960s and 1970s, were very significant in providing one source of the crisis of capital. Workers' struggles (those of both men and women) in the center led to increased exploitation of workers in the periphery in the late 1970s and 1980s.

3. This point was thoroughly grasped by Marx, who analyzed capital in all phases of its development, beginning with the period of "primitive accumulation," as a

global process. Some important aspects of Marx's analysis have been developed in the world-systems approach.

4. The falling rate of profit tendency should not be understood as a mechanistic formula, but as one index (or summary) of the many complex variables which enter into the class struggle. The seminal discussion is in Marx's *Capital*, vol. 3, chaps. 13–15. For an interpretation see Bell & Cleaver 1982.

5. This implies that wages are below the normal subsistence level and survival depends on finding additional subsistence goods outside of the wage-labor market (Frank 1981: 161–74).

6. See Smith et al. 1984.

7. For further discussion of the theoretical distinction between the industrial reserve army and relative surplus population (stagnant, latent, floating, and *lumpen*, see Marx's *Capital*, vol. 1, chap. 25.

REFERENCES

Bell, Peter F. (1977). "Marxist Theory, Class Struggle and the Crisis of Capitalism." In Jesse Schwartz, ed., *The Subtle Anatomy of Capitalism*. Santa Monica, Calif.: Goodyear, 170–94.

―――― (1978). "'Cycles' of Class Struggle in Thailand." In A. Turton et al., eds., *Thailand: Roots of Conflict*. Nottingham: Spokesman, 51–79.

―――― (1982). "The Centrality of Feminism in Marxist Theory." Paper presented to Political Economy and Friends of Women Groups, Bangkok, Chalalongkorn University, August.

―――― (1986). "The Thai State, the Development of Capitalism and the Rural Areas in Thailand." *Journal of Political Economy*, 5, 3–4, 155–74

Bell, Peter F., and Harry M. Cleaver (1982). "Marx's Theory of Crisis as a Theory of Class Struggle." *Research in Political Economy*, 5, 189–62

Benería, Lourdes, ed. (1982). *Women and Development*. New York: Praeger.

Cleaver, Harry M. (1978). *Reading Capital Politically*. Austin: University of Texas Press.

Dalla Costa, Maria Rosa, and Selma James (1972). *The Power of Women and the Subversion of the Community*. Bristol: Falling Wall.

Elson, Diane, and Ruth Pearson (1981). "The Subordination of Women and the Internationalization of Factory Production." In K. Young et al., ed., *Of Marriage and the Market*. London: CSE Books, 144–66.

Frank, Andre Gunder (1981). *Crisis in the Third World*. New York: Holmes & Meier.

Fröbel, Folker, Jürgen Heinrichs, and Otto Kreye (1980). *The New International Division of Labor*. Cambridge: Cambridge University Press.

Halim, Fatimah (1983). "Workers' Resistance and Managerial Control: A Case Study of Male and Female Workers in West Malaysia." *Journal of Contemporary Asia*, 13, 2, 131–50.

Karnjanauksorn, Teeranat (1987). "Gender Relations, Sex-Related Services and the Development of the Thai Economy." Paper presented to the Association for Asian Studies, annual meetings, Boston, April 11.

McLellan, Susan (1985). "Reciprocity or Exploitation: Mothers and Daughters in the Changing Economy of Rural Malaysia." Working Paper No. 93, Women in International Development, Michigan State University.

Marx, Karl (1973). *Capital, Vol. 1*. New York: International.

Mies, Maria (1982). "The Lace Makers of Narsupur." In L. Benería, ed., *Women and Development*. New York: Praeger, 1–28

_____ (1986). *Patriarchy and Accumulation on a World Scale: Women in the International Division of Labor*. London: Zed.

Nash, June, ed. (1983). *Women, Men and the International Division of Labor*. Albany: SUNY Press.

Smith, Joan, Immanuel Wallerstein, and Hans-Dieter Evers, eds. (1984). *Households and the World-Economy*. Beverly Hills: Sage.

Yun, Hing Ai (1984). "Women and Work in West Malaysia." *Journal of Contemporary Asia*, 14, 2, 204–18.

6

"A Tailor Is Nothing without a Wife, and Very Often a Child": Gender and Labor-Force Formation in the New York Garment Industry, 1880–1920

Kathie Friedman Kasaba

Women entered the industrial labor force as the lowest-paid, most vulnerable, and severely exploited workers next to children. This has become an axiom of the feminist study of women and work, buttressed, of course, by an enormous amount of historical and empirical documentation. Scholars and activists, over the past twenty years or so, have drawn upon and generalized from these kinds of historical experiences, and come up with a set of varying perspectives purporting to explain, not merely women's exploitation in the labor force, but the perpetuation of women's subordination in society at large.

Some researchers have focused nearly exclusively on the structure and social relations of the workplace. Seen from this perspective, employers attempted to rationalize and/or enhance their control over the production process by substituting the cheaper labor of women for the more expensive labor of men.[1] Other scholars have looked into the problems of overcrowding in a sex-segregated labor market and stressed the determinant factors of gender ideology and gender conflict in the very structuring of employment opportunities. Accordingly, the crowding of women into a very few "women's trades" intensified the competition for work which had the further consequence of increasing women's special vulnerability to wage cutting, overwork, and marginalization.[2] Still others, who were unhappy with the existing unions or divorce settlements between productive and unproductive labor or production and reproduction, made an effort to fuse everything together in one grand reconciliation. These researchers sought to connect the manufacturing process with a labor market fragmented according to the dictates of family ideology and household economic practices for the purpose of explaining women's subordinate role in capitalist production.[3]

The debates eventually wound down, in part because of the increased recognition that the diversity of perspectives could themselves be linked to the historically complex and variable ways in which women were drawn into waged labor. But above all, the various viewpoints had been reduced to one simple common denominator. Accordingly, the common characteristic of female employment has been its price. Women, quite simply, have had the unenviable capacity throughout history to underbid, undercut, replace, and displace more skilled and thus higher-waged male workers. This unique vulnerability of women whenever and wherever they have entered the labor market has been considered the basis for the weakening of labor's overall bargaining power.

This is an admittedly oversimplified portrayal of debates on the use of female labor power in manufacturing industry. The objective of this chapter is to use some of the insights derived from these analyses of women and work in order to clarify the social processes by which a category of particularly vulnerable laborers is created and maintained. I will attempt this broader task by examining a historical situation that is probably considered unlikely and anomalous from the previously mentioned perspectives, or at least unorthodox.

During the course of the nineteenth and early twentieth centuries it became clear to at least New York garment manufacturers that all women were not the same, insofar as their labor-force behavior was concerned. Married women and mothers seemed to prefer to combine waged industrial homework with their unwaged domestic obligations. Unmarried teenage daughters could be increasingly spared from unpaid household drudgery and released to earn their keep in the relative liberty of the factory workroom among girlfriends. Similarly, during this period, it became clearer to garment manufacturers, as well as to their increasingly displaced female employees, that not all male wage earners were the same. Some men were clearly in a more vulnerable position than other men with regard to the price of their labor. But even more challenging to the simplest-common-denominator perspective on female labor was the existence, in the last quarter of the nineteenth century, of a group of men who fortuitously appeared on the New York City labor market just when ready-made garment manufacture was set to take off. These men, the "Columbus tailors" to-be, the "green immigrants," were more attractive as an exploitable labor force than even the victimized sewing woman, combining her housework with wage work, and her own labor with her children's labor.

In the earliest days of the production of custom-made clothing, the workers were nearly all men. With the development of "outside shops" from the "outwork system" the employment of women began, leading eventually to their monopoly over the production of fitted waistcoats and trousers. Similarly, in the larger "inside shops," especially in the manufacture of pants, vests, and coats, women were employed almost exclusively. In 1860, out of a total of 397 persons employed in New York and Brooklyn in the manufacture of cloaks and mantillas, 379 were women. In the German immigrant-dominated "family system" of clothing production women workers were numerous, just as they were in the more isolated homework system (Pope 1905: 28, 55; Stansell 1986: 105–29).

But in report after report on conditions in the New York garment industry toward the end of the century, investigators noted the increasing competition between male and female employees, as men gradually replaced women workers at a variety of tasks. According to New York Factory Investigators, in the shops manufacturing pants, vests, coats, and cloaks the percentage of women to the total number employed was: in 1888, 41 percent; in 1891, 28 percent; in 1896, 26 percent; and in 1900, 25 percent (Pope 1905: 57).

Writing in 1902, Mabel Willett tried to understand why, in New York, which was by far the largest center of garment production in the country, women constituted the smallest percentage of employees, next to children. If "the work of women is cheaper," Willett reasoned, then we would expect the low cost production of garments to be characterized by an especially large percentage of women workers (1968: 53–54).

Testimony to the fact that New York specialized in low-cost clothing production were the threats meted out to labor organizers in other states by their employers: "We will get our work made in New York" (USIC, 1901: 319). By 1919, commenting on the previous twenty-five years of proportional decline for women workers in the clothing industry, Edith Abbott explained it in these terms: "The chief influence . . . which has tended to diminish the proportion of women employed has been the invasion of the industry by the Russian Jews, which began shortly before 1880" (1919: 229). Abbott was just one of the many public and private social investigators to comment on the peculiar fit of the Jew in the garment industry.

The industry itself was peculiarly fitted for the employment of the grade of labor which they could furnish. It suited their lack of capital and physical strength, yet it offered excellent opportunity for the exercise of the dexterity which has been mentioned as one of their prominent characteristics. Furthermore, it did not interfere with their peculiar religious customs. It is not surprising, therefore, that the clothing industry absorbed the great majority of the newcomers. (Pope 1905: 50)

According to the 1901 Industrial Commission on Immigration,

The Jew occupies a unique position in the clothing trade. His physical strength does not fit him for manual labor. His instincts lead him to speculation and trade. His individualism unsuits him for the life of a wage-earner, and especially for the discipline of a labor organization. For these reasons, when the Jew first lands in this country he enters such light occupations as sewing, cigar making, shoemaking, etc. Only about 11 percent of the Jewish immigrants were tailors in Europe. The reason why so many of them take up that occupation in America is because the work is light. (USIC 1901: 325)

As Russian Jews increasingly entered the trade, one scenario was that former employees, the young German, Irish, and native-born American women workers, refused to accept the reduced wage which would have been necessary to compete with and exclude the immigrant. Instead, about 1500 to 2500 women were driven out of the trade and moved into other lines of work which they found more remunerative, particularly work in department stores and offices (Pope 1905: 56). Those who remained, however, the finishers and edgebasters, who had not yet been replaced by men, saw their wages decline by one-fifth, while their hours of labor rose (USIC 1901: 368).

In the remainder of this chapter I will address why and how these male Russian Jewish immigrants found themselves in a position to undercut and replace women workers at a typically "female trade," and in contradistinction to the expectations of the perspectives outlined previously. Was it because of their unique Jewish racial characteristics—a question we would without hesitation reject at present—despite the arguments of the Industrial Commission that the Jewish people, after all, "are peculiarly eager to earn a big day's wages, no matter at what sacrifice" (USIC 1901: 346). Willett observed that "the Jewish tailor is quick, alert, and above all, ambitious to rise from the grade of laborer to that of controller of labor . . . and with this object in view . . . the Jewish coatmaker will work with tireless energy" (1968: 38). Or could the position of the Russian Jewish tailors have been the consequence of their distinctly *masculine* characteristics when exercised in the labor process—a question we would unfortunately only hesitantly reject today.

The "task system" of clothing manufacture which accompanied immigrant Jews to New York between 1876 and 1882 became known as "the most ingenious and effective engine of overexertion known to modern industry" (USIC 1901: 346). A combination of cooperation between increasingly specialized and speedy workers on a team, a fixed piece-rate payment system, and increasing numbers of coats per task and tasks per day may have explained to some investigators why women lacked the endurance to hold their own in the trade (USIC 1901: 368). But this image of the superiority of male strength, speed, and dexterity in the 1880s and 1890s was contradicted by the very harsh demands of needlework prior to 1880, on the heavy and cumbersome foot-powered machines and the physically taxing hand irons used for pressing (Pope 1905: 43).

Oddly, but perhaps not entirely coincidentally, the "image" of the Jewish tailor promoted by social investigators sharply contradicted the dominant view of masculinity in this era as embodied by the male manual laborer. Preceding comments by contemporaries on the peculiar fit of the Jew in the clothing industry stand out in this context, not so much for their racist sterotyping, as for their attributing of traditionally feminine characteristics to immigrant men. Nimble fingers and a penchant for endurance made up for the frail physiques Jewish immigrant men supposedly, like women, presented in the labor market. Just as motherhood was said to naturally and universally constrain women's labor-force behavior and direct it toward maternally compatible occupations like homework, Jewish religious proscriptions against Saturday work were said to particularly suit them for sweatshops. Finally, neither women nor Jewish men were expected by contemporaries to unionize as a consequence of their common lack of devotion to permanent wage-earning status.

In the search for more acceptable and comprehensive explanations we need to inquire into the historical processes and social relationships that allowed Russian Jewish men to be categorized as a particularly vulnerable, powerless, controllable, and low-cost labor force. In this endeavor insights from the feminist study of women and work should not be scrapped, but instead broadened and extended to account as well for the labor-force position of men. The notion that the allocation of women's labor to various tasks is determined within a "family economy" and related to the activities of other family or household members, in particular, should have been applied to the study of men's labor-force behavior long ago. The household or family influences on the use of male labor should be equally scrutinized. The already documented importance of the diversity of women's nonwaged contributions to the reproduction of proletarian households should be linked to the waged labor-force position of their brothers, husbands, fathers, and sons.

Insights derived from the study of the development of the capitalist world-economy, and the interstate system, specifically concerning household income-pooling practices, could also be broadened and extended to the analysis of male Russian Jewish participation in the New York garment trades (Smith, Wallerstein & Evers 1984). How was it that specifically *Russian Jews* arrived en masse at the port of New York just in time to participate in the enormous expansion of the ready-made clothing industry?

The economic destiny of a Russian-Jewish tailor "sweating" himself, his family, neighbors, and *"landsleit"* on New York's lower east side began to be determined in nineteenth-century Europe. The effectiveness of these individuals in the competition to secure a livelihood from sewing was structured, in part, by the global processes, political and economic, that organized their European departure, entry into the United States, and incorporation into New York City's "great immigrant metier."

Imperial Russia's defeat in the Crimean War during the mid-nineteenth century considerably reduced her position within the European states-system, leading to intensified competition with France and Great Britain. Highlighting certain inadequacies of the multiethnic imperial system, the defeat spurred a series of domestic reforms designed to stabilize imperial rule and meet the international military competition. One of these reforms involved formally emancipating the serfs in 1861, a necessary precondition for population movement. Russian policy on migration until the 1860s had been dominated by a net inflow of immigrants, mostly German settlers. Emigration was severely restricted.

The unification and rapid industrialization of Germany in the 1870s challenged Russia, pushed her into a Western alliance, and severely threatened the security of her western borders. In the attempt to defend this multiethnic western frontier from the 1880s on, Russia shifted to a policy of the selective release of certain social groups. State emigration policies became one means to strengthen "the state" by additionally defining it as "a nation." Increased "Russification" of the state promoted the exodus of non-Russians. The emigration of ethnic Russians continued to be formally prohibited. The differential rate of emigration between the various nationalities was ultimately a combined product of the individual minority's sense of historical persecution or disadvantage and of intensifying discriminatory imperial policy as earlier edicts on minority "privileges" were invoked and enforced (Skocpol 1979: 82–94, 128–30; Pearson 1983: 100; Aronson 1977: 361–62).

In the 1880s and 1890s, Jews almost monopolized emigration from the empire, reaching 91.6 percent of the total in the peak year of 1891. Between 1899 and 1901 the Jewish proportion of the total outflow averaged nearly 44 percent, compared to the Russian, at 4.4 percent (Pearson 1983: 101). Imperial Russia's strategies for achieving industrial development and dominance in the global competition involved, in part, the defining and selective targeting of particular social groups for elimination, whether through the liberalization of emigration policy for minorities only, the concentration and overcrowding of minorities in one locale (as in the Pale of Settlement), the sponsoring of pogroms, or other forms of Russification. Russian Jews were created as an economically and politically vulnerable social group prior to their arrival at New York port.

The next question that must be answered in an analysis of the labor-market position of Russian Jewish men is why they entered the United States at all. Why did they not remain in Germany rather than board the ships for New York? Mary Antin, reminiscing about her youth in Polotsk, Russia, provided a simple but clear response with her comment, "America was in everybody's mouth" (1912; as quoted in Raphael 1979: 102). Of equal importance was the fact that, despite many decades of nativist movements and domestic political pressure to protect its borders from new immigrant arrivals, the United States had left them relatively open until the 1920s, and was thus able to profit from the European power conflict.

Since the 1840s Jews had been immigrating in fairly large numbers to New York. By the 1880s, despite official denials of assisting their brethren, German and central European Jews in New York and elsewhere, through a number of organizations, were sponsoring and organizing Russian Jewish immigration. The Jewish Colonization Association (Baron de Hirsch Fund) arranged with the governments of Russia and Romania to have passports provided without cost to Jewish emigrants who were recommended by the association, on the condition they would swear never to return to their native land. Such passports could be obtained within a few days compared to the weeks or months of waiting to pay for one as an isolated individual. Local branches of the association also gave advice on where to settle in the United States and issued tracts detailing these locations (USImC 1911: 66). "Frequently, members of immigrant aid committees were employers and would combine philanthropy with business. In a mixture of self-interest and genuine concern, they would conduct the immigrants directly to their shops" (Tcherikower, 1961: 143).

The continuous supply of vulnerable "green immigrant" labor to the shops of their so-called brethren fueled the expansion of the clothing industry and provided some Russian Jewish men the experience and contacts necessary to move from the position of wage earner to that of controller of labor. In the process they exploited each other, themselves, and their families in order to support those they had left behind in Europe. A Galician newspaper reported in 1900 that almost every Jewish family in Taronberg had a relative in America who helped support them. Between 1908 and 1910, 58 percent of Jewish immigrants landing in New York had prepaid tickets from American relatives, compared to only 30 percent for all immigrants (Raphael 1979: 99).

It is in the very process of migration, as well as in the formation and maintenance of immigrant households in immigrant communities that income pooling becomes operative. In the case of migrant labor systems and immigrant labor, it is essential to look beyond the confines of the co-residential family unit for income pooling. The basis for the low-waged controllable nature of male Russian Jewish labor resided, in part, in income pooling between family members in Russia and those on New York's lower east side. It resided in the practice of nominally similar groups assisting and organizing the emigration of their so-called co-ethnics. And once in America, the "Columbus tailor," although not necessarily willing, was able to offer himself up on the labor market for reduced wages because he continued to receive a degree of material assistance from the various immigrant benevolent societies, or *Landsmanshaftn*.

About half of all Jewish immigrants who arrived in New York between 1880 and 1923 belonged to an independent *landsmanschaft* at one time in their lives. Garment employers, at various levels, also manipulated *landsleit* sentiments as a means of keeping labor discipline in their shops and shutting unions out (Weisser 1985: 5, 83; Kaganoff 1986). Not infrequently, contractors and employees belonged to the same societies that would loan out small sums of money to tide a worker over during slack seasons of the trade (Pope 1905: 188; Tenenbaum 1986).

Finally, but scarcely incidentally, within the first-generation immigrant clothing worker's household the tailor knew he could control the labor and command the income of his wife and children. During the busy season he "sweated" himself, his wife, and particularly his daughters, just as he was "sweated" within the contractor's web. Later, during the dull seasons of the trade, he knew he could rely on family members' contributions from peddling and other kinds of self-employment and nonwaged income, thus completing the circuit of income pooling (Pope 1905: 172–73; Eaton 1885; Ewen 1985: 94–109).

Although "a tailor is nothing without a wife, and very often a child," the social relationships creating and sustaining this category of particularly vulnerable laborers extend well beyond the confines of the co-residential family unit.[4] They extend well beyond the organization and social relations of the sweatshop, and beyond the crowding of Jews into light industry. They extend beyond the New York City labor market and the political boundaries of the United States. The historical processes and social relationships underlying the relative vulnerability of the male Russian Jewish garment worker were to be found in the construction of subordinate ethnicities and genders in a world-economy.

NOTES

1. For an extensive statement of this position, see Rubery 1980. Continuing debates on how to analyze the workplace once gender is recognized as a significant variable may be found in Crompton & Mann 1986.

2. For an excellent review and critique of labor-market perspectives on sex inequality see Blau & Jusenius 1976. A sophisticated historical treatment of gender ideology and conflict at work may be found in Rose 1986.

3. Louise A. Tilly (1981) puts this approach to work in order to understand the conditions under which women engage in collective action.

4. Conrad Carl, a German-born New York tailor, testified to the pervasiveness of this household economic strategy before a Senate investigating committee (USCEL 1885: 414; quoted in Stansell 1986: 117).

REFERENCES

Abbott, Edith (1919). *Women in Industry*. New York: Appleton.

Antin, Mary (1912). *The Promised Land*. New York: Houghton Mifflin.

Aronson, I. M. (1977). "The Prospects for the Emancipation of Russian Jewry During the 1880s." *Slavonic and East European Review*, 55, 3, July, 348–369.

Blau, Francine D., and Carol L. Jusenius (1976). "Economists' Approaches to Sex Segregation in the Labor Market: An Appraisal." *Signs*, 1, 3, part 2, 181–200.

Crompton, Rosemary, and Michael Mann, eds. (1986). *Gender and Stratification*. New York: Basil Blackwell.

Eaton, Isabel (1885). "Receipts and Expenditures of Certain Wage-Earners in the Garment Trades." *Quarterly Publications of the American Statistical Association*, June.

Ewen, Elizabeth (1985). *Immigrant Women in the Land of Dollars: Life and Culture on the Lower East Side, 1890–1925*. New York: Monthly Review Press.

Kaganoff, Nathan M. (1986). "The Jewish Landsmanschaftn in New York City in the Period Preceding World War I." *American Jewish History*, 76, 1, September, 56–66.

Pope, Jesse E. (1905). *The Clothing Industry in New York*. University of Missouri, Social Science Series, No. 1.

Raphael, Marc Lee (1979). *Jews and Judaism in a Midwestern Community: Columbus, Ohio 1840–1975*. Columbus: Ohio Historical Society.

Rose, Sonya O. (1986). "'Gender at Work': Sex, Class and Industrial Capitalism." *History Workshop Journal*, No. 21, Spring, 113–31.

Rubery, Jill (1980). "Structured Labor Markets, Worker Organization and Low Pay." In Alice H. Amsden, ed., *The Economics of Women and Work*. New York: St. Martin's, 242–70.

Skocpol, Theda (1979). *States and Revolutions*. Cambridge: Cambridge University Press.

Smith, Joan, Immanuel Wallerstein, and Hans-Dieter Evers, eds. (1984). *Households and the World-Economy*. Beverly Hills: Sage.

Stansell, Christine (1986). *City of Women: Sex and Class in New York, 1789–1860*. New York: Knopf.

Tcherikower, Elias (1961). *The Early Jewish Labor Movement in the United States*. New York: YIVO Institute for Jewish Research.

Tenenbaum, Shelly (1986). "Immigrants and Capital: Jewish Loan Societies in the United States, 1880–1945." *American Jewish History*, 76, 1, September, 67–77.

Tilly, Louise (1981). "Paths of Proletarianization: Organization of Production, Sexual Division of Labor, and Women's Collective Action," *Signs*, 7, 2, Winter, 400–17.

U.S. Congress, Senate Committee on Education and Labor (USCEL). (1885). "Testimony as to the Relations between Labor and Capital," 48th Congress.

U.S. Immigration Commission (USImC) (1911). *Emigration Conditions in Europe*. Reports of the Immigration Commission, 4, 61st Congress, 3d session, S. Doc. 748. Washington, D.C.: U.S. Government Printing Office.

U.S. Industrial Commission (USIC) (1901). *Reports of the Industrial Commission on Immigration*, 15. Washington, D.C.: U.S. Government Printing Office.

Weisser, Michael R. (1985). *A Brotherhood of Memory: Jewish Landsmanshaftn in the New World*. New York: Basic Books.

Willett, Mabel Hurd (1902). *The Employment of Women in the Clothing Trade*. New York: Columbia University Studies in the Social Sciences, No. 42 (reprinted edition, New York: AMS, 1968).

PART III

Race and Gender and the Creation of Work in the World-System

7

GENDER RELATIONS IN THE WORLD–ECONOMY: COMPETITION IN THE TEXTILE INDUSTRY, 1850–1900

Ann E. Forsythe and Roberto P. Korzeniewicz

This chapter examines changes in the organization of textile production in the period from 1850 to 1914. In particular, we will focus on the relationship between gender differentiation and transformations in the organization of textile production in Argentina, England, France, and Germany. We will show that the development of the social division of labor in the textile industry entailed the creation of new competitive forces both between enterprises and households located in different regions of the world-economy, and between women and men within the labor force. Furthermore, we will argue that processes of gender differentiation were integral to the development of the textile industry within the world-economy.

We begin by examining the basic features of the textile industry in the provinces of the interior of Argentina over the first half of the nineteenth century. During that time, the textile industry involved primarily the production of woolen goods destined for popular consumption. Production was carried out in households, where women did most (or all) of the spinning and weaving.

Women's handicraft textile production in Argentina was undermined after the 1850s. Most accounts explain the timing of this decline as an outcome of railroad expansion in the interior provinces of the country. According to these accounts, railroad expansion brought the competition of British imports to weigh heavily upon household production.

Rather than look only at conditions within Argentina to explain what happened to textile producers, we look at the changes within the organization of textile production in Europe that brought new competitive pressures to bear upon women handicraft producers in Argentina.

Capitalist entrepreneurs throughout Europe, facing the pressure of innovations in England's woolen industry after the 1850s, introduced mechanization and factory production in their own woolen industries during the 1860s and 1870s. Technical innovation and increased competition among European enterprises increased demand for Argentine wool in the world market, led to a significant decline in the price of European woolen goods, and resulted in dramatic increases in European woolen imports into Argentina. Great Britain lost the Argentine woolen market to other European competitors (such as France and Germany) at precisely the same time that we find evidence of a dramatic decline in handicraft textile production within Argentina.

The second part of the chapter focuses on mechanization in the European textile industry. Customary relations in the industry had severely constrained the growth of textile production prior to mechanization. In particular, these customary relations involved household control over the content and pace of work, as well as a division of labor involving all family members. Mechanization generated resistance by handicraft workers, who rapidly formed organizations to defend customary arrangements, as well as to restrict competition which had intensified with the breakdown of household control over the supply of labor.

Facing this resistance, and to offset the expense of investing in machines, capitalist entrepreneurs introduced women (and children) as nonskilled, low-paid, unorganized workers into the wool industry. Craft organizations were both cause and effect of new competitive pressures within the labor force: reacting to competition, male craft workers moved to restrict the employment and organization in craft associations of certain groups of workers (women and children), thereby creating reserves of workers that could be tapped by employers to avoid craft resistance to innovations.[1]

The new competitive pressures exerted by textile enterprises in England forced producers in the global textile industry to specialize, separating commodity-producing enterprises from labor-supplying households,[2] and competition was intensified both among enterprises and among suppliers of labor. The consequences of these developments were not evenly distributed among enterprises or suppliers of labor. In the latter case, they were clearly uneven by gender. For instance, women handicraft workers in the interior provinces of Argentina were rapidly impoverished by competition in textiles and the development of a wage-labor market centered around urban areas and commercial agriculture. There were new employment opportunities for women in the new textile and garment enterprises that grew around Buenos Aires after the late 1870s, but these were a restricted number of subordinate and lower-paid (relative to men) positions in a reconstituted social division of labor on a world scale. As in Europe, this outcome was in many respects shaped by the efforts of organized (male) workers to regulate competition in the labor market.

What we observe in this chapter is the process of the global divisioning of labor in the textile industry. As capitalist enterprises and households differentiated in the production of textiles—enterprises producing commodities, households supplying labor for enterprises—competition was intensified within each sphere.

On the one hand, competition intensified among textile producers, inducing two concurrent sets of processes: (1) further differentiation of households and enterprises in the textile industry globally; and (2) specialization among enterprises themselves. The latter, in turn, produced regional differentiation among enterprises, those specializing in raw wool production in Argentina and those specializing in textile production in Europe.

On the other hand, competition intensified among households, both as sites of manufacturing and as suppliers of labor. Again, competition occurred at two levels. First, the relatively higher level of wages in Argentina made industrial production relatively unprofitable there, while Argentina's global competitive advantage in commercial agriculture allowed the raw wool industry to flourish even in the context of high wages. This set in motion, but limited, the specialization of households and enterprises. Limited competition, which accounted for the (relatively high) level of wages in Argentina, was predicated upon a shortage of labor. The shortage of labor was itself relative, however; as the global division of labor deepened, competition became global. In the subsequent period, regional differentiation led to a relative decline in wages, and (relatively) low wages were sustained by the very lack of specialization in wage labor (see Smith et al. 1984).

Secondly, in Europe and Argentina the very competitive relations that compelled individual suppliers of labor to pool income and form households (or sustain them) created inequalities among households' members as competition structured claims on resources, including waged labor itself, and the level of wages. The results are rigid stratification systems by sex and age, organized around a new norm, the (adult male) family wage earner.

HOUSEHOLD PRODUCTION IN ARGENTINA IN THE EARLY NINETEENTH CENTURY

By the early nineteenth century, textile production in Argentina involved primarily the manufacture of woolen goods. Earlier, textile production in the northern areas of Argentina had involved cotton cultivation and cotton textile production as well. However, labor costs undermined the position of domestic producers of cotton textiles vis-à-vis their Peruvian counterparts and led to the virtual disappearance of cotton production by the early 1800s.[3] In the few pockets where it persisted, cotton production was either for personal use or was limited to the manufacture of traditional clothing.

By contrast, wool production presented a much more vigorous picture. Platt points out that "(t)he Argentines were a pastoral people" (1972: 21), and abundant references to wool production and trade confirm that much of the textile production in Argentina was in wool.[4] Most common was the production of clothing, woolen ponchos, saddle cloths, and blankets—in other words, goods intended for popular consumption. Oriented toward the production of wage goods, the wool industry maintained a "vitality" past the mid-nineteenth century, and was "more effectively defended against Peruvian competition" (Halperín Dongui 1975: 12). In short, whereas the cotton industry was confronted by intense competition from cheap Peruvian goods, wool production dominated domestic industry.

The interdependence of woolen textiles and sheep breeding in the economies of the provinces led to plentiful supplies of raw materials (including native *llama* and *vicuña*) and ensured the place of wool spinning and weaving early on. Both before and after independence in the 1810s, wool production in the provinces also faced little competition from abroad. There were limited imports of woolen goods, and these consisted of high-quality textiles for landowning and merchant classes.

Detailed information on the internal organization of textile production and the household is scant and inconclusive, although it is certain that production was centered in households, and that textile production was organized largely for sale in the market.[5] Yet it is difficult to ascertain the extent to which market production coincided with or was distinct from production for use, and the available historical data are insufficient to specify the sources of raw materials, the division of labor in the household, the system of payment for and collection of cloth, the relative contribution of textile production to the economy of the household, and the procurement of tools and machinery.

However, the available data suggest that there was little specialization between households, and that there were no major changes in the internal organization of textile production in Argentina during the period under consideration. For example, no historical sources mention the existence of any local or intraprovincial trade in yarn that would imply a division of labor among households between spinning and weaving. And one of the few studies that focuses on the organization of domestic textile production argues that in Córdoba there were no changes in production techniques during the nineteenth century (Assadourian 1983: 269).

Finally, household textile production appears to have involved primarily "individual women who slowly turned out coarse flannels on single-person handlooms after spinning the yarns on hand-spindles" (Brown 1979: 223). However, further elaboration of the division of labor in spinning and weaving and the allocation of labor within the household (men's, women's and children's) awaits a more thorough investigation of household production.

The extent to which the textile industry endured throughout the nineteenth century is the subject of some debate. Authors disagree on when and where the textile industry faltered and then crumbled. Many argue, for example, that soon after independence in the 1810s a sudden influx of cheap British imports rapidly ruined the domestic textile industry.

Some of these disagreements can be resolved by taking into account differences between cotton and wool. Many authors fail to acknowledge that there were minimal amounts of cotton textile production in Argentina by the time of the revolution,[6] and that the domestic textile industry was specialized in the production of specific items of popular consumption. British imports, on the other hand, were composed primarily of cottons and expensive, by popular standards, woolens. These British imports competed directly with Peruvian cottons, but not with domestic production of woolen textiles.

The information available on the survival/decline of the textile industry through the 1850s and 1860s is more inconclusive, and claims for the persistence as well as the ruin of the industry during those decades are each in some respects plausible. Halperín Dongui is probably the most accurate in summarizing the data from the 1869 census as follows: "The growing consumption of imported textiles does not seem to have struck a decisive blow at local handicraft production, for the census of 1869 was able to demonstrate, in the occupational structure of Northern and Central provinces, the part which domestic textile production still played in their economy" (1975: 90).

On the other hand, between 1869 and 1895 there was a virtual collapse of the textile industry. "In total, the number of weavers in Argentina declined by 54,653 in twenty-six years while the total population doubled" (Guy 1981: 76). By comparing data from the censuses of 1869 and 1895, we find that in the span of thirty years, women in the interior wove themselves into destitution.

When did textile household producers in Argentina succumb to the pressures of competition? Many have argued that the turning point occurred around mid-century with the arrival of the railroads.[7] Paul Goodwin (1977), on the other hand, shows that there already was an extensive commodity exchange between Buenos Aires and the interior prior to the railroad era.[8] Also, the railroads did not begin to reach the provinces of the interior until the 1870s, after competitive pressures in textiles had affected domestic producers.[9] Finally, emphasis on the railroad implies that the survival of domestic industries depended primarily on the margin of protection offered by transportation costs and that patterns of competition between domestic and foreign products were a function of transport costs alone.

The impact of the railroad must be considered in light of two concurrent developments in the social division of labor in the textile industry within the world economy.[10] First, in the 1850s, mechanization was widely implemented in the production of woolen textiles in England, reducing their price and expanding exports. Mechanization in the wool industry in France and Germany followed over the next two decades and had the same effect. As a consequence, in a context of intensive competition among European producers in the world-economy, European wool imports increased rapidly in Argentina. Secondly, from the point of view of the local textile producers, the price and availability of raw wool in Argentina was adversely affected by the introduction of sheep breeding for export purposes, which began in the 1840s and spread rapidly in the 1860s.

The increase in exports of raw wool from Argentina was matched by an increase in imports of woolen textiles from Europe. But while raw wool prices rose substantially in the world market, "product prices did not necessarily respond rapidly to increases in raw materials prices" (Jenkins & Ponting 1982: 144). It is probable that the prices of woolen goods were held down by competition among European manufacturers, which was intensified by the increasing uniformity of technological conditions in the European wool industry after 1860. In any case, this situation spelled doom for the women in the interior provinces of Argentina.

MECHANIZATION OF WOOL TEXTILE PRODUCTION IN EUROPE

Mechanization was part and parcel of three significant, concurrent developments. First, by launching an offensive against customary arrangements, mechanization allowed for capitalist enterprises to separate from, and compete against, household production. In the same stroke, mechanization allowed capitalist entrepreneurs to attack customary relations which had limited competition among producers in the textile industry. Thirdly, as these customary arrangements restricting competition among producers were undermined, new arrangements took shape through which workers in the textile industry were able to regulate competition anew. These arrangements were predicated upon the restructuring of gender relations. Altogether, these changes brought new and intense competitive pressures to bear upon textile production in the world-economy.

The destruction of customary arrangements simultaneously involved the creation of a market for labor, distinguishing waged from unwaged labor. Within the labor market, workers quickly moved toward limiting competitive pressures within the supply of labor by appealing to customary arrangements whereby men's labor was defined as skilled and higher-waged (than women's).

Clearly, women were not "unskilled" prior to mechanization in the textile industry, but the social and historical significance of skill, as a social category, derived from its relationship to the organization of guild production and apprenticeship: "skill" was itself defined customarily. On the other hand, women's labor was defined customarily as "natural" to them, and this was posed as the antithesis to skill.[11]

The introduction of mechanized wool production relied overwhelmingly on women's labor, and was in fact accomplished through the rigid use of gender differentiation. Based on the division of labor in household textile production and customary gender relations, relations between newly specialized suppliers of labor and entrepreneurs in the textile industry designated women as subordinate, and in this sense, unskilled labor. Craft workers—and this category itself is reconstituted over the period we are discussing—were able to restrict competitive pressures within the supply of labor by dividing workers into more or less noncompeting segments, first skilled and unskilled, later waged and unwaged. These new customary arrangements made unskilled female labor a sector of the labor force that could be paid substantially less than skilled/male labor. Moreover, women workers had little history of organizing to protect or preserve a craft, could be employed without loss of skills to attend machines, and eventually could be legitimately excluded from the waged-labor force altogether. The unwaged/nonworking woman was created toward the end of this period.

These characteristics were essential in the transition to factory production in Europe. Craft traditions, in which only men were involved, were a primary source of labor's resistance to mechanization. Guilds and households fought against losing control over the content and pace of work and even more against a loss of control over access to trades—hence to the labor market—which possession of craft skills conferred on labor. For their part, capitalists insisted that low wages were necessary to compensate for investments in machinery. The use of women's labor—unskilled and low-waged—addressed both of these constraints to mechanization (Forsythe 1983).

Mechanization of wool production began in England and quickly spread to the continent. In this sense, enterprises in England, having displaced household producers, set the pace of competition for textile production as a whole, and other producers either "caught up" or were displaced entirely.[12] In England, the peak rate of mechanization in the wool industry came in the 1850s and 1860s (Deane 1965: 169), and it consisted of two primary innovations: the introduction of machinery for the combing of wool (the process which prepares long wool for spinning and replaces the older carding methods) and the initiation of powerloom weaving (Jenkins & Ponting 1972: 102). Each of these processes employed predominantly women and children, and in general, despite the already low percentage of men in the cotton mills, "the demand for male labor in the wool industry was relatively lower than in cotton" (Jenkins & Ponting, 1972: 161). In fact, until the cost of steam-powered engines was reduced substantially in the 1850s, the use of women's labor, in place of men's labor, was a primary cost-reducing mechanism. "All the time that women earned much less than men, it was possible for manufacturers to make substantial economies by substituting one for the other in certain jobs, and this had a direct bearing on the profitability of technical innovation" (Gregory 1982: 76).[13]

As steam power secured the place of factory production over household production, so the place of women in the wool industry was similarly secured. While in 1850 male employment considerably exceeded the employment of women in the industry as a whole, well over half of the factories' workers were women, and from mid-century that proportion increased.

Women workers were consistently paid one-half to two-thirds the wages of male workers, and their positions in the production process were subordinate and unskilled.

Mechanization in France followed. Mechanized combing of wool was introduced in French industry in the 1850s, and between 1848/51 and 1860/62, the price of a kilo of combed wool fell 34%; it fell another 33% by 1880, and altogether it fell by 76% over the second half of the century (Levain, Rougerie & Straus 1984: 61). The impact of improvements in combing can be seen in the increase of wool production in its wake. Between 1850 and the end of the 1860s, the volume of wool textiles doubled, increasing another 42% from 1868/72 to 1891/96 (Levain, Rougerie & Straus 1983: 61).[14]

Not only did wool textile production accelerate from the 1850s, but wool exports increased 227% in the two decades following mid-century. However, the export of wool fabric increased even more dramatically— 286% in this period—representing further competitive gains from the mechanization of weaving in the French wool industry from the 1860s on (Levain, Rougerie & Straus 1983: 95). While the first mechanized looms were employed in Roubaix, which in turn became the center of French wool production, weaving on powerlooms was generalized throughout the industry in the 1870s. From this date, the quality, composition, and price of wool textiles changed. Equally important, by the late 1860s, production in factories overtook household production; for instance around Roubaix domestic production continued, but only in periods of expansion in the industry (Levain, Rougerie & Straus 1983: 111).

From 1870 until the eve of World War I, French production increased in response to world-market demand (Levain, Rougerie & Straus 1983: 60). French firms mechanized both in response to British competition and simultaneous with France's thrust toward the world-market.[15]

As in England, mechanized textile production marked the entry of women into wage labor in the factory; here again, women's wages were one-half to two-thirds of men's wages, and their positions unskilled and subordinate (Tilly & Scott 1978: 80).[16] In Roubaix, the census of 1872 showed that 50% of females over 15 were employed, 55% of these worked in the textile industry, and most of the latter were young and single, 82% under 30 years of age (Tilly & Scott 1978: 82). In the nation as a whole, 25% of all women worked for wages in 1860, and this proportion increased steadily throughout the century (Tilly & Scott 1978: 71). Of these, 10% were working in textiles in 1866. Women were 32% of the total waged-labor force in 1860, but 45% of workers in the textile industry in 1861 (Tilly & Scott 1978: 70, 152).[17]

A somewhat similar situation existed in Germany, where mechanization of the wool weaving industry proceeded from the late 1860s (Clapham 1923: 243).[18] Mechanization was more erratic than in France or England, and handicraft production of wool textiles persisted even into the twentieth century.

In Saxony, where "textile employment alone was responsible for (its) position as a relative 'industrial' region in 1861," wool production moved into factories after 1880; from this point, the overall number of textile workers increased as the number of handicraft workers declined (Tipton 1976: 125). In both Silesia and Westphalia, the wool industry declined substantially from around the 1840s to the 1860s, although the decrease in wool production was accompanied by an increase in cotton spinning in this period (Hamerow 1958: 242). However, the wool industry grew overall from the 1870s. Between 1875 and 1895, the labor force in wool production increased 35 percent. While spinners and weavers accounted for 65% of this increase, the number of workers in the preparatory processes grew a full 348% (Dawson 1908: 56). In 1875, the ratio of spinners and weavers to preparatory workers was 36.7 to 1; in 1895, it was 13 to 1. This is important to the extent that it reflects the subdividing of work and deskilling. While we don't have detailed information on the division of labor in textile enterprises in Germany, we suspect that these "auxiliary," subordinate positions were filled by women (and children).

Women's employment increased from mid-century (Quataert 1974: 37). In 1905, the only date for which we could find data, women were 46% of the textile labor force in Germany (Dawson 1908: 44).[19] Furthermore, "female employment remained predominantly unskilled labor and the 12 years between 1895 and 1907 recorded a decline in skilled working women from 6.1% to 5.8%" (Quataert, 1974: 42). Women's employment in industry generally increased faster than men's from 1882 to 1907 (35% to 28%). While women's employment in industry increased 38.3% from 1895 to 1907, compared to 35% for men (Quataert 1974: 41), the labor force in wool production more than doubled (Dawson 1908: 45). Women's participation increased more rapidly than men's precisely as the textile industry was increasingly centered in capitalist enterprises. Again, we can only hypothesize that this correlations means women comprised proportionately more of the labor force in capitalist enterprises in textiles.

Renate Bridenthal (1973) claims that overall wage differentials between men and women before World War I were on the order of 50 to 60 percent.[20] In the last quarter of the nineteenth century, "women's work life in factories tended to follow life- and family-cycle patterns. As single women, they took on factory work and later, after marriage and children, swelled the ranks of home industry in consumer goods production," principally garments (Quataert 1974: 271).

HOUSEHOLD PRODUCTION IN ARGENTINA IN THE MID- AND LATE-NINETEENTH CENTURY

Mechanization in Europe increased demand for raw wool, providing incentives for shifting commercial agriculture in Argentina toward the production of wool. In 1837, wool accounted for 7% of the value of exports from Buenos Aires, but from the 1840s onwards, the export of wool grew spectacularly, rising by 1875–1879 to half the value of Argentina exports (Diaz Alejandro 1970: 17). Horacio Giberti tell us: "The growth of exports was fabulous. In 1850, 76.8 tons of wool left the country, and this quantity was five times greater than that of a decade before; however, 12,445 tons were exported in 1855, and the amount reached 18,950 tons three years later. In 1875, these exports reached 90,720 tons. In 25 years exports had increased over a thousand times!" (1961: 152). Exports went chiefly to the United States and England, although wool was redistributed throughout Europe from England at this time.[21]

The increased consumption of Argentine wool in European markets was largely the result of the use of long wool made necessary by the intricacies of applying machinery to wool production (Clapham 1923: 172). The pace of growth of export production varied among different provinces in Argentina,[22] but around the mid-1850s the price of wool within Argentina rose prohibitively for local handicraft textile producers. According to Hilda Sábato, "The growing popularity of Argentine wool in European markets raised its price locally to such an extent that the manufacture of ordinary cloth by the primitive methods available in the old centers . . . ceased to make sense where British or French woolens were so much less expensive. Some very fine blankets were still being made in Córdoba in the 1860s, but they were enormously dear" (1982: 70).

Germany imported an increasing share of its yarn from abroad, England in particular, although the collapse of its sheep-breeding industry also occasioned an increase in its imports of raw wool,[23] of which Argentina was a major provider.

In 1860, the French government abolished tariffs on wool imported on French vessels, and France became the main consumer of Argentine wool. For example, Elbeuf increased its consumption of Argentine wool from 4000 bales in 1859 to 40,000 in 1869 (Levain, Rougerie & Straus 1983: 82).[24]

The expansion of raw wool exports from Argentina was part of the deepening of a social division of labor of the increasingly world-scale textile industry. In Europe, low-waged labor in manufacturing enterprises produced finished textiles. In Argentina, territorial expansion allowed for commercial agriculture to develop further around wool production, attracting wage workers through relatively high wages. In both Europe and Argentina, households increasingly engaged in the production of labor supplies.[25]

As the textile industry in the interior provinces of Argentina was undermined by these transformations in the global division of labor—through both the diversion of raw wool toward the world market and the changing volume and composition of imports—women in those regions lost their sources of livelihood. The deterioration of employment opportunities for women in the provinces of the interior had preceded the decline of the textile industry.[26] But Cacopardo's analysis of the transformation in the period between 1869 and 1895 "concludes that high levels of female participation fell markedly because of decreased economic activity for all ages, resulting from socio-economic factors, especially urbanization, for women'' (Knaster 1977: 375).[27]

The wool-processing industries, for example, did not offer women steady employment or wages comparable to the incomes earned in the heyday of handicraft textile production. Sheep shearing, for example, appears to have occupied primarily men; women in the interior were only sporadically employed in sheep shearing in the 1840s and 1860s, usually to substitute for men who had joined the civil wars or had migrated to the cities (Gibson 1893: 138).[28] More women were employed in wool washing,[29] but the major part of the wool exported from Argentina in the second half of the nineteenth century was dirty (Sábato 1982: 69).[30]

From the 1890s on, the expansion of manufacturing in and around Buenos Aires generated a significant increase in the work available for women, but it was in low-paying, unskilled, gender-specific jobs. Women were concentrated in domestic service such as laundering. Women's work in the Litoral provinces and Buenos Aires was organized predominantly in outwork or sweatshops; gender became a primary determinant of wages, occupations, degrees of authority, skill exercised in the labor process and levels of labor-force participation.

The production of ready-made clothing provided an opportunity to undermine craft relations that had previously restricted entry into the job market through skill control.[31] For instance, the sewing machine and the subdivision of tasks allowed producers of ready-made clothing to displace custom tailors (Sofer 1982: 100).

Both sweatshop owners and external contractors increasingly moved toward employing workers who had no craft tradition; thus, "the garment industry became the employer of women, children, semiskilled workers, and unemployed intellectuals with no skills at all'' (Sofer 1982: 100).[32] The sewing machine and the subdivision of tasks also facilitated the spread of external subcontracting, relying primarily on women workers.[33]

This does not mean that large factories became predominant. In the mid-1890s, *La Vanguardia* (May 30, 1896) argued that "[tailors are] spread out by themselves or in small groups, because the production of clothing has not yet fallen in the hands of big industry.'' However, the nature of these small enterprises had been transformed; they no longer produced independently, but were integrated into a subdivision of tasks within textile production as a whole. Large commercial enterprises, for example, now relied primarily on external subcontracting for their supplies of ready-made clothing (Patroni 1898: 79).[34]

But primarily, the spread of the sewing machine and the subdivision of labor allowed for the use of unskilled workers both in sweatshops, or on a take-home, piece-rate basis. As stated by Eugene Sofer: "As each task became more well-defined, tailors needed less skill'' (1982: 100). In fact, with the introduction of new techniques of production, capitalist entrepreneurs could claim that the nature of the work had become thoroughly transformed, requiring qualitatively new types of workers, a majority of whom were women.

By the 1890s, most textile factories in Argentina employed a large proportion of women.[35] Indeed, it appears that a majority of workers in mechanized textile factories at the turn of the century were women and children.[36] Even in 1910, inspectors from the Departamento Nacional de Higiene reported that many of the factories inspected by them employed a majority of women.[37]

There are difficulties in estimating the size and composition of the textile and clothing labor force, but a census of the *Capital Federal* in 1911 reported there were over 52,000 workers in these activities.

In clothing, a 1906 study of 60 firms producing clothing showed a total labor force of 11,308 workers, the overwhelming majority of whom (99%) were women (*Boletín del Departamento Nacional de Trabajo*, 3 December 31, 1907: 323-24).[38] Most of these workers were employed by large establishments: 48% of the labor force was employed by just one enterprise, and the ten largest firms together employed 86% of the total work force (*Boletín del Departamento Nacional de Trabajo*, 3 December 31, 1907: 323-24). However, according to one study, 69% of the total labor force in the clothing industry worked at home and not in factories. This made it difficult to organize garment workers; they were geographically dispersed and lacked the constant daily contact experienced by workers in the factory. This was also reflected in wage levels, for evidence suggests that factory workers earned higher wages than home workers.[39]

Table 7.1
Gender and Workers in Textile and Clothing (1911)

	#Workers	#Women	% Women
Seamstresses	16,316	16,316	100.0
Dress Makers	16,086	16,086	100.0
Tailors	10,358	715	6.9
Weavers	1,929	1,395	72.3
Corset Makers	1,049	1,049	100.0
Pant Makers	901	901	100.0
Coat Makers	692	692	100.0
Laundresses	572	556	97.2
Shirt Makers	560	467	83.4
Ribbon Makers	216	216	100.0
Tie Makers	189	173	91.5
Cap Makers	166	94	56.6
Glove Makers	141	101	71.6
Total	*49,175*	*38,761*	*78.9*

Source: Boletín del Departamento de Trabajo, 16 (March 31, 1911:24-27).

In textiles, according to a 1910 study of 34 weaving and spinning factories by the Argentine Department of Labor, there were 7142 workers employed in these industrial establishments, of whom 56% were adult women, at least 14% women under 16, and 29% men.[40] Wages for men, according to the same study, were generally 33% to 100% higher than wages for women.[41]

Not all the unskilled were women. The category included recent immigrants with no technical skills, children, and so forth. More important, not all the women were unskilled.[42] Ultimately, jobs were defined as "skilled" and "unskilled" depending on who performed them (i.e., males or females), so that the reconstruction of a hierarchy of job positions involved, at the same time, the reconstruction of a gender hierarchy.

Women's labor in the textile factories in Buenos Aires replicated, in important respects, the experiences of women in European textile factories. Their employment was central to the deskilling of labor, to the erosion of craft controls over the labor process, and to the undercutting of men's wages. Of course, women were channeled into specific sectors that included the poorest working conditions and lowest-paying jobs. But the scale of factory textile production was much smaller than in Europe, enterprises were unstable, and Argentina continued to import increasing volumes of textiles produced predominantly by women in Europe.

Does this contradict Guy's assertion that women in Argentina were marginalized from factory production?[43] It may well be that women and children were displaced and/or kept away from many factory jobs after the late 1880s. For example, the handlers of Bonsak machines in cigarette-making were women in the late 1880s, but men by the early 1900s.[44] In fact, women were already being marginalized from some jobs,[45] and they faced various forms of institutional discrimination as well.[46]

Gender divisions within industry were gradually introduced through the creation of a hierarchy of job positions, partly promoted by male workers themselves to limit competition for industrial jobs. "Protective" legislation at the turn of the century played a key role in this respect, restricting the access of women to factory jobs.[47] Thus, after congressional approval of a bill restricting the working day of women, large commercial houses producing garments closed their shops and moved toward reliance on outwork (Panettieri 1984: 71). In this sense, the strong presence of women in textile factories at the turn of the century should be seen as part and parcel of a process of transition that in many industries led to the gradual marginalization of women from the factory floor.[48]

CONCLUSION

Prior to the early nineteenth century, the structure arrangements that prevailed within the European textile industry entailed little or no competition among household-based handicraft producers. These customary arrangements imposed significant constraints upon capitalist expansion in textiles. Most importantly, they prevented the development of any substantive differentiation between households and capitalist enterprises. This was significant:

The propensity [of the enterprise] to perform functions and use means typical of states and households prevents or restrains its specialization as a commodity-producing, profit-making institution. And this lack of specialization, in turn, prevents the capitalist enterprise from developing strong competitive advantages vis-a-vis households and states in the provision of means of livelihood and means of protection. (Arrighi 1986: 17)

After the nineteenth century, capitalist entrepreneurs undercut and by-passed customary arrangements through the introduction of major innovations in the organization of production by virtue of which they increasingly specialized in producing "means of livelihood, means of protection, and means of production" (Arrighi 1986: 2). Competitive pressures on household production progressively increased as a result, thereby both eliminating the production of handicrafts within households and "freeing" portions of the population for employment.

These innovations were unevenly distributed through the world-economy. Among the locales considered in this chapter, the extension of capitalist control over the labor process advanced rapidly in Great Britain, more slowly in France and Germany. In each of these, innovations in the labor process were the key mechanism through which capitalist enterprises gained a competitive edge over handicraft household-based textiles.

In a process of deepening differentiation, households began to abandon handicraft production and to specialize instead in producing labor supplies. For example, textile enterprises in core areas of the world-economy competed for raw materials and markets in Argentina; in the process, new incentives were created in the rural areas of Argentina for labor to seek income outside the household, while handicraft production in the provinces of the interior was undermined through falling prices for finished textiles and rising prices for wool.[49] This led to a transformation in the very nature of the household in Argentina.

Over the period we have considered in this chapter, as one set of customary arrangements was undermined, another came into place. We have seen how innovations such as mechanization and deskilling allowed capitalist entrepreneurs to circumvent the control of households over the labor process. The destruction of customary arrangements simultaneously involved the creation of a market for labor, distinguishing waged from unwaged labor. Within the labor market, workers quickly moved toward limiting competitive pressures within the supply of labor by appealing to customary arrangements whereby men's labor was defined as skilled and higher-waged (than women's).

Clearly, women were not "unskilled" prior to mechanization in the textile industry, but the social and historical significance of skill, as a social category, derived from its relationship to the organization of guild production and apprenticeship; "skill" was itself defined customarily. On the other hand, women's labor was defined customarily as "natural" to them, as opposed to being "skilled."

As women and men began to compete with one another for wages, rather than cooperate in a division of labor internal to the household, women's and men's labor were distinguished, according to custom but with an innovative twist, as "skilled" and "unskilled" labor. There was little inherent in the new jobs in the textile enterprises themselves to determine whether tasks were to be performed by "skilled" or "unskilled," male or female labor. Rather, custom met innovation, resulting in the creation and enforcement of new customary arrangements.

These new customary arrangements were activated primarily by the creation of exclusionary craft organizations based on differences between skilled and unskilled workers. As we have argued, the introduction of innovations in the labor process generally went hand-in-hand with the escalating employment of women and children. This allowed employers both to lower the overall new costs of production and to avoid craft resistance to these innovations. Craft organizations, in the wake of "excess competition," soon restricted access to these jobs by reconstructing mechanisms of control over the labor process and access to trades. They created in effect conditions under which men and women (as well as children and adults) did not compete for the same jobs, where men were assured higher wages, and unwaged labor was as appropriate ("natural"), if not more appropriate, for women.

By the end of the period we are studying, the call for a family wage was generalized throughout England, Germany, France, and Argentina. This suggests that over the long term, intensified competition generated resistance. In the late nineteenth century, this took two forms: labor movements and the first wave of feminism.

NOTES

The authors wish to thank Terence K. Hopkins for the substantial comments he made on an earlier version of this chapter.

1. Competition within the labor force, in the sense that we will use it in this paper, is meant to signify the transformations in the structural position of suppliers of labor vis-à-vis one another in the world-economy. Competition is inherent in this relationship as a consequence of the economic insecurities that producers face with the development of a labor market—that is, with the breakdown of the self-sufficiency of households, and with their specialization in supplying labor to enterprises. The development of wage labor involves the simultaneous generation of social mechanisms to restrict the expansion of market mechanisms in regulating labor. For instance, in the late nineteenth century, in the face of the eradication of skills and craft traditions as a defense against what Marx called the "levelling" tendency of capitalist development, gender, a customary mechanism of social differentiation, took on a new meaning and the process of social stratification supplanted the place of skill in regulating competition. Also, as we will show, competition within labor is not limited by national boundaries.

2. For a broader analysis on the separation of enterprises, households, and states, see Arrighi 1986.

3. "The composition of output (in the interior provinces) underwent some changes during the colonial period. Perhaps the most significant were the disappearance of cotton farming and cotton cloth manufacture as a result of the dying out of Indian labor and the introduction of sheep and wool production" (Ferrer 1967: 27; see also Halperín Dongui 1975: 13).

4. Many authors discuss wool production since it was so central to the economic livelihood of the provinces. See Dorfman 1970; Guy 1980; Gibson 1893; Halperín Dongui 1975; Platt 1972; Ferns 1960; Giberti 1961.

5. In the province of Córdoba, for example, "domestic weaving offered an additional source of income to the destitute rural population, which subsisted thanks to the advances of merchants, who went the rounds of 'hills and dales' selling to the weavers on credit, and collecting their debts when the work had been done" (Halperín Dongui 1975: 10).

6. Except for isolated pockets of production, such as in Catamarca.

7. See, for example, Ferrer:

Imports easily reached into the Interior, and their competition dealt a death blow to the shaky local industries. For example, the production of cloth succumbed completely to imported textiles. Railroads not only enabled imported manufactures to penetrate the regional markets of the interior, but also doomed the traditional, albeit modest, trade between regions. With all the railroads leading from the peripheral zone to the Litoral center, the regions remained uncommunicated, and their reciprocal trade declined even further (1967: 129).

8. See his article in the *Hispanic American Historical Review*:

Overland transportation, even though slow and expensive, had not prevented significant economic growth. Rather, the carters in no small way contributed to Argentina's eventual transformation into an export-oriented country long before the laying of the first steel rails. With the gradual integration of Argentina into a wider world-economy, the carters were able to shift their emphasis from servicing local markets to participation in an emerging world trade pattern in which they carried Argentine products to the ports and foreign merchandise from the port to the interior. . . . The carts, not the railroad, provoked the disintegration of local artisan industries and helped prepare Argentina for its role as exporter (1977: 617).

Goodwin's is an important contribution, and points out that economic development and profitable opportunities preceded, and attracted, railroads in the first place.

9. The line from Rosario to Córdoba opened in 1870—the only significant length of track in the interior—and was not connected to Buenos Aires, although the river traffic from Rosario to Buenos Aires was well established at this point. The Córdoba-Tucumán section of the North Central Railroad opened to traffic in 1876, and the Buenos Aires-Mendoza line in the 1880s. See Ferrer 1967: 92, and Platt 1972: 68.

10. Each of these developments was profoundly influenced by the Civil War in the Unitet States, which resulted in greatly increased wool prices in the transatlantic trade (see Jenkins & Ponting 1982: 158).

11. "Skill," socially, as an attribute of a job or an occupation, need have no necessary relation to manual dexterity or technical knowledge. Rather, jobs or occupations are often socially labeled "skilled" or "unskilled" depending on the gender of those who occupy them. See Phillips and Taylor 1980 for further discussion of this point. That men were associated with skills, and women with unskilled labor, was seen as "natural" by many observers in the nineteenth century and historians in the twentieth century. The "problem" to be explained involved low wages, mechanization, male unemployment, and so forth. From our persepective, gender differentiation is not natural, and the historical problem is why competition took the form of gender differentiation in the supply of labor.

12. With the relatively cheaper labor of women applied to the cost-reducing innovations in weaving and combing, Great Britain's textile exports grew considerably. While woolen imports from England remained relatively stable from the 1820s through the 1840s, they began to increase from the 1850s on. Proportionately, however, from this same date, British firms exported to Argentina less than other European manufacturers, and the British Consul in Argentina commented in 1867 that "French, German and Belgians are striving hard to obtain the control of this important branch of trade and are rapidly improving their position, except in plain goods, in which they can not compete" (Jenkins & Ponting 1982: 252–53). Belgium's exports to Argentina increased from three million francs in 1870 to eleven million in 1881 (Mitchell 1975: 506).

British entrepreneurs lost a part of the Latin American market to producers in France and Germany from the 1870s on. Thus, "in Argentina, where imports of woolens increased over 130% between 1876 and 1884, British imports remained stationary so that their share fell from 21% to 11%" (Platt 1972: 150). In other words, Britain was facing increasing competition from other European states that were catching up with mechanization.

13. Gender relations in this sense contributed to the competitiveness of British woolen textiles in England prior to the introduction of mechanized production, that is, gender relations enhanced their competitiveness vis-à-vis imported woolens and cotton goods. British producers did not export significant volumes of woolen goods before the advent of mechanization.

14. In 1891/96, the volume of production reached 100,000 tons, its highest point in the century. Consumption of raw wool in France increased from 99,000 metric tons in 1862 to 163,000 metric tons in 1875, and 230,000 by 1892 (Mitchell 1975: 444–45)

15. "The powerloom made headway especially after the treaty of 1860 had scared French manufacturers with the prospect of Bradford competition. . . . But towards the end of the Second Empire, there were still twice as many handlooms in the country around Riems as there were powerlooms in the town" (Clapham 1923: 249). Levain, Rougerie and Straus comment: "Pour réagir à la concurrence britannique, Roubaix opera une 'véritable révolution' en trois ans en construisant de vastes établissements de peignage et de filature, en achetant à Bradford des métiers à tisser mécaniques, en important enfin de nouveaux procedes d'apprets. Alors qu'en 1855 les roubaisiens ne faisaient batre que quelques centaines de métiers mécaniques, en 1867, la fabrique en possedait 10.000 et 12.000 en 1869 (1983/84: 82). See also Landes 1969: 213.

16. Competitive pressures on labor were exacerbated in Roubaix by immigration from Belgium. From the 1860s to the 1880s, the population of Roubaix was more Belgian than French (Levain, Rougerie, & Straus 1984: 73).

17. Compared with data for England, these numbers are low. In England in 1860, women were 31% of the total labor force, but in 1861 52.5% of the textile labor force. In 1851, 22% of all working women worked in the textile industry, 17% in garments. However, the proportion of working women in the garment industry in France was higher than in textiles, 11% in 1866. In this year, 78% of all workers in the French garment industry were women; they were 89% in 1906, when they were 56% of textile workers. (The figures for England are given on the same pages in Tilly and Scott as the French figures.) The higher proportion of women in the garment industry (11% over 10% in 1866) in combination with the smaller proportion of

women among textile workers, than in England for example, could reflect the relative success of French workers in curtailing women's factory work. While more married women worked in France than in England, the overall tendency was for women to stop working in factories after marriage. This did not mean that married women ceased to produce an income. Many were absorbed into outwork, particularly in the garment industry from the 1870s onwards (Tilly & Scott 1978: 124).

18. Quataert writes: "Between 1800 and 1860 mechanization encroached on the home textile industry; increasingly, products earmarked for distant markets were commissioned by employers, factories sprang up, and large numbers of artisans found their livelihood precarious. By 1870 the machine had replaced hand spinning, although mechanization was slower in weaving. There, low wages reduced the cost advantage of machine over hand looms and in the late 1860s textile handicraft still coexisted with factories" (1970: 40). Kitchen (1978: 62) claims that by 1860 spinning and auxiliary processes were mechanized but weaving was still by hand.

19. Landes also comments that wool spinning remained "little developed," and "survived past mid-century on the cheap labor of old men, women and children" (1969: 174).

20. Dawson states: "In general the maximum rates are still considerably below those usual in the same trades in the United Kingdom until the unskilled occupations are reached, when only a narrow margin divides the two countries" (1908: 129).

21. See Sábato 1982; Brown 1979; Giberti 1961; Gibson 1893; Reber 1979.

22. Assadourian shows that in Córdoba, for example, production of wool for exports accelerated from the 1840s. He shows that long before the railroad made its appearance, the textile industry in Córdoba was irrevocably transformed, not by the presence of imports from the interior, but by two related factors: first, the inability of Cordobese manufactures to establish a market in Buenos Aires, at a time when markets were lost in and en route to Potosí; secondly, by the export of wool to the world market (1983: 272). In 1869, Córdoba had 13,694 weavers; by 1895, the census only registered 4812.

23. Output of raw wool in Germany declined from 34,200 metric tons in 1872 to 23,800 metric tons by 1892, and 13,300 metric tons by 1913. On the other hand, net imports of raw wool rose from 53,400 metric tons in 1880 to 151,400 by 1892, and 182,200 by 1913 (Mitchell 1975: 445).

24. Argentine wool for a long time was so dirty it had to be slowly, painstakingly cleaned by hand, by poorly paid female workers to be usable (Levain, Rougerie & Straus 1983/84: 83). That entrepreneurs would decide to ship dirty wool from Argentina to be cleaned in Europe suggests that low-waged women's labor in Argentina was relatively more expensive than low-waged women's labor in France. In 1867 a chemical process for cleaning wool was invented.

25. The process was extremely uneven within Argentina because of drastic regional differences: growth in Buenos Aires and the Litoral, and stagnation—for example among former textile-producing households—in the interior.

26. Already in 1869, nearly three out of five women (over the age of ten) were recorded in the census as practicing an occupation, but "evidence suggests that a greater proportion of women participated in artisan trades in 1810." The 1869 census also revealed "that half the adult female population waits with uncertainty for daily sustenance" (Hollander 1977: 184).

27. Guy argues that for most of the nineteenth century, women in the interior were in a better economic position than women in the Litoral or Buenos Aires,

but from the 1890s on the balance shifted in favor of women in and around Buenos Aires. It is difficult, however, to draw the comparisons that Guy (1981) or Hollander (1977) want to draw about changes over time in the relative position of women versus that of men in either region because of the lack of information on gender relations in the early nineteenth century, most importantly information on the household age and gender, division of labor, and income-pooling and resource distribution practices within the household. Without this information, we are limited in the estimates we can make about changes in gender relations attendant with industrialization in Argentina.

28. Gibson (1893) notes, however, that these women were paid wages below subsistence levels.

29. It is not clear how many women were employed in this occupation, or under what conditions. In Córdoba, according to Assadourian, most of the work force in wool washing was composed of women (1983: 269).

30. Assadourian (1983: 269) claims that 65 percent of the wool leaving for Buenos Aires from Córdoba in the 1847–1853 period was washed, but this may have been an exceptional case. Thus, Ezequiel Paz commented in 1869 that: "An industry here has completely disappeared and the workforce of thousands of women who earned their livelihood washing wool and the large investments in ranches and equipment for this operation are today left unutilized. This has been the greatest consequence (of the wool crisis) that Cordobese people have suffered. Working women, unable to continue their traditional work, have no other employment possibilities, so suited to their conditions. These unfortunate facts would not be so important if Córdoba had some other industrial activity whose productive needs were suited to female labor, but in our interior provinces it is impossible to diversify suddenly the use of this type of labor as it is in the coastal provinces where the cities need women workers" (quoted in Guy 1981: 73).

31. The widespread introduction of the sewing machine was an important factor in the reorganization of textiles taking place at the time. According to Dorfman, the first sewing machine was brought to Buenos Aires in 1854, generating fears among seamstresses that they would become unemployed (1970: 71). It is difficult to ascertain the subsequent evolution of imports of sewing machines, but the *South American Journal* noted in the late 1880s that 19,083 sewing machines had been imported in 1886, 24,440 in 1887, and 25,027 in 1888. Most of these sewing machines were imported from Germany (63% in 1886, 68% in 1887, and 62% in 1888); the second major source of sewing machines at the time was the United States (22% in 1886, 20% in 1887, and 19% in 1888) (*The South American Journal*, December 28, 1889). The presence of the sewing machine was an essential part of the spread of the sweatshop in Buenos Aires: "The sewing machine's wide availability helped spread the sweatshop through the working-class neighborhoods of Buenos Aires. It provided workers with a source of savings; in time of extreme need they could pawn their machines. Because of its low cost, the sewing machine was also a favored form of work-stimulating charity in the Jewish community" (Sofer 1982: 102). Another favored form of charity among the wealthy was to pawn off worker's sewing machines from the bank.

32. Of course, sweatshop owners and external contractors also continued to employ displaced craft workers who were unable to find jobs in the custom-made tailor shops.

33. In a survey made in 1907, of 9972 out-workers employed in 60 shops, only 4

were male. (Panettieri 1984: 67). By 1912, of 86,732 workers recorded in the census under the category *Vestido y Tocador*, 74,177 worked at home, and 60,000 of these were women (Panettieri 1984: 68).

34. A particularly large employer was the *Intendencia de Guerra*, directly hiring between 2300 and 2400 seamstresses for the production of army uniforms (*La Prensa*. February 23, 1899).

35. The factory "San Martin," producing socks and shirts, employed primarily women (*La Prensa*, April 3, 1895). The weaving factory of "Dell'Acqua y Cia." employed primarily women on some looms, a mix of men and women on others, and men on a third section of looms, but three-quarters of the total work force were women (*La Prensa*, January 24, 1896, and March 19, 1896). The weaving factory of "Baibieni y Antonini" produced different types of undergarments, and employed 300 women out of a total work force of 350 (*La Prensa*, July 4, 1894). The looms were also operated by women in the small weaving shop of "Soumet & Rivas" (*La Prensa* July 27, 1889). On the other hand, the large weaving factory of "A. Prat" employed primarily male workers, but the press found this fact to be worthy of comment: "Against the custom of many factories in which the looms are run by women, here it is men that are in charge of this work due to the great difficulty there is in finding women workers. However, the work of women would be preferable, according to the director of the factory, not only because it is generally cheaper, but also because of the greater care with which they attend a work that does not need effort, but patience" (*La Prensa*, June 25, 1890). The only other instance we have been able to find of a spinning and weaving factory employing primarily men is that of *El Lanificio Argentino de Prandina y Compañia*, whose owner remarked to the press that it was easy to find workers trained in Spain and Italy (*La Prensa*, August 7, 1895).

36. One important exception was the *Intendencia de Marina*, which in the late 1890s moved to produce its own uniforms in a large shop that employed 150 workers and three supervisors, all of whom were male. *La Prensa* opposed the establishment of such a shop, arguing that it was a mistake to employ men in a "class of work that is fit for women, who do not have any other profession that allows them to make a living" (*La Prensa*, February 23, 1899). On the subject, see also *La Prensa*, February 19, 1899.

37. Inspector Mendez reported that 2 weaving factories visited by him employed 99 workers, of which 87 were women, 2 were children and 10 were men (Palacios 1910: 214–15). The presence of women in factories was not limited to textile production; early factories in Argentina, as elsewhere, in general relied a great deal on child and female labor.

38. Three-quarters of those employed in these firms were women of eighteen years of age, and one-quarter were women between the ages of fourteen and eighteen.

39. See "Trabajo de la mujer a domicilio," in *Boletín del Departamento Nacional de Trabajo*, 19 December 31, 1911: 788–96). Of course, it is very difficult to find reliable data on wage differentials. However, the *Anuario Estadístico del Trabajo* published in 1914 by the Argentine Department of Labor included two sets of data on wages, one on wages of female factory workers, and another on average wages for female home workers over the age of 16. The data on factory wages were gathered on the basis of an extremely small sample of the working population, but they show wages for seamstresses to be $2.23 in the factory and $1.13 for home workers; while *modistas* at the factory earned $2.98 as opposed to $1.65 at home (*Anuario Estadístico del Trabajo*, 1914: 142–43, 194–95).

40. As indicated by a Department of Labor inspector reporting at the time, the proportion of minors was higher. "I can assert, with no exaggeration, that one can increase by 30% the number of [minors] that should be registered, because I have observed that employers very often hide the truth when providing this information" (*Boletín del Departamento Nacional de Trabajo*, 12 March 31, 1910: 206).

41. It is not clear the extent to which wage differentials were accompanied by an exclusion of women from weaving, although an inspector for the Department of Labor noticed that one particular factory employed "62 workers, of whom 5 are men who work the weaving machines and 57 [are] women who work in *confección*, ironing and packing" (*Boletín del Departamento de Trabajo*, 12 March 31, 1910: 201).

42. Patroni claimed, for example, that as early as 1890 some skilled positions in the custom-made tailor shops were occupied primarily by women, such as the *pantaloneras* and the *chalequeras* (1898: 78).

43. "Women . . . had no contact with machinery other than sewing machines, and even those were often operated by men. Furthermore, many never saw the inside of a factory, as they worked at home and were paid by the piece" (1981: 77).

44. See *La Prensa*, December 24, 1889.

45. Such as shearing; see *The South American Journal*, January 4, 1890.

46. For example, the Argentine General Commission of Immigration announced in 1897 that "single women, with no family" would not be accorded the usual benefits received by other immigrants, such as temporary shelter. A few days later, the press complained that as a result of the measure many recently arrived single women were forced to wander around the city, looking for some form of shelter (*La Prensa*, March 13, 1897).

47. For a review of this protective legislation, see Guy 1981: 80–84.

48. This marginalization did not extend to all lines of production. In 1910, 60 percent of the personnel of cigarette factories were women and children; they also accounted for 52 percent of workers employed in *alpargatas* factories; and two-thirds of the workers employed in the production of matches (Panettieri 1984: 84–85).

49. Of course, there were subsequent attempts to limit competitive pressures through the introduction of protectionist policies; even here, the elimination of customary arrangements provided a new meaning to these policies. As indicated by Pollard, "whereas the mercantilist body of doctrine to which much of the pre-1860 structure owed its existence was essentially premised on a static world, holding on or increasing the share of a constant total, the politicians of the post-1879 era seemed to be attempting to hold up, or at least divert, an irresistible flood. It was change and increase which (subsequently) forced the hands of governments, not loss and stagnation" (1981: 270).

REFERENCES

Arrighi, Giovanni (1986). "Custom and Innovation: Long Waves and Stages of Capitalist Development." Unpublished paper presented at the International Workshop "Technological and Social Factors in Long Term Fluctuations," Certosa di Pontiguano, Siena, December 15–17.

Assadourian, Carlos (1983). *El sistema de la economía colonial: el mercado interior, regiones y espacio económico*. México: Nueva Imagen.

Bridenthal, Renate (1973). "Beyond Kinder, Kirche, Küche: Weimar Women at Work," *Central European History*, 6, 2, 148–66.

Brown, Jonathan (1979). *A Socio-Economic History of Argentina, 1776–1860.* Cambridge: Cambridge University Press.

Clapham, John Harold (1923). *The Economic Development of France and Germany 1815–1914.* Cambridge: Cambridge University Press.

Cortés Conde, Roberto, and Shane J. Hunt, eds. (1985). *The Latin American Economies: Growth and the Export Sector 1880–1930.* New York: Holmes & Meier.

Dawson, William H. (1908). *Evolution of Modern Germany.* London: T. Fisher Unwin.

Deane, Phyllis (1965). *The First Industrial Revolution.* Cambridge: Cambridge University Press.

Diaz Alejandro, Carlos F. (1970). *Essays on the Economic History of the Argentine Republic.* New Haven: Yale University Press.

Dorfman, Adolfo (1970). *Historia de la industria argentina.* Buenos Aires: Solar/Hachette.

Ferns, H. S. (1960). *Britain and Argentina in the 19th Century.* Oxford: Clarendon.

Ferrer, Aldo (1967). *The Argentine Economy.* Berkeley: University of California Press.

Forsythe, Ann E. (1983). "The Factory Act of 1844," unpublished manuscript.

Giberti, Horacio (1961). *Historia económica de la ganaderia argentina.* Buenos Aires: Solar/Hachette.

Gibson, Herbert (1893). *The History and Present State of the Sheep-Breeding Industry in the Argentine Republic.* Buenos Aires.

Goodwin, Paul B., Jr. (1977). "The Central Argentine Railroad and the Economic Development of Argentina, 1854–1881." *Hispanic American Historial Review,* 57, 1, 613–33.

Gregory, Derek (1982). *Regional Transformation & Industrial Revolution: A Geography of the Yorkshire Woolen Trade.* Minneapolis: University of Minneapolis Press.

Guy, Donna J. (1980). *Argentine Sugar Politics: Tucumán and the Generation of Eighty.* Tempe: Arizona University Press, Center for Latin American Studies.

———— (1981). "Women, Peonage and Industrialization: Argentina, 1810–1914." *Latin American Research Review,* 16, 1, 65–89.

Halperín Dongui, Tulio (1975). *Politics, Economics and Society in Argentina in the Revolutionary Period.* Cambridge: Cambridge University Press.

Hamerow, Theodore (1958). *Restoration, Revolution, Reaction: Economics and Politics in Germany 1815–1871.* Princeton: Princeton University Press.

Hollander, Nancy Caro (1977). "Women Workers and Labor Force Participation of Latin American Women: The Domestic Servants in the Cities." *Signs,* 3, 1, 129–41.

Jenkins, D. T., and K. G. Ponting (1982). *British Wool Textile Industry 1770–1914.* London: Heinemann Educational Books-Pasold Research Fund.

Kitchen, Martin (1978). *The Political Economy of Germany, 1815–1914.* Montreal: McGill-Queen's University Press.

Knaster, Meri (1977). *Women in Spanish America: An Annotated Bibliography from Pre-Conquest to Contemporary Times.* Boston: G. K. Hall.

Landes, David (1969). *The Unbound Prometheus.* London: Cambridge University Press.

Levain, Janine, Jacques Rougerie, and André Straus (1983/84). "Contribution à l'étude des movements de "longue durée": la croissance de l'industrie lainiere en France au XIXe siècle, ses allures et ses déterminants," *Rech. Trav. Inst. Hist. Econ. Soc. Univ. Paris*, 1, 12, 59–96; 1, 13, 59–125.

Mitchell, B. R. (1975). *European Historical Statistics 1750–1970.* New York: Columbia University Press.

Palacios, Alfredo L. (1910). *Por las mujeres y niños que trabajan.* Valencia: Prometeo.

Panettieri, José (1984). *Las primeras leyes obreras.* Buenos Aires: Centro Editor de América Latina.

Patroni, Adrián (1898). *Los trabajadores en la Argentina.* Buenos Aires: Imprenta, Lit. y Enc.

Phillips, Anne, and Barbara Taylor (1980). "Sex and Skill: Notes Towards a Feminist Economics." *Feminist Review*, 6, 79–88.

Platt, D. C. M. (1972). *Latin America and British Trade, 1806–1914.* London: A. & C. Black.

Pollard, Sidney (1981). *Peaceful Conquest: The Industrialization of Europe 1760–1970.* Oxford: Oxford University Press.

Quataert, Jean H. (1974). "The German Socialist Women's Movement 1890–1918: Issues, Internal Conflicts and the Main Personages." Ph.D. diss., U.C.L.A.

Reber, Vera Blinn (1979). *British Mercantile Houses in Buenos Aires, 1810–1880.* Cambridge, Mass.: Harvard University Press.

Sábato, Hilda (1982). "Wool Trade and Commercial Networks in Buenos Aires, 1840s–1880s." *Journal of Latin American Studies*, 15, 1, 49–81.

Smith, Joan, Immanuel Wallerstein, and Hans-Dieter Evers, eds. (1984). *Households and the World-Economy.* Beverly Hills: Sage.

Sofer, Eugene (1982). *From Pale to Pampa: A Social History of the Jews of Buenos Aires.* New York: Holmes & Meier.

Tilly, Louise, and Joan Scott (1978). *Women, Work and Family.* New York: Holt, Rinehart & Winston.

Tipton, Frank (1976). *Regional Variations in the Economic Development of Germany During the 19th Century.* Middletown, Conn.: Wesleyan University Press.

Journals and Official Documents

Argentine Republic. Departamento Nacional del Trabajo, *Anuario Estadístico del Trabajo*, 1914.

Argentine Republic. Departamento Nacional del Trabajo, *Boletín*, 1907–1913.

La Prensa, 1887–1907.

South American Journal, 1889–1890.

La Vanguardia, 1896.

8

FEMALE RESISTANCE TO MARGINALIZATION: THE IGBO WOMEN'S WAR OF 1929

Kathryn B. Ward

This chapter details the events leading to and the consequences of the 1929 Igbo Women's War in Nigeria (Van Allen 1972, 1976a, 1976b). This war is an example of how world-systems processes limited women's as compared with men's access to valued economic resources and of how women have actively resisted socioeconomic marginalization. A crucial concern for world-systems research should be how women are affected by the processes of incorporation into the world-economy—in particular, what determines women's access (relative to men's) to socioeconomic resources within a society. Under capitalism, these valued resources are jobs and wages to which women as a group need access for their survival. The distribution of such resources is a competitive and dynamic process that can lead to women organizing as a group to compete more effectively with men for these resources. Under these conditions, women and men may have competing or conflicting socioeconomic interests. Researchers' use of the household or only women's informal labor as a unit of analysis may obscure this competition process.

The processes of incorporation into the capitalist world system, the resulting underdevelopment, and imposed patriarchal institutions from the core led to a decline in women's status.[1] Classical dependency or cash cropping and mineral extraction introduced cash economy and wage labor in peripheral areas. Due to patriarchal structures and/or core ignorance of women's socioeconomic roles before the arrival of colonial officials, women were denied access to the monetary economy and paid labor in agriculture, extraction, and trading. Many women remained within the subsistence or informal labor sectors. During later periods of foreign investment, women have had lower access than men to industrial and better paying service-sector jobs. Instead, many women have remained in the subsistence or informal economic sector (Ward 1984).

Within an economy or niche, women and men compete for control over valued resources such as jobs and earnings (Rosenfeld & Ward 1985, 1986). In turn, this competition can generate organizational and collective activity by women. As discussed below, economic and demographic change affects competition in the niche and collective behavior.

What happened to Igbo women is an example of what has happened to women during classical dependency. The marginalization of Igbo women from socioeconomic resources set the stage for their later marginalization during import substitution. The inclusion of the Igboland into the global economy resulted in women's lower socioeconomic position relative to men's. Before colonization, Igbo women were socially expected by men to be economically self-supporting (Van Allen 1972, 1976a, 1976b; Wipper 1982). Women had separate political structures that governed the relations between women and men. For example, recalcitrant men who ignored women's rules had to deal with the women's disciplinary ritual of "sitting on a man." Further, women had separate marketing and political organizations that enabled them to compete economically and control the profits from their production. The arrival of the global economy and colonial officials meant that men were given greater access to the international trading networks and cash crops. Meanwhile women remained in subsistence agriculture and local trading. Thus, men acquired access to the expanding cash economy. The British colonial officials instituted regional governmental posts that were exclusively given to men. Eventually, women's economic and political organizations were unable to compete effectively.

With the rumored imposition of a palm oil tax in 1929, Igbo women found themselves in a perilous position. They had limited access to the monetary economy and were potentially unable to pay taxes. Therefore, Igbo women went to war against the British by sitting on and eventually destroying the local government buildings. Their demands were simple: women should occupy one-half of the administrative units, and all white men should return from whence they came. Eventually, the war spread to a six hundred-square-mile area. All area British troops and even the Boy Scouts were called out to put down the rebellion. The British could not believe that only women were behind the rebellion and instituted reforms in administrative units that further solidified the power of Igbo men. Furthermore, they banned many women's organizations and the ritual of sitting on a man, thereby depriving women of their relative economic and social power (Van Allen 1972, 1976a; Wipper 1982).

Although the women's organizations were able to organize economically active women, the collective activities of the women's groups were unable to overcome the repressive strength of colonial officials and the global economy. Given the threats to their competitive position within the monetary sector or niche, the women organized against the political symbols of colonial intrusion rather than against the economic changes in their lives. Thus, the Women's War exemplifies how the global economy negatively affects women's access to monetary economy and how these processes generate women's collective behavior. Furthermore, vis-à-vis the world-system, women and men had competing socioeconomic interests.

Using the example of the Igbo Women's War, I trace a model of the effects of the world-system on women's status along with a competitive model of women's collective behavior (Ward, 1984; Rosenfeld & Ward 1985; Ward & Rosenfeld 1986). First, I examine women's lives within precolonial Igbo society using both the competitive framework and the work of Sanday (1974) and Ward (1984) on female status. Second, I outline the negative effects of the world-system through colonial intrusion or classical dependency on the status of Igbo women in the public domain and women's subsequent collective behavior. My competitive explanation extends the political perspective of Van Allen (1972, 1976a, 1976b). Finally, I examine the consequences of the resolution of the Igbo Women's War for women's status relative to men's.

THE COMPETITIVE MODEL

Ward and Rosenfeld (1985, 1986) and Weiss (1978) derive their competitive model from the human ecology framework (Hawley 1950; Hannan & Freeman 1977). This model assumes that populations compete for access to resources within a niche or niches. Competition is affected by the attributes of and the constraints on competing populations by organizational structures and external forces. Within a niche, competition results from a demand for access to finite or environmentally limited resources.

Organizational structures within the niche reflect both interaction with their environment and the nature of competition. As such these organizations shape the relative means of allocation and distribution of niche resources. Populations organize to compete more effectively within the niche and environmental limits.

Constraints and attributes of competition come about through the allocation of resources based on distinct population characteristics such as sex, the capacity to bear children, or achieved characteristics such as education. Competitive constraints (such as pregnancy) and attributes (education) along with population organizational efforts are important factors in determining a population's ability to compete successfully in the niche.

Finally, external forces such as the intrusion of the world-system may disrupt the environment, thereby leading to changes in the effectiveness of organizations competing for resources in a particular niche. A change in the environment through the arrival of colonial officials may thus result in the introduction of new resources necessary for survival (such as money) and a change in the relative competitive abilities of populations, utilization of attributes, and influence of constraints on populations.

In our competition model, we operationalize the key theoretical concept of the niche as the total number of economic activities necessary for survival. Organizational structures include the state or some form of polity for the entire niche and separate organizations of women and men to compete more effectively (e.g., unions). Finally, women's constraints are childbearing capacities and probability of marriage, while competition attributes are education or training programs necessary for competition within the niche.

Igbo Women's Niche

In precolonial days, Igbo societies were organized around a loosely connected series of kinship group villages or compounds where the niche consisted of primarily rural/subsistence economic activities (Uchendu 1965). Within the niche, women and men conducted their own separate, but complementary, activities. Men cleared the bush, grew their ceremonial yams, and sold palm oil in long-distance trading. Women engaged in subsistence farming and palm oil processing. They also received the profits from their surplus production from trading in farm products and the palm products received from men (Van Allen 1976a).

Constraints. Unlike middle-class married women of the core during the Victorian period, Igbo married women were expected to be economically independent and support themselves and their children. The marital system was polygamous with a virilocal residence after marriage. Each wife was expected to support herself and offspring and also rotate with other wives in the cooking activities for the husband during the week. A major difference between this system and that of other ethnic groups was that while the husband paid an appropriate bride price for his wife or wives, he was also expected to supply each wife with tools, implements, and land. Further, the profits from surplus produce or trading were the woman's rather than belonging to the husband. Although these provisions strengthened the socioeconomic position of wives vis-à-vis husbands, women's meager profits from trading never exceeded men's economic assets. In return, Igbo husbands received possession of the children and the right to the return of the bride price if the marriage was not successful (Van Allen 1976a).

Children were an economically valuable resource within Igbo society because they were expected to engage in agricultural activities and child care (Caldwell 1976). The high fertility of Igbo women was not necessarily a constraint per se on economic activities. Women's work was combined easily with caring for children. More children (to counteract high mortality) led to greater agricultural production. However, children constrained long-distance trading. Hence, children were a partial constraint on women's competitive abilities.

Attributes. Formal education is one of the major attributes for enhancing a group's competitive ability within the niche in most countries in the periphery and the core. For Igbo women, education was informal and took place as socialization into the female role at their mothers' sides. According to Rosaldo (1974), women's lives are their education and preparation for women's prescribed social roles. Men's education is for achievement within the public and formal institutions.

With the arrival of missionary schools, some educational facilities became available—primarily to men. Mothers used their already meager profits to provide education for their sons rather than daughters, who were utilized for child care, subsistence, and trading activities. As Huntington (1975) has noted, girls' economic activities with their mothers' have provided a major barrier to women's gaining access to education. Meanwhile, boys are generally released from economic activities for their education.

Due to their early involvement in productive activities and cultural values, Igbo women had limited access to education and remained largely illiterate. Additionally, if they received any formal education at all, their education was from Christian schools for domestic duties (Leith-Ross 1939). While education was not a prerequisite for active participation in Igbo society (as we shall see later), the early preference for educating males and the presence of certain forms of missionary school education for women had negative effects on Igbo women.

State/Polity. As Weiss (1978) and Parpart (1986) have argued, the organization of polity (especially the state) can affect the nature of competition within the niche. In precolonial Igbo societies, especially west of the Niger River, a diffuse form of (nonstate) polity existed under the rule of area monarchs (Okonjo 1976; Van Allen 1972, 1976a). Elements of political, social, and economic organizations were loosely but intricately connected within Igbo society. No individual spoke for or had authority over others unless this authority was achieved by virtue of leadership, work, and wealth.

This framework was reflected in the dual sex polity and relations between women and men (Okonjo 1976). For example, the male monarch (*obi*) and his cabinet (who dealt with the male section of the community) had their counterparts in the female *omu* and her *ilogo* (cabinet). Omus did not achieve their position by being spouses of monarchs, but rather were acknowledged as mothers of the communities. Women achieved authority positions through verbal and leadership abilities in everyday life, not through wealth or status. This system emphasized leadership via women's participation and consensus. Okonjo (1976) notes that the omu and ilogo were in charge of regulating the local market through establishing rules, rights, and peace within the marketplace after consulting with representative groups of women. In addition, the omu and her cabinet could settle disputes between women in their relations to men.

At the local kinship level of Igbo society were two important institutions for women: *otu umnada* (daughters of the village) and *otu inyemedi* (daughters of a lineage). The umnada held the highest status among the women of their natal village (Okonjo 1976; Van Allen 1976a). Although located in exogenous residence as a function of virilocal marriage patterns, the umnada still maintained close ties with their villages of origin. The umnada met periodically (*ogbu*) to keep the peace within their villages of origin.

The otu inyemedi provided day-to-day rules and organization for women of the village. The meeting of the wives (*miriki*) performed the major networking function within the village, since, as a group, inyemedi would organize marketing activities and make social rules that could be applied to both women and men (e.g., punishment of a recalcitrant husband).

The ultimate sanction by the miriki to maintain their competitive position within the niche was their procedure or institution of "sitting of a man." This process, recognized as serious and legitimate by men,

involved gathering at his [i.e., the derelict male's] compound at a previously agreed-upon time, dancing, singing scurrilous songs detailing the women's grievances against him (and often insulting him along the way by calling his manhood into question), banging on his hut with the pestles used for pounding yams, and, in extreme cases, tearing up his hut (which usually meant pulling the roof off). This might be done to a man who particularly mistreated his wife, violated the women's market rules, or who persistently let his cows eat the women's crops. The women would stay at his hut all night and day, if necessary until he repented and promised to mend his ways. (Leith-Ross 1939: 109; Harris 1940: 146–48; Van Allen 1976a: 61–62)

The use of "sitting on a man" by women against men (and sometimes against other women) symbolized an important facet of the dual sex system contrasted with similar systems. Women had a legitimate and recognized means of enforcing their rules and reinforcing their competitive position within the niche. Under the diffuse political, economic, and social structure of the Igbo, women particpated fully in society with institutionalized political/economic roles in the public domain. Thus, for external entities to deal exclusively with one sex as representative of the entire group was reprehensible to men and in particular to women who would take steps to correct the situation.

Organizations

Within the niche, one group may organize to compete more effectively in the niche vis-à-vis other groups for access to economic and political resources (Weiss 1978). In a similar manner, women of West Africa have organized women's associations. These associations have taken the form of a miriki for Igbo women, marketing associations among women of the Ivory Coast, the Yoruba in western Nigeria (Lewis 1976), or the Anlu in the Cameroons (Wipper 1982).

The Igbo women formed marketing associations along a miriki-ogbo-market nexus. The omu was the head of the regional market. She set prices, made rules, and allotted space with the help of the ilogo. At the local level, the miriki served as the regulating mechanism for women's and men's marketing and farming behavior.

The market and women's associations served two important purposes. First, they enabled women to organize selling prices to maximize slender profits and provide essential goods and services. Secondly, they served as a major information network among diverse groups of women.

Women were able to compete effectively with men through the relatively high degree of organizational strength achieved by Igbo women's marketing and local associations. Consequently, in precolonial Igbo society, these associations were an essential element in Igbo women's status and power base.

Igbo Women's Precolonial Status

According to Sanday (1974: 192), there are four crucial elements to women's status in the public domain:

I. *Female material control.* Females have the ability to act effectively on, to allocate, or to dispose of things—land, produce, crafts, and so on—beyond the domestic unit.

II. *Demand for female produce.* Female produce has a recognized value either internally—beyond the local family unit—or in an external market.

III. *Female political participation.* Females, even if only through a few token representatives, may express opinions in a regular, official procedure and may influence policy affecting people beyond the domestic unit.

IV. *Female solidarity groups devoted to female or economic interests.* Females group together in some regular way to protect or represent their interests, and are recognized and effectual in this activity.

According to my ecological analysis and Sanday's (1974, 1981) criteria, precolonial Igbo women had high status in the public domain. First, due to their essential role in subsistence food production, Igbo women had control over the products and profits of their surplus crops in the niche. Secondly, female marketing activity reflected a societal or external demand for female products and economic activity. Thirdly, Igbo women had an officially sanctioned voice in village affairs, for example, speaking at public meetings on issues that affected the village (Van Allen 1976a). Finally, through mirikis and women's marketing associations, Igbo women were organized into a number of strong and powerful solidarity groups that provided rules for women's and men's conduct. Consequently, precolonial Igbo women had achieved a high degree of status in the public domain vis-à-vis men.

Colonial Intrusion/Unrest Among Women

One of the basic assumptions of the competitive/ecological model is that the processes of competition within a niche occur in a stable environment.

However, external forces can introduce changes in the environment that may result in a change in the nature and organization of competition. Under such changing conditions, one group may gain the competitive edge and become dominant over another group in the new niche.

In 1900, Nigeria and, in particular, Igboland became annexed as part of a larger British colony. This annexation eventually resulted in classical dependency and underdevelopment. These events in turn had negative consequences for Igbo women and Igbo society.

Ecological Change. The world-system represented an external force entering the environment or colonial intrusion[2] that led to a change in the niche structure. New economic resources necessary for survival were introduced along with new political institutions. A new monetary niche became differentiated from the older subsistence (or noncash) niche. As a consequence, the nature of competition changed as women and men adapted to the new environment and set of resources. For example, because of colonial intrusion and dominance imposed by colonial officials, local men were able to compete more effectively within the new niche. Thus, men were able to dominate the new niche.

A second consequence of a change in the environment is change in the political and organizational structures and their effectiveness in competition. Previously women and men occupied the subsistence niche in a symbiotic manner within their own political and organizational structures. The dominance of men over women relative to access to new resources led to the rise of new organizational structures. These structures reflected the dominance and control of men over the allocation and distribution of resources. Older women's organizations found they were less effective in competing for resources in the new environment.

External Forces and Resources. When the British conquered Igboland, they represented an external force or colonial intrusion bringing Igbos into contact with the world-economy's cash or monetary system. The British colonial system had a policy of colony self-sufficiency through taxation (Van Allen 1976a). In this way the colonial administration introduced new monetary resources necessary for survival. Igbo men controlled the long-distance trade of a major export product, palm oil. Subsequently, the men were brought into the monetary niche through their trading activities and the necessity of meeting tax obligations. In addition, the British gave Igbo men access to the production of cash crops, an additional means of acquiring the new monetary resources. Meanwhile women continued in their subsistence agriculture and local/regional market practices without the benefit of new agricultural techniques. Women were left by men and colonial officials with only limited access to the resources of the new monetary niche controlled by men.

Changes in Organizational Structure. The British also introduced a system of colonial administration into the monetary niche based on the taxation of the economic resources of men along with the control of political and legal posts by men. The officials assumed that political activity and administration was a male domain (Van Allen 1976a). They installed an administration governed by the indirect rule of a warrant chief. A single person (male Igbo) had control over a large district area (Afigbo 1972). While the concept of one person in authority was antithetical to the Igbos, certain enterprising Igbo males took over these posts. Since the warrant chief controlled taxation and British-imposed native courts in the area, the position was a means of acquiring greater economic resources. Thus, one group, males, exerted greater control over the organizational structures of the monetary niche. Further, the native courts usurped the traditional judicial powers of the women's organizations, particularly the omu and her court. Finally, a number of kinship lineages and villages were subsumed under each administrative district. This restructuring meant the loss of the traditional autonomy of each kinship group. Therefore, colonial intrusion resulted in changes in the niche and in the organizational structures of the economy and polity which became dominated by men to the detriment of women.

Women found their prior competitive and organizational opportunities threatened in several different ways. Women's competitive abilities within the new niche were hindered because women's associations were specifically organized for effective competition in the older subsistence niche. The structure of women's groups was ill-suited for competition for long-distance trading or cash-cropping resources. The traditional enforcement power of women's associations dissipated under the new administrative structure of indirect rule. Finally, Christian churches forbade both polygamous marriages and participation in the pagan rituals of women's associations (Van Allen 1976a). Ultimately, these restrictions weakened the solidarity of village women in political participation, rule making, and marketing subsistence activities.

Colonial Intrusion and the Status of Women

This perspective on the loss of female status during colonial intrusion can be compared with Van Allen's (1976a) political explanation of the situation. Van Allen (1976a) argued that the decline of traditional Igbo women's political institutions and power was due to the ideological "invisibility" of women in Victorian England. Since English women were invisible in national policy, colonial policy ignored Igbo women. I extend Van Allen's explanation by offering a broader socioeconomic perspective based on a competitive model and incorporating Sanday's (1974, 1981) work into a world-systems model.

At first examination, Igbo women's activities within their subsistence niche remained relatively the same before and after colonial intrusion. They engaged in subsistence agriculture, local marketing, cottage industries, and women's trading associations, and had some political participation. According to Sanday's criteria of female status, Igbo women should have maintained their high status. However, Sanday (1974) noted that women may lose status within the public domain if men are able to achieve an external sphere of control, perhaps as a function of war. From the competitive and world-systems models, colonial intrusion affected competition between women and men for the niche resources, for example, through the monetary economy, opening up of long-distance trade markets for men, infusion of British products, cash crops, a change in political organization, and the imposition of male-oriented ideology. These changes led to men's gaining an external sphere of control or a competitive advantage over women (Ward 1984, forthcoming). Therefore, British ideology was a sufficient but not necessary condition for the decline in women's status. Instead, the systemic effects of colonial intrusion and classical dependency provided the major impetus for the decline of women's status.

Reexamining the new alignments of Sanday's criteria after colonial intrusion illustrates this point. Two factors are important. First, the terms and resources for competition within the monetary niche have shifted to where men were the dominant group within the new niche. This occurred through the intrusion of the new economic system and the imposition of male hegemonic attitudes from Great Britain. Secondly, women's activities within the subsistence niche were largely unpaid or generated meager profits. In precolonial times Igbo women were able to gain relatively high status through their organizations and economic activities in the dual sex system. However, colonial intrusion and resultant changes in the economic/political structure of the niche meant that women competed less effectively with men. Consequently, women found themselves losing status due to their predominant location in the older subsistence niche and constrained position in the monetary niche, a relatively powerless position compared to Igbo women's previous status. Therefore, while part of this shift in location may have occurred as a function of British Victorian ideology, the major factors in Igbo women's status were the structural changes in competition that accompanied colonial intrusion and imported male dominance.

UNREST AMONG WOMEN

After approximately thirty years of British colonization, Igbo women had gone from a position of relatively high status within the public domain to less profitable activities in the monetary niche. However, they did not accept this situation passively. Instead, in 1929, they went to war against the British in the Aba area. This collective behavior of tens of thousands Igbo women occurred on a massive scale (Wipper 1982). Eventually a six hundred-square-mile area was involved. The Igbo women's behavior was both a reaction to the imposition of male polity upon a dual sex system (Van Allen 1976a) and collective behavior due to the negative influence of colonial intrusion on women's competitive abilities.

Igbo women were concerned about maintaining their economic independence in this system through their less profitable niche activities. They had been stymied in their access to the various means of acquiring monetary resources, and their profit margins were almost nil (Van Allen 1976a). Faced with this economic threat to their competitive abilities and status relative to men, women's organizations responded by invoking their rules and engaging in coordinated behavior—the *Ogu Umumwanyi* or the "Women's War." They sat on the symbols of British intrusion: the warrant chiefs and the native courts.

Taxation Without Representation

According to Van Allen (1976a) and Wipper (1982), in 1925, British officials had levied a tax on men when the price of palm oil was high in the world-economy. By 1929, the price had fallen dramatically. Shortly thereafter rumors spread that women, who participated in palm oil processing and essentially nonmonetary activities, were to be taxed. Since the men had been told previously that males in the palm oil district would not be taxed, women were concerned that the officials were lying once again. The women's associations demanded more evidence. The action of colonial officials then started the women's war, as Van Allen (1976a: 72) describes:

On November 23, an agent of the Oloko Warrant Chief, Okugo, entered a compound and told one of the married women, Nwanyeruwa, to count her goats and sheep. She replied angrily, "Was your mother counted? at which "they closed, seizing each other by the throat" (Perham 1937: 207). Nwanyeruwa's report to the other Oloko women convinced them that they were to be taxed. Messengers were sent to neighboring areas, and women streamed into Oloko from all over the Owerri Province. They "sat on" Okugo and demanded his cap of office. They massed in protest at the District Office and succeeded in getting written assurances that they were not to be taxed. After several days of mass meetings . . . Okugo was arrested, tried and convicted of "spreading news likely to cause alarm" and of "physical assault on the women" (Gailey 1970: 108–13).

The news about these activities moved through the women's associations-market network (Leith-Ross 1939; Van Allen 1976a, 1976b), as other women moved on native courts in their districts. The rebellion spread to the Owerri and Calabar districts and eventually involved the burning of most native courts within the area. The British and Boy Scouts, confronted by the sight of angry women making war, responded violently. Over fifty women were killed (Wipper 1982).

After the women were dispersed, the British administration instituted a series of reforms that continued the dominant competitive edge of men. The warrant chief system was continued, only now with jurisdiction over smaller districts. The demands of the women for all white men to leave and for women to be appointed warrant chiefs were ignored. In addition, the native courts were strengthened in their power (Van Allen 1976a; Wipper 1982).

Although the women's associations organized a large body of economically active women, the collective action of the women's groups failed to overcome the repressive strength of the state. Shaped by their weakened competitive position in the monetary niche, the women chose to organize against the political symbols of colonial intrusions rather than against the economic changes in their lives per se. The ultimate irony of the women's war was this: because the British officials believed that Igbo men were behind the uprising, they instituted reforms only within the system of indirect rule. These reforms only further decreased women's competitive abilities and status. Therefore, collective behavior produced by economic and political forces in Igbo women's lives only led to greater domination of women's economic and political lives by men—a situation that exists in an even greater degree today in Nigeria (see Akande 1979; Awosika 1976).

CONCLUSION

This chapter has used a competitive framework to study the effects of colonial intrusion on the status and collective behavior of Igbo women. The specific structural relationships between world-system, colonization, and the status of women in the public domain (Sanday 1974) have been examined as well as the relation of these factors to the collective behavior of Igbo women in their Women's War. In doing so, this framework has expanded the political analysis of Van Allen (1972, 1976a, 1976b).

The implications of this research for future studies of women and development are threefold. First, the interaction of colonial intrusion and patriarchy has resulted in a decline in women's status relative to men's. The preference for male-paid labor in colonization (and dependency) is related to the current structure of underdevelopment. Due to their informal-sector location, women still lack access to the monetary economy and resources for competing in agriculture, trading, and other economic activities. As a consequence, women become dependent on men and therefore subject to men's control over their reproductive and productive roles. Hence, world-system researchers need to add the concept of patriarchy and male dominance to their theories and research. Secondly, the negative influence of the world-system on the status of women has meant that the resources generated by women's economic activities have been ignored in the development effort. In fact, some researchers are now rediscovering women's subsistence contributions in their research on the crucial role of the informal sector in the maintenance of the world system (see, e.g., Portes 1985). Women are now the major participants in the informal sector around the world (ICRW 1980; Ward forthcoming; Simms & Dumor 1976/77). Thus, it is important for researchers to examine how women are denied access to paid employment or economic resources. The ecological-competitive model outlined in this chapter should be useful for studying these problems of women in underdevelopment and the informal sector.

Thirdly, this research points to the competitive relationship between women and men. Often women and men have competing socioeconomic interests that should not be subsumed or ignored while studying households. This emphasis on households obscures how patriarchal relations interact with the processes of the world-system to perpetuate women's subordination, dependency on men, or to lower women's status relative to men's (for a historical discussion of this perspective, see Hartmann 1976).

In conclusion, the case of Igbo women and the Women's War in 1929 has provided a good example of the effects of the world-system and colonial intrusion on women's status. The consequences of the world-system for women's competition spurred the collective behavior of women. Meanwhile, African women have continued to actively resist the erosion of their political and economic activities (for other examples, see Boserup 1970; Wipper 1982). For example, in the Cameroons, the Kom women brought down the government in the late 1950s. Finally, Igbo women's use of sitting on a man provides contemporary women with a potential ritual for organizing against patriarchal power (e.g., sexist professors, sexual harassers, and so forth). However, there is also a lesson to be learned: women should collectively act against the male-dominated economic structures that bind all women and not organize solely against political symbols.

NOTES

Parts of this chapter were presented at the meetings of the American Sociological Association, Toronto, 1981. The author thanks Rachel Rosenfeld and Davita Silfen Glasberg for their comments, and acknowledges the intellectual inspiration and contribution of the late Jane Allison Weiss (1946–1981) through her work on competition theory and women's economic roles.

1. At the 1987 PEWS conference, June Nash argued that we should distinguish between preexisting patriarchy and male hegemony imposed from outside the particular society or culture. In the case of Igbo women, I will be examining the imposition of patriarchal relations from the core on the Igbo culture.

2. Some researchers refer to such a process as "colonial penetration," but I prefer to avoid such terms so as not to replicate sexist imagery. Thus, I use the term *colonial intrusion*.

REFERENCES

Afigbo, A. E. (1972). *The Warrant Chiefs: Indirect Rule in Southeastern Nigeria, 1891–1929*. London: Longman.

Akande, J. O. (1979). The Law and the Status of Women in Nigeria. ECA/ATRLW/RESO1/79. Addis Ababa: UNECA, African Training and Research Center for Women.

Awosika, K. (1976). "Nigerian Women in the Informal Labor Market: Planning for Effective Participation." Paper presented at the Conference on Women and Development, Wellesley College, Wellesley, Mass., June 2–6.

Boserup, Ester (1970). *Women's Role in Economic Development*. New York: St. Martin's.

Caldwell, John C. (1976). "Toward a Restatement of Demographic Transition Theory." *Population and Development Review*, 2, 3-4, September–December, 321–66.

Gailey, Harry (1970). *The Road to Ava*. New York: New York University Press.

Hannan, Michael T., and John Freeman (1977). "The Population Ecology of Organizations." *American Journal of Sociology*, 82, 5, March, 929–64.

Harris, J. S. (1940). "The Position of Women in a Nigerian Society." *Transactions of the New York Academy of Sciences*. Series 2, 2, 5. New York: New York Academy of Sciences.

Hartmann, H. (1976). "Capitalism, Patriarchy, and Job Segregation by Sex." *Signs*, 1, 3, part 2, 137–69.

Hawley, A. (1950). *Human Ecology*. New York: Ronald Press.

Hungtington, S. (1975). "Issues in Women's Role in Economic Development: Critique and Alternatives." *Journal of Marriage*, 37, 4, 1001–13.

International Center for Research on Women (ICRW) (1980). *Keeping Women Out: A Structural Analysis of Women's Employment in Developing Countries*. Washington, D.C.: Agency for International Development.

Leith-Ross, S. (1939). *African Women. A Study of the Ibo of Nigeria*. New York: Praeger.

Lewis, B. (1976). "The Limitations of Group Action Among Entrepreneurs: The Market Women of Abidjour, Ivory Coast." In N. Hafkin and E. Bay, ed., *Women in Africa*. Stanford: Stanford University Press, 136–56.

Okonjo, K. (1976). "The Dual-Sex Political System in Operation: Igbo Women and Community Politics in Midwest Nigeria." In N. Hafkin and E. Bay, eds., *Women in Africa*. Stanford: Stanford University Press, 45–58.

Parpart, J. (1986). "Women and the State in Africa." *Women in International Development Working Papers*. East Lansing, Mich.: Office of Women in Development, 117.

Portes, Alejandro (1985). "The Informal Sector and the World Economy." In M. Timberlake, ed., *Urbanization in the World-Economy*. Orlando: Academic Press, 53–62.

Rosaldo, Michelle (1974). "Women, Culture and Society: A Theoretical Overview." In M. Rosaldo and L. Lamphere, eds., *Women, Culture and Society*. Stanford: Stanford University Press, 17–42.

Rosenfeld, R., and Kathryn Ward (1985). "The Rise of the U.S. Women's Movement After WWII." Paper presented at the annual meetings of the American Sociological Association, Washington, D.C., August.

Sanday, P. (1974). "Female Status in the Public Domain." In M. Rosaldo and L. Lamphere, eds., *Women, Culture and Society*. Stanford, Calif.: Stanford University Press, 189–206.

_____ (1981). *Female Power and Male Dominance*. Cambridge: Cambridge University Press.

Simms, R., and E. Dumor (1976/77). "Women in the Urban Economy of Ghana." *African Urban Notes*, 2, 3, 43–64.

Uchendu, V. (1965). *The Igbo of Southeast Nigeria*. New York: Holt, Rinehart and Winston.

Van Allen, J. (1972). "Sitting on a Man: Colonialism and the Lost Political Institutions of Igbo Women." *Canadian Journal of African Studies*, 6, 2, 165–82.

———— (1976a). "'Aba Riots' or Igbo 'Women's War'? Ideology, Stratification, and the Invisibility of Women." In N. Hafkin and E. Bay, eds., *Women in Africa*. Stanford: Stanford University Press, 59–86.

———— (1976b). "African Women, 'Modernization,' and National Liberation." In L. Iglitzin and R. Ross, eds., *Women in the World: A Comparative Study*. Santa Barbara: Clio, 25–54.

Ward, Kathryn (1984). *Women in the World-System: Its Impact on Status and Fertility*. New York: Praeger.

———— (1985a). "Women and Urbanization in the World-System." In M. Timberlake, ed., *Urbanization in the World-Economy*. Orlando: Academic Press, 305–24.

———— (1985b). "The Social Consequences of the World-Economic System: The Economic Status of Women and Fertility." *Review*, 8, 4, Spring, 561–94.

———— (forthcoming). Women in the Global Economy." In B. Gutek, L. Larwood, and A. Stromberg, eds., *Women and Work #3*. Beverly Hills: Sage.

Ward, Kathryn and R. Rosenfeld (1986). "The Contemporary Women's Movement: A Test of Competition Theory." Paper presented at the annual meeting of the American Sociological Association, New York.

Weiss, J. (1978). "A Competitive Model of Women's Labor Force Participation." Unpublished paper, University of Iowa.

Wipper, A. (1982). "Riot and Rebellion Among African Women." In J. O'Barr, ed., *Perspective on Power*. Durham, N.C.: Duke University Occasional Paper No. 13.

9

DEGRADED WORK AND DEVALUED LABOR: THE PROLETARIANIZATION OF WOMEN IN THE SEMICONDUCTOR INDUSTRY

John Horton and Eun-Jin Lee

WOMEN IN THE PERIPHERY ENTER THE GLOBAL ASSEMBLY LINE

The increased proletarianization of undervalued female labor in the Asian peripheries has been a recent tendency within the capitalist world economy. Over the last two decades, transnationals, most notably in the textile and electronics industries, have transferred their routine assembly work from relatively high-waged core regions to low-waged workers in the peripheries, overwhelmingly to young women who are entering the waged labor force for the first time (Fröbel et al. 1980; Fuentes & Ehrenreich 1984; Lim 1978; Nash et al. 1983; Taplin 1986; UNIDO 1980). These changes reflect, on the one hand, a dramatic restructuring of the division of labor in manufacture—the increased reorganization of the labor process by standardizing its component tasks and imposing this discipline on the workers (Taylorization)—and, on the other hand, the restructuring of the social division of labor—the reassignment of unequal tasks to unequal people within the regional, ethnic, and sexual divisions of labor.

In this study, we examine the proletarianization of women in the Asian subsidiaries of the U.S.-owned sector of the semiconductor industry (classified as SIC 3674). This industry makes the discrete components (diodes and transistors) and, increasingly, the more technologically sophisticated integrated circuits that are destined to be the brains of modern machinery—from cheap calculators to computers and enormously expensive military and space hardware.

Several characteristics of the semiconductor industry make it an attractive candidate for a world-systems analysis of proletarianization. First, the industry has a single labor process whose components are unevenly dispersed within a global economic and social division of labor. Therefore, the industry provides us with data on core/peripheral, gender, and ethnic divisions within a single production process.

Secondly, the semiconductor industry is paradigmatic of the restructuring of postwelfare capitalism. As such, it is a key to understanding present and future trends in the exploitation and subordination of the working classes. The industry represents the high-tech forms of reindustrialization that have rapidly developed since the 1960s in a climate of world recession, increased militarization, and Reaganomics. Its technological development has clearly benefited from the research priorities of the new Cold War era: increased militarization of the world and space. Its volatility, mobility, and relentless search for innovation and cost cutting exemplify the spirit of competitive, antilabor supply-side economics. Finally, its product, the semiconductor, is revolutionizing work and accelerating mechanization, Taylorization, and proletarianization.

What conditions made possible the historical entry of Asian women into the semiconductor industry and have determined the nature of their labor control and exploitation as wage labor? While the answer obviously requires detailed historical studies, within the limited scope of our research and speculation we have tried to focus on several factors that may be an important part of that history. Our major hypothesis is that the entry of Asian women in the peripheries into the global assembly line was made possible by the historical intersection of two capitalist strategies aimed at reducing the costs of labor power: (1) the deskilling of productive work through Taylorization within the technical division of labor: and (2) the sexist and racist devaluation of labor power within the social division of labor.

Our first research objective was to investigate the labor process or the technical division of labor in the manufacture of semiconductors. Specifically, we investigated the hierarchical organization of tasks involved in the conception and execution of production work. Following Harry Braverman (1976), we expected that Taylorism would be a major factor in the hierarchical organization and proletarianization of work. Taylorism involves three principles of work organization and labor control: (1) "the dissociation of the labor process from the skills of the workers" (its form therefore depends on the practices of management rather than the abilities of workers); (2) "the separation of conception from execution"; and (3) "the use of this monopoly over knowledge to control each step of the labor process and its mode of execution" (Braverman 1974: 112–19).

This separation of execution and performance in the labor process is an aspect of proletarianization, understood broadly as the uneven historical process of the subordination of labor to capital. "The parameters of proletarianization are defined not only by the social relations of production (a person's relationship to the ownership of capital or labor power) but by the relations in production (what a person does and his/her relation to the immediate labor process in which s/he is involved) as well" (Herman 1982: 10). Moreover, this parameter of proletarianization in the labor process is also expressed in class terms as a polarization between, on the one side, relatively highly paid technical and supervisory workers (an "intermediate stratum") who monopolize conception and planning in the interests of capital, and, on the other side, low-paid, low-skill workers who neither plan, control, nor organize their own work (the most proletarianized workers from Braverman's viewpoint).

Our second research objective was to investigate the social division of labor within the semiconductor industry, that is, the way particular tasks within the labor process are allocated to particular workers and regions. Following Wallerstein, we expected to find that the social division of labor was hierarchically organized according to the social characteristics of workers. "What was new under historical capitalism was the correlation of division of labor and valuation of work" (Wallerstein 1983: 25). Valued and devalued tasks tend to be allocated according to invidious distinctions based on region, race, sex, age, and so on (Wallerstein 1983: 25).

One implication of this for an understanding of proletarianization is that its parameters include, in addition to the social relations of production and the social relations in production, the social division of labor (the subordination of labor to capital through the devaluation of labor power on sexist, racist, and other grounds). A more controversial implication of this expanded definition of proletarianization is that position in the social division of labor must also be included in our understanding of class (Wallerstein 1981: 47–52).

Our data for this investigation were based on available occupational statistics, technical studies of the labor process, and reports on women's work in the semiconductor industry. Our conclusions are suggestive and speculative. Detailed historical studies of the proletarianization of women in the new export industries remain to be done.

Above all, our aim is theoretical: to develop a tentative framework for future research on the process of proletarianization within the capitalist world-system. Rather than emphasize the separate role of the technical and social divisions of labor in the subordination of labor, we argue for their unity within the capitalist world-system. In our opinion, world-systems theory offers the most promising framework for understanding that unity. According to this perspective, in addition to relying on forms of exploitation and labor control built into the relations of production and relations in production, historical capitalism continually transforms and profits from inequalities in the social division of labor and develops ideological and coercive forms of labor control on that basis (Wallerstein 1974, 1983; Mies 1986). At least in the case of the semiconductor industry, we need to address the capitalist form of the two divisions of labor in order to understand the historically specific character of women's proletarianization.

PROLETARIANIZATION IN THE
SEMICONDUCTOR INDUSTRY

The pattern of proletarianization, exploitation, and labor control within the semiconductor industry is established vertically by the highly Taylorized and hierarchical organization of the labor process associated with making electronic circuits (the division of labor in manufacture or the technical division of labor) and horizontally by the uneven distribution of deskilled Taylorized work to devalued populations within the social division of labor as defined by economic regions (core/periphery), gender, and ethnicity.

Vertical Proletarianization: The Taylorized Labor Process

The Taylorized separation of conception and execution is built into the four basic stages of manufacture in the semiconductor industry: design of the chips, mask making (transferring the computer design to photomasks), chip fabrication (with the aid of photomasks and carefully controlled chemical processes, silicon wafers produced in-house or bought from subcontractors are transformed into circuits), and assembly. Assembly is the most deskilled phase of the labor process. It involves several separate stages. In the first, the wafer or chip, which may now contain hundreds of devices, is sectioned into individual chips. With the aid of microscopes or videoscreens, workers bond tiny gold or aluminum wires to electrodes in the circuits. Finally, the unit is packaged and sealed. At the second stage, integrated circuits are "stuffed" into printed circuit boards for assembly into computer systems. Testing is an important unskilled task in assembly as well as earlier stages of the labor process (UNCTC 1986: 144–86).

These stages of the labor process clearly define the hierarchy of skill, control, and remuneration. At one pole stand the professional and technical workers who monopolize research, design, and planning in the interests of capital; at the other side stands a mass of semiskilled and unskilled workers who perform routine tasks of assembly, testing, and monitoring machines and who neither command, control, nor organize the labor process. Above these are the corporate planners, the ultimate decision makers whose profit decisions set limits on all subordinate planners.

Although correctly considered high-tech and employing large numbers of technical personnel, the semiconductor industry, at least in its initial stages of development, depends on many labor-intensive processes and the exploitation of semiskilled and unskilled labor. If we measure labor intensity by the proportion of production workers, one survey put the figure in 1978 at 63 percent for domestic semiconductor firms and at 78 percent for this U.S. industry as a whole, including foreign subsidiaries (see table 9.1).

Of course, the semiconductor industry is changing rapidly: capital investment is increasing, former skills are becoming obsolete, and new skills require retraining. However, automation and technological advances tend to

Table 9.1
Employees in U.S. Firms Engaged in Producing Integrated Circuits, 1978

	Domestic	Foreign Subsidiary	Total
All Persons Employed in Producing Integrated Circuits	66,426	65,152	131,578
Production and Related Workers	41,746 (62.9%)	60,677 (93.1%)	102,423 (77.8%)

Source: ITC, 1979: 100-1

reinforce the basic pattern of polarization between professionals/technicians and deskilled labor. In the United States, increased automation means that semiskilled production workers are being replaced by highly skilled design, test, and inspection personnel, and assembly workers are being turned into even less skilled machine operators (Ernst 1983: 62).

Horizontal Proletarianization: The Unequal Social Division of Labor

The pattern of proletarianization and labor control in the semiconductor industry does not stop with the process of Taylorism and the vertical organization of work. The subordination and exploitation of labor are maximized by the horizontal distribution of devalued tasks to devalued populations within the global social division of labor. By the social division of labor we mean the way particular workers are allocated to particular tasks within the labor process of the semiconductor industry. This generalization applies to the past two decades of global expansion: workers in the core and men in general get the best jobs, while the most Taylorized components of the labor process are assigned to women, mainly to Asian women in the peripheries, but also to Asian immigrants and other minority women in the core of the capitalist world-system.

Thus, the semiconductor industry exemplifies the "new" international division of labor. The highest decision-making functions and the most capital-intensive and sophisticated labor processes tend to be located in the core. The majority of labor-intensive assembly operations have shifted to the peripheries. Specifically, management, design, fabrication, and assembly of custom circuits and circuits destined for military use, as well as some "stuffing" of circuit boards, take place in the core. Workers in the peripheries receive wafers fabricated in the core or peripheries. They are assembled into circuits, then sealed and tested, and shipped back to the United States or even remain in the periphery to become parts of consumer goods.

The labor process begins and usually ends in the core. Dominant in the industry until the mid-1970s, U.S.-based firms still accounted for 66.8% of world production in 1985, followed by Japan with 26.7% and western Europe with 5.1% (OECD 1985: 21). Within the United States, the core of the core, the innovative center of the semiconductor industry rapidly developed in the 1960s and 1970s outside of the traditional manufacturing regions: outside of the "Frostbelt" and inside the "Sunbelt" in Orange County, California, Dallas and Fort Worth, Texas, and most importantly in California's "Silicon" Valley.

Within the periphery, the major extensions of the U.S.- and Japanese-based semiconductor industry are in Asia, particularly Hong Kong, Singapore, Korea, Taiwan, and, more recently, the Philippines, Sri Lanka, and Indonesia. There has also been expansion into Latin America and the peripheries of Europe. (For a discussion of the spatial organization of the semiconductor industry see Scott 1986; Scott & Angel 1986; Ernst 1983.) While technologically sophisticated processes are developing in the more industrialized peripheries, much of the work remains Taylorized and low-skilled.

Exact data are hard to come by, but two pieces of evidence typify the inequalities in the core/periphery division of labor in the semiconductor industry. First, the four labor processes are very unevenly distributed when we compare the United States as a major core region with nations at different levels of development within the periphery: India, South Korea, and Singapore. As we would predict, the majority of U.S. plants have facilities for all phases of the production process, while few plants in Asia have the capacity of design or wafer fabrication. They are dependent parts of a labor process that has been planned and designed in the core. However, we note that the pattern is complex. For example, Korea has developed testing facilities on a scale comparable to core regions (table 9.2).

Table 9.2
Production Capacities of Production Facilities by Region, 1984

Production Capacities	U.S.	Asia excluding Japan			
		Total	India	S.Korea	Singapore
Design	83.2%	19.2%	16.7%	25.0%	57.1%
Diffusion	85.9	12.5	12.5	37.5	14.3
Assembly	91.9	93.3	100.0	100.0	100.0
Test	94.6	52.9	37.5	87.5	42.9
Production Facilities	(149)	(104)	(24)	(8)	(7)

Source: Wilson, 1985: 153-376

Secondly, comparative data on employment in core and peripheral regions show that production workers clearly predominate in the foreign subsidiaries of U.S.-based semiconductor firms. In 1978, they comprised 93% of the employees in foreign subsidiaries as compared to 63% in the United States (see table 9.1). Compiling data from more recent sources, we find that in Korea in 1984 the figure was 85% for all semiconductor firms as compared to 37% in U.S. firms. This shows a decline in the percentage of production workers in the core, but not in the periphery of the semiconductor industry (table 9.3).

Thus, following the pattern predicted by world-systems theory, the brains and control of the semiconductor industry are located in the core, in the United States, but increasingly in Japan and to a lesser extent in western Europe. More labor-intensive and less sophisticated labor processes have been assigned to the peripheries and are dependent largely on design, conception, and markets located in the core. Subsidiaries of transnational firms are like "puppets on a string." They carry out plans that have been decided in the core (Scriberras 1977: 83).

The Unequal Sexual Division of Labor

The story of proletarianization within the semiconductor industry has historically been about the subordination and superexploitation of women. Men manage and dominate; women do the routine, labor-intensive assembly work. This division of labor is also found in the textile industry and repeats the pattern of women's employment in manufacturing in Europe and the United States during the early stages of the Industrial Revolution.

Today in the semiconductor industry, women constitute the largest and lowest segment of the industrial proletariat in both the core and periphery, although they are concentrated in the latter. In the Silicon Valley at least 75% of the assembly-line workers are women. Of these, 40% are immigrants or women of color: Filipinos, Thais, Samoans, Mexicans, and Vietnamese (Howard 1981: 25). Their sisters in the peripheries (mainly Asia) constitute over 90% of the unskilled and Taylorized work force (Fuentes & Ehrenreich 1984: 16, 54; Scott 1986: 19; Siegel 1980: 14). If we take just the case of one firm, Signetics Korea, women constitute almost 99% of the unskilled work force, 41% of clerical workers, and about 1% of technical and skilled workers. The sexual division of labor could hardly be more stark (table 9.4).

Labor Control in the Peripheries: "Bloody Taylorism"

With the growth of export industries, women are becoming a preferred labor force in the peripheries. But does their entry into the labor force convert them into "free" wage labor, controlled and exploited on the basis of

Table 9.3
Occupational Structure in the Semiconductor Industry by Region

Occupational Categories	U.S.		S. Korea		Singapore
	(1) Semi-conductor	(2) Survey of 5 Plants	(3) Semi-conductor	(4) Motorola	(4) Signetics	(5) Survey of 6 Firms
	1986	1977	1984	1981	1980	1976
Production Workers	37.1%	54.3%	85.3%	90.4%	93.3%	n.a.
Managerial, Supervisory, Clerical & Technicians	n.a.	42.3	n.a.	9.6	6.7	5.0%

Source: Bureau of Labor Statistics, 1986: 62; Bernstein et al., 1980: 108; Economic Planning Board, 1986: 202-3; Park 1982: 545, 548; Fong & Kim 1977: 22

Table 9.4
Sex Composition by Skill Levels at Signetics Korea, 1980

Skill Levels	Male Employees	Female Employees	Total
Clericals	86(59.7%)	59(40.7%)	145(100.0%)
Technicians	43(100.0)	–(0.0)	43(100.0)
Skilled	211(99.1)	2(.9)	213(100.0)
Unskilled	30(1.3)	2,366(98.7)	2,396(100.0)
Total	370(13.2%)	2,427(86.8%)	2,797(100.0%)

Source: Park, 1982: 557

their Taylorized work? Or is their labor power further devaluated on sexist and racist grounds? Reports largely from feminists have confirmed the latter. The generic portrait of the Asian assembly worker is a young, unmarried woman, probably of rural origin, who contributes significantly to the support of her family. She starts her career in her late teens and works at the same low-skilled, routine tasks for up to seven or eight years until she is married or replaced by younger workers. She starts her assembly career with perfect vision. But she may soon lose her good eyesight because she spends her days peering through a microscope while bonding hair-thin wires to the miniature silicon chips. Her hours are long, from 40–60 per week. Her wages are low, from less than a $1.00 per day in Sri Lanka to $8.00 per day in South Korea. Her work is unhealthy due to eye strain and exposure to chemicals.

Her job has probably been designed in the Silicon Valley with a plan for exactly what routine movements she should perform, how she should perform them, and for how long. The goal is to minimize her decision making and to turn her into a machine-like motion minutely supervised and continually evaluated by line-persons and managers in the factory. Her so-called unskilled work, which may in fact take months to master, involves skills, dexterity, healthy vision, and the stamina to survive routine, constant supervision, exposure to chemical and environmental hazards, long hours, rapid pacing by machines, insufficient wages, no chance of mobility, and the possibility of lay-offs in a job ever sensitive to recessions and the geographical mobility of capital (Chi 1984; Fuentes & Ehrenreich 1984; Grossman 1979; Lim 1978; Mies 1986; Nash & Fernandez-Kelly 1983; Ong 1985; Siegel 1980; Sudworth 1985).

This portrait confirms what Alain Lipietz has called "bloody Taylorism": systematic labor control built into Taylorized work, plus harsh work conditions enforced by direct political and sexist forms of coercion (Lipietz 1984). Major agents of these direct forms of labor control superimposed on the labor process are the transnational companies. As one observer put it: "Multinational companies which manage local factories and service industries operate as agents of cultural imperialism, reconstituting unequal relations between local men and women, while reinforcing the unequal relations between host societies and advanced capitalist societies'' (Ong 1985: 2).

Unequal relations between core and periphery are continually reinforced by direct, imperialized forms of control and direction of production: the subtle and not so subtle assumption of inferiority to justify low wages; production for export rather than for domestic consumption and development; and production designed and centered in the core and soldiered by weak, dependent states using repressive measures to control workers.

Core-based companies have also reconstituted sexist relations in order to justify their superexploitation of women. Some of these strategies reinforce old patterns. Women are paid less than men for the same jobs, occupy the least skilled categories, and unlike men rarely increase their skill or mobility during their careers. Moreover, their assembly work, although sex-blind, is defined as women's work performed by the small, nimble fingers of dutiful, docile, Asian daughters (Salaff 1981; Lutz, this volume).

But capitalist strategies do not rely merely on some "backward" Asian "culture of patriarchy"; they introduce new and foreign ideologies to mystify the economic motives for hiring young, female labor. Maria Mies argues that one consequence of capitalist development for women in Europe and now in the peripheries has been their redefinition primarily as housewives while men acquire the status of wage workers and chief breadwinners. "This means that their work, whether in use value or commodity production, is obscured, does not appear as 'free wage labor,' is defined as an 'income-generating *activity*,' and can hence be bought at a much cheaper price than male labour" (Mies 1986: 116). American firms add to "housewifization" the reproduction of new roles of female consumerism and individuality by promoting beauty contests, make-up classes, and company T-shirts.

The re-creation of gender inequalities goes far beyond the enclaves of export manufacturing. Young women who are laid off or otherwise cannot afford to support themselves and their families by their low factory wages may end up in the so-called informal sectors or even find employment in the large entertainment and prostitution industry fostered by transnational capital for their managerial strata and visiting tourists (Ong 1985). On the other hand, expanded opportunities for women's work, however devalued, also upset gender hierarchies at a historical moment when men face unemployment and men and women must adjust to the social implications of women's becoming major breadwinners.

CONCLUSION

Our task has been to locate women within the process of proletarianization in the Asian subsidiaries of the semiconductor industry. Our data confirm our initial hypotheses and show: (1) the Taylorization of the labor process and the extreme polarization of mental and manual work within the technical division of labor of the semiconductor industry; (2) the assignment of Taylorized and deskilled work to the most devalued sectors of the social division of labor as defined by geographical location (core/periphery), gender (men/women), and race (white/non-white); and (3) the particularly sexist and exploitative nature of peripheral Taylorism.

Women *are* the proletariat of this industry. They are located at the bottom of the hierarchically organized division of labor in manufacture and division of labor in society. They perform the routine Taylorized tasks designed by men. They perform these degraded tasks not as abstract "free wage laborers," but as *women* whose labor has undergone a historical process of devaluation. The ways in which they are superexploited and controlled bear the stamp of their contradictory status as women wage workers in the peripheries. Although in fact they are major breadwinners for their households, employers can justify paying them less than the value of their labor power by defining them primarily as dependent women.

Thus, the proletarianization of women in the semiconductor industry is defined by the Taylorized work that they perform (deskilled, Taylorized labor) and by their devalued status in the social division of labor. Capital profits from both. Their entry into the labor force and their proletarianization are consequences of two interrelated strategies of capital accumulation: surplus value gained, on the one hand, by degrading work and, on the other, by devaluing labor power of particular workers and then justifying this devaluation on sexist and racist grounds.

The Unity of the Two Divisions of Labor in the Process of Accumulation and Proletarianization

Throughout our discussion we have argued for the unity of the two divisions of labor in the process of accumulation and proletarianization. This unity is clearly apparent in the accumulation process of the semiconductor industry. Paradoxically, this industry, which epitomizes the latest capitalist strategy of accumulation through innovation and revolutionizing work, has depended on what can only be described as a form of "primitive accumulation," combining labor-intensive Taylorized work and a coercive and sexist devaluation of labor power.

The unity of the two divisions of labor within the capitalist world-system must also be invoked to explain why Asian women in particular became the preferred labor force in the semiconductor industry. We reject the position that postulates two separate divisions of labor with different "laws" of motion, one based on wage labor and capital, the other on patriarchal exploitation, which happen to coincide under certain historical circumstances. More likely, there is one capitalist "law" of maximizing accumulation which manipulates and transforms both divisions of labor under specific historical conditions.

Some Marxist theorists have emphasized the role of the technical division of labor in the feminization and ethnicization of work. In particular, Marlene Dixon (1978), Susanne Jonas & Marlene Dixon (1980), and Gabriel Kolko (1976) have argued that Taylorism, by deskilling work and rendering social characteristics abstractly irrelevant, has fostered the proletarianization of diverse populations within the global social division of labor. Thus, in nineteenth- and twentieth-century America, mechanized and Taylorized work helped convert an ethnically diverse, "unskilled" immigrant work force of largely rural origin into unskilled wage labor. Today, in addition, highly mobile capital also emigrates to the peripheries where a transplanted and Taylorized labor process can work the miracle of proletarianization on a newly emerging "unskilled" immigrant work force of largely rural origin.

However, theorists who claim that the feminization and ethnicization of work come about as a result of Taylorism cannot explain why Taylorized jobs are assigned to specific populations within the social division of labor. Why to men in core industries? Why to women in the export-oriented industries of the peripheries? The theoretical problem can be traced in part to the Marxist tendency to analyze the capitalist character only of the labor process, while exiling the division of labor in society to a precapitalist or ideological limbo outside the framework of capitalist accumulation. (See, e.g., Marx's own interpretation of the two divisions of labor in the first volume of *Capital* [1973: 350–58] and Braverman 1974, 1976.)

The lack of a satisfactory Marxist theory of the social division of labor has in turn encouraged complaints about the unhappy marriage of feminism and Marxism (Hartman 1981) as well as dualist theories that trace the subordination of women to a patriarchal division of labor predating and separate from capitalism. However, patriarchy does not explain the specifically capitalist process of the proletarianization and subordination of women. We cannot deduce the recent preference for Asian women workers from some abstract principle of sexism in the social division of labor. If sexism had been the sole cause, why did the transnationals not select poor black female labor in the United States? Why Asian women? If we take into account the availability of deskilled jobs (in the case of the semiconductor industry already sex-typed as "women's work") and capital's search for cheap labor, the answer can be found, not in an abstract sexism, but in the particular historical position of Asian women within the capitalist world-economy at a particular point in its development. Asian women (immigrants to urban areas in both the core and periphery) were preferred because they were available, cheaper, and more open to control than their sisters elsewhere.

Their availability was one specific consequence of the "green revolution," the capitalist transformation of agriculture that set women "free" and drove them to the cities where Taylorized work processes in the export industries accelerated their proletarianization. Such has been the case for many women in southeast Asia in the 1970s, for women in Korea and Taiwan in the 1960s, for their sisters in the Philippines and Bangladesh today, and for all the women of the world who have provided cheap assembly labor for new manufacturing industries (Hamilton 1983).

Their cheapness was also a consequence of recent changes in the social division of labor. To move on even more speculative grounds, we suspect that the rapid creation of a needy and available labor force in Asia meant the devaluation and cheapening of female labor, which capital creates, then exploits, and subsequently justifies through a mixture of new and old sexist ideologies. We are thinking about the immiseration of a newly created working class. For women the "progressive" transition to wage work can be experienced as a demotion in the social division of labor, a transition from being productive workers in self-sustaining subsistence households to being both dependents and wage earners in semiproletarian households.

The sexist devaluation of women's labor is a historical product of capitalist development. Capital does not merely take advantage of traditional sexism, it creates it and gives it distinctly capitalist forms. To quote Immanuel Wallerstein:

Men may often have done different work from women (and adults different from children and the elderly), but under historical capitalism there has been a steady devaluation of the work of women (and of the young and the old), and a corresponding emphasis on the value of the adult male's work. Whereas in other systems men and women did specified (but normally equal) tasks, under historical capitalism the adult male wage-earner was classified as the "breadwinner," and the adult female home-worker as the "housewife." (1983: 25)

Housewives were a historical creation of capitalism (Mies, 1986: 100–44). This status emerged over one hundred years ago in the core. Today, it is emerging in the semiconductor and other export industries in the peripheries where the requirements of Taylorized assembly work are defined as feminine.

Thus, at one moment in historical capitalism and in one industry, patterns of work and social domination change and combine with capital's cost-cutting strategies to make Asian women a preferred labor force. We do not assume the stability of any of these patterns. Asian women workers may not necessarily accept with docility their new responsibilities as breadwinners and new and continuing forms of coercion. Indeed the transnationals may even decide to ship their routine assembly back to more docile workers in the core rather than face the militancy of women workers in Asia (Cho 1985). What we have been analyzing is instability rather than stability of a process of female proletarianization within a larger framework of the immiseration of the working class as a whole.

REFERENCES

Bernstein, Alan, et al. (1980). "Silicon Valley: Paradise or Paradox." In Magdelena Mora & Adelaida R. del Castillo, eds., *Mexican Women in the United States.* Los Angeles: Chicano Studies Research Center, Univ. of California.

Braverman, Harry (1974). *Labor and Monopoly Capital: The Degradation of Work in the Twentieth Century*. New York: Monthly Review Press.

―――― (1976). "Two Comments." *Monthly Review*, 28, 3, 119–24.

Bureau of Labor Statistics (1986). "Employment and Earnings." Washington, D.C.: United States Department of Labor.

Chi, Young-Sun (1984). "Short of Simple Labor: Imbalance in the Demand and Supply of Women's Labor." *On Dong-A Daily*, December 12.

Cho, Soon Kyoung (1985). "The Labor Process and Capital Mobility: Limits of the New International Division of Labor." *Politics and Society*, 14, 2, 185–222.

Dixon, Marlene (1978). "Abstract: The Degradation of Waged Labor and Class Formation on an International Scale." *Synthesis*, 2, 3, 46–53.

Economic Planning Bureau, Republic of Korea (1981). *Report on Mining and Manufacturing Survey 1979*. Seoul: EPB.

Ernst, Dieter (1983). *The Global Race in Microelectronics*. Frankfurt am Main: Campus.

Fong, Pan Eng, & Linda Kim (1977). *The Electronics Industry in Singapore: Structure, Technology and Linkages*. Singapore: Economic Research Center, Univ. of Singapore.

Fröbel, F. J., J. Heinrichs & O. Kreye (1980). *The New International Division of Labor*. New York: Cambridge Univ. Press.

Fuentes, Annette, & Barbara Ehrenreich (1984). *Women in the Global Factory*. Boston: South End.

Grossman, R. (1979). "Women's Place in the Integrated Circuit." *Radical America*, 14, 1, 29–49.

Hamilton, Clive (1983). "Capitalist Industrialization in East Asia's Four Little Tigers." *Journal of Contemporary Asia*, 13, 1, 35–73.

Hartman, Heidi, ed. (1981). *The Unhappy Marriage of Marxism and Feminism: Debates on Class and Patriarchy*. London: Pluto.

Herman, Andrew (1982). "Conceptualizing Control: Domination and Hegemony in the Capitalist Labor Process." *Insurgent Sociologist*, 11, 3, 7–22.

Howard, Robert (1981). "Second Class in Silicon Valley." *Working Papers Magazine*, 8, 5, 20–31.

International Trade Commission (ITC) (1979). *Competitive Factors Influencing World Trade in Integrated Circuits*. Washington, D.C.: ITC.

Jonas, Susanne, & Marlene Dixon (1980). "Proletarianization and Class Alliances in the Americas." In T. K. Hopkins and I. Wallerstein, eds., *Processes in the World-System*. Beverly Hills: Sage, 224–48.

Kolko, Gabriel (1976). *Main Currents in Modern American History*. New York: Harper & Row.

Lim, Linda Y. C. (1978). "Women Workers in Multinational Corporations: The Case of the Electronics Industry in Malaysia and Singapore." University of Michigan, Michigan Occasional Paper No. 9.

―――― (1983) "Capitalism, Imperialism, and Patriarchy: The Dilemma of Third-World Women Workers in Multinational Factories." In June Nash and Maria Patricia Fernandez-Kelly, eds., *Women and Men in the International Division of Labor*. Albany: State University of New York Press, 70–91.

Lipietz, Alain (1984). "Imperialism or the Beast of the Apocalypse." *Capital and Class*, No. 22, Spring, 81–109.

Marx, Karl (1973). *Capital, I.* New York: International.

Mies, Maria (1986). *Patriarchy and Accumulation on a World Scale.* London: Zed.

Nash, June, and Maria Patricia Fernandez-Kelly, eds. (1983). *Women and Men in the International Division of Labor.* Albany: State University of New York Press.

Ong, Aihwa (1983). "Global Industries and Malay Peasants in Peninsular Malaysia." In June Nash and Maria Patricia Fernandez-Kelly, eds., *Women and Men in the International Division of Labor.* Albany: State University of New York Press, 426–41.

——— (1985). "Industrialization and Prostitution in Southeast Asia." *Southeast Asia Chronicle*, No. 96, 2–6.

Organization for Economic Cooperation and Development (OECD) (1985).*The Semiconductor Industry: Trade Related Issues.* Paris: OECD.

Park, Se Il (1982). "Electronics Industry II." In Kim Su-Kon and Tai-Hyu Ha, eds., *Case Studies in Labor Relations (in Korea).* Seoul: Korea Development Institute, 518–621.

Salaff, Janet W. (1981). *Working Daughters of Hong Kong.* New York: Cambridge University Press.

Scott, Allen J. (1986). "The Semiconductor Industry in South-East Asia: Organization, Location and the International Division of Labor." Los Angeles: University of California, Los Angeles, Institute for Industrial Relations, Working Paper No. 101.

Scott, Allen J. and D. P. Angel (1986). *The U.S. Semiconductor Industry: Locational Analysis.* Los Angeles: University of California, Los Angeles, Graduate School of Architecture and Urban Planning.

Scribberas, Edmond (1977). *Multinational Electronics Companies and National Policies.* Greenwich, Conn.: JAI.

Siegel, Lenny (1980). "Delicate Bonds: The Global Semiconductor Industry." *Pacific Research*, 11, 1, First Quarter, 1–26.

Sudworth, Elizabeth (1985). "Let the Robber Barons Come, Free Trade Zones." *Connexions*, No. 15, Winter, 3–5.

Taplin, Ruth (1986). "Women in World Market Factories: East and West." *Ethnic and Racial Studies*, 9, 2, 168–95.

United Nations Center on Transnational Corporations (UNCTC) (1986). *Transnational Corporations in the International Semiconductor Industry.* New York: United Nations.

United Nations Development Organization (UNIDO) (1980). *Export Processing Zones in Developing Countries.* New York: UNIDO.

Wallerstein, Immanuel (1974). *The Modern World-System. I. Capitalist Agriculture and the Origins of the European World-Economy in the Sixteenth Century.* New York: Academic Press.

——— (1981). "Race Is Class?" *Monthly Review*, 32, 10, March, 47–52.

——— (1983). *Historical Capitalism.* London: Verso.

Wilson, Kenneth, ed. (1985). *Profile of the Worldwide Semiconductor Industry.* London: Benn Electronics.

10

"Ethnicity" and "Race" in the Small Business Literature: Some Lessons from the World-Systems Perspective

Richard Williams

Stereotypes occur as the result of a fixed attitude and an assumed relationship. The fixed attitude is that a group of people who are defined by one common attribute (e.g., physical features, geography, religion, language) have characteristics and behaviors that are affiliated with that attribute. The assumed relationship is that *all* individuals with the defined attribute have the characteristics (Sagarin 1975: 343).[1]

The term *racist stereotype* is therefore here used to refer to a fixed attitude and assumed relationships about a group of people who are defined by having the attribute "race" in common. To assert that the ethnic small business literature perpetuates racist stereotypes is therefore to imply that the literature reenforces the notion that there are racially and ethnically defined groups with permanent characteristics that are exhibited by all members of the group. The roots of racist stereotypes are precisely rooted in the naive use of ethnic and racial categories.[2]

The world-systems perspective allows us to see how to move beyond the racial stereotyping of the literature by shifting from its reliance upon status-groups (defined as primordial and homogeneous within a national context) toward world-class categories (defined as having an interaction within the international arena). The basis of this reconceptualization is rooted in the notion that ethnic groups are created and re-created within the context of the modern world capitalist system (Wallerstein 1980), even though they appear to be primordial groups. This notion is combined with the understanding of status-groups developed by Arrighi, Hopkins, and Wallerstein (1983).

The first section of this chapter presents a general description of the ethnic small business literature, which points to the traditional explanations for low rates of small-business participation among blacks in the United States. Out of that will come a discussion of some of the assumptions that are critical to the explanations in that literature.

In the second section I discuss the use of ethnic and racial categories as cases for the comparative method. There I demonstrate that some of the problems that arise from their use are related to the abuse of the rules of the comparative method. This leads to a discussion of those categories as specific instances of the general concept *status-groups*.

The third section goes further into the discussion of status-groups and reconceptualizes ethnicity and race from the world-systems perspective. Further examples from the literature are used to demonstrate the validity of this reconceptualization.

My conclusion elaborates upon the fact that the use of ethnic and race categories (status-groups) serves to re-enforce racism within the society. It also elaborates upon the notion that the way to change that type of re-enforcement is to root those categories in their world-historical context. This is the contribution of the world-systems perspective.

THE ETHNIC SMALL BUSINESS LITERATURE

The general discussion in this literature is about differential rates of small-business participation among ethnic and racial groups. Its theoretical emphasis is located in explanations for low rates of black participation as compared with other groups. An important assumption in this literature is that small-business participation has historically provided a path toward social mobility for lower-class groups within the United States (Glazer & Moynihan 1963; Lieberson 1980).

It is possible to divide this literature into two groups: early studies (pre-1970s), which tend to concentrate on comparisons between whites and Negroes (Myrdal 1944; Drake & Cayton 1945; Frazier 1957; Glazer & Moynihan 1963), and present studies (1970s–present), which tend to concentrate on comparisons between blacks and nonwhites, primarily Asians (Light 1972; Bonacich 1973; Bonacich & Modell 1980; Auster & Aldrich 1984; Waldinger, Ward & Aldrich 1985).

The early explanations for why people of African descent in the United States had low rates of small-business participation are summarized by Glazer and Moynihan. Writing about the black population of New York City, they assert that "there were in 1940 only small groups of professionals and clerical and sales workers. But perhaps most striking was the almost complete absence of a business class, and this is still true today" (1963: 30). Their initial explanations for this phenomenon are: (1) The black population had no experience with money, due to slavery. (2) The population had no skill in planning and foresight, again due to slavery. (3) Slavery prevented that population from having financial resources. (4) That population faced prejudice and discrimination when attempting to get stock, capital, or space for rent (1963: 30).

The authors do not leave the issue to those explanations, however. They go on to say that "surely there were in the great Negro city that grew up in Harlem in the 1920s *opportunities* for the business-minded to get a foothold by serving their own, as so many ethnic groups had done before them" (1963: 32). Thus this position held that despite the specific historical and societal conditions that distinguished the "black" population from the "white" population, there were opportunities for people of African descent that were similar to those for ethnic Europeans. This shift of focus explicitly states that the explanations for differences in rates of small-business participation are to be found in attributes that are internal to groups, rather than in the historical and societal factors that are external to them. More specifically, the attributes relate to the differential ability of groups to take advantage of existing opportunities.

Therefore other factors are used to explain different rates of small-business participation (ability to take advantage of existing opportunities). (1) There were no special markets in the black migrant community, because they did not have a foreign culture. (2) Blacks did not develop "the same kind of clannishness" as other ethnic groups. (3) Blacks did not develop the same close and strong family ties as did other groups. (4) "In the end, the most important factor is probably the failure of Negroes to develop a pattern of saving" (1963: 33).

The essence of the other factors is based upon comparing the black population with the white population. Thus, prejudice, discrimination, and assumptions about the historical effects of slavery are replaced by implicit and explicit comparative statements.[3] "The black community lacked special markets because they lacked a foreign culture" can also be read as "European ethnics had special markets because they had a foreign culture." "The failure of Negroes to develop a pattern of saving" can also be read as "European ethnics were able to develop a pattern of saving." While the above are implicit comparisons, the issues of clannishness and strong family ties need no elaboration, because they are explicitly comparative.

What should be noticed is that special markets, clannishness, strong family ties, and a pattern of saving have not been demonstrated to be more significant in relationship to small-business participation than prejudice, discrimination, and the impact of slavery. It could even be argued that making such comparisons between blacks and whites is not legitimate precisely because slavery, prejudice, and discrimination are causally related to the existence of markets, clannishness, family ties, and saving patterns.

It is in addressing this issue that the break between early and present in the literature can be defined. With Ivan Light (1972), the essential phenomenon to be explained (low rates of small-business participation among people of African descent in the United States) is the same, but there is a shift in one of the units that are compared in order to address that issue. In his work, blacks are compared with Asians rather than with whites. Waldinger, Ward and Aldrich (1985) argue that a methodological advance was achieved by shifting the comparisons to those among nonwhites. The basic assumption of this argument is that the racial characteristics of non-whites make them more similar to each other than to whites. Therefore, with the use of "nonwhite" units for analysis, the results should reflect a closer adherence to the rules of the comparative method. Such is the case, they assert, because all such groups face discrimination (blocked opportunities) due to their physical distinctiveness from the white majority population. The chances for success within U.S. society, they continue, are therefore more similar for these groups than they are for ethnic whites and blacks. The legitimacy of the shift therefore depends upon the validity of the notion that the physical distinctiveness of nonwhites is the dominant causal factor in determining chances for success within the society.[4]

In their attempt to explain different rates of small-business participation between blacks and Asians, Ellen Auster and Howard Aldrich (1985) isolate two causal variables. One is the opportunity structure; the other is organizing capacity. The logic of their explanation rests upon the assumption that all nonwhites face similar restrictions of opportunity. This assumption of commonality (physical features and opportunity) logically leads to the question: How then do we account for the highly variable rates of movement by "ethnic" groups into self-employment and small business? (Auster & Aldrich, 1984: 47). The assumption of commonality therefore serves as a conceptual bridge by which to direct the reader to internal group characteristics and away from external social phenomena.[5]

Using the bridge, groups—"blacks" and "Asians"—are first defined as similar due to their opportunity structures, and then organizing capacities are used to make distinctions between them. Auster and Aldrich state:

Opportunities are irrelevant unless taken advantage of, and people vary widely in their ability to seize opportunities and make the most of them. Bonacich (1973), Light (1972) and others have argued that the possibility of exploiting opportunities is linked to a group's internal organizing capacity. Ethnic groups with a high level of self-organization provide co-ethnics with a collective capacity for organizing new ventures. (1985: 47)

Following Light (1972), they characterize mutual aid societies (e.g., rotating credit systems) as key internal (cultural) variables for explaining Chinese and Japanese rates of small-business participation (Light 1972, 1980). Blacks, on the other hand, are characterized as lacking the cultural traditions that would generate the types of mutual aid that have helped the Chinese and Japanese. It is thus their lack of internal means for generating funds that makes the black population in the United States vulnerable to discrimination on the part of banks and other sectors of society.[6] The issue of causality is absolutely ignored here and in this literature in general (Auster & Aldrich, 1984: 48).

To sum up, the pre-1970s literature asserts that blacks and whites were similar because there "must have been opportunities for both groups to serve their own." The present literature asserts that blacks and Asians (minorities) are similar because of their parallel opportunity structures. In the early literature, low rates of black small-business participation are explained by a lack of clannishness, a lack of strong family ties, and an inability to save. The present literature explains the low rates of small-business participation by the lack of mutual aid societies (self-help groups) that can generate funds for the group. There are therefore incredible similarities in the basis upon which groups are defined as well as in the explanations for differential rates of small-business participation between the pre-1970s and the present literature (Auster & Aldrich 1984: 48).

Thus, we can conclude that the shift from comparing whites with blacks to comparing Asians with blacks has added nothing to our theoretical understanding of ethnic small business in the United States. After all, we knew before 1972 that explanations for low rates of small-business participation among blacks were to be found in factors that are internal to the group.

THE COMPARATIVE METHOD: "ETHNIC" AND "RACE" CATEGORIES

The early literature ultimately relied upon racial groups as units of comparison, while the present literature relies upon ethnic/national and racial groups to do so. In this section I will look at some of the problems that are generated when status-groups are utilized to generate theory through the comparative method.

In her discussion of comparative historical analysis, Theda Skocpol provides the basis of our discussion:

Basically, one tries to establish valid associations of potential causes with the given phenomenon one is trying to explain. There are two main ways to proceed. First, one may try to establish that several cases having in common the phenomenon one is trying to explain also have in common a set of causal factors (the method of agreement). Second, one can contrast the cases in which the phenomenon to be explained and the hypothesized causes are present to other cases in which the phenomenon and the causes are both absent, but which are otherwise as similar as possible to the positive cases (the method of difference). (1979:36)

When utilizing the comparative method our concerns therefore are threefold. We must specify our cases, the phenomenon to be explained, and our hypothesized causes.

Looking at these three concerns through the methods of agreement and difference it can be seen clearly how problems arise in the use of "ethnic" and "racial" categories. The method of agreement can be characterized as in figure 10.1.

The purpose of this approach is to establish whether or not there is a relationship between causes and an observed phenomenon for the cases being studied. Its strength, therefore, is in allowing us to determine whether there is any validity to our hypothesized causes.

The cases in the ethnic small-business literature are, not surprisingly, ethnic and racial groups. It would therefore be expected that the categories *Asian*, *black*, and *white* are entities that give support to the hypothesized causes upon which the literature is based. For instance, when those categories are used, it is expected that they are representative of a number of individuals with similar blocked economic opportunities and organizing capacities. As a result, the composite group will have a rate of small-business participation that correlates, as hypothesized, with the causes.

But how valid is the assumption that the status-group categories (e.g., "ethnicity" and "race") are actually representations of individuals with similar blocked economic opportunities and organizing capacities? While it is difficult to even address this question in regard to organizing capacity, an attempt can be made in regard to blocked economic opportunities. Max Weber describes status-groups as collectives that are organized outside of the market (1978: 932). This means that status-group categories are not always homogenized, especially in regard to economic life chances.

But it is precisely the use of those status-groups, with their assumption of homogeneity, that precludes the necessity of investigating the extent to which similar status-groups in fact correlate with similar economic opportunities.[7]

Figure 10.1
The Method of Agreement

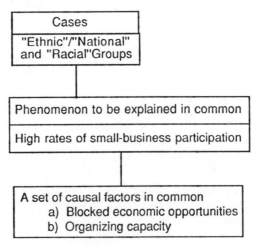

Within the context of the method of agreement the use of the status-group categories *ethnicity* and *race* result in problems that require further analysis.

The method of difference is based upon the contrast of cases established by the method of agreement with cases in which neither the phenomenon nor the causal factors exist. The method of difference can be characterized as in Figure 10.2.

Ideally the method of difference concentrates upon contrasts between cases in which the phenomenon to be explained and the causal factors exist and cases in which neither exists. The present data on ethnic small-business

Figure 10.2
The Method of Difference

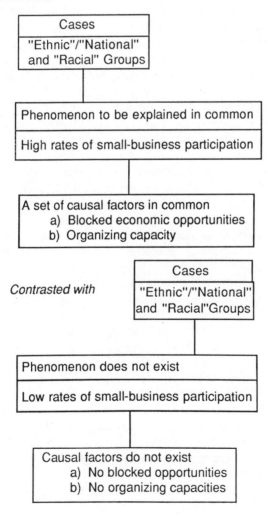

participation indicates that whites and Asians have high rates of participation while blacks have low rates of participation. The logic of this method would lead us to believe, however, that groups with blocked economic opportunities and organizing capacity will have high rates of participation, while those without blocked economic opportunities and without organizing capacities will have low rates of participation.

But within this framework there is an inconsistency in regard to the links between the phenomenon to be explained and the set of causal factors. Rather than having two distinct instances (causal factors exist, phenomenon exists), we in fact have muddy instances. The Asian group, as presented in the literature, has high rates of participation and causal factors exist. The black group, again according to the literature, has low rates of participation. Given the relationship between the causal factors and the existing phenomenon we would expect to find no blocked economic opportunities and no organizing capacity for the black group. A critical feature of the literature, however, has been its insistence upon similarity of opportunities for the groups being compared.[8]

Here the methodological problem arises out of the fact that the literature utilizes "blocked opportunity" as a mechanism to equate groups, while at the same time it insists on using that notion as one of the explanations for participation in small business. But obviously blocked opportunity (an external factor) is not related to participation in the manner asserted. "Organizing capacity" (an internal factor as defined in the literature), which appears much more consistent in that regard, then becomes utilized as the actual explanation for rates of participation. This shift of explanation is achieved, however, because blocked opportunity, it is asserted, fails to explain differences among group rates of participation.

There are, therefore, problems when the ethnic small-business literature is looked at in the context of the method of agreement, and there are problems when it is looked at via the method of difference. The focus of the problems is the same, however. In both cases they revolve around the relationship that is alleged to exist between blocked opportunities and the status-group's ethnicity and race.

When analyzing the literature from the perspective of the method of agreement, we have shown that it assumes that individuals within status-groups have similar blocked opportunities. But such an assumption is precisely ruled out by the definition of status-groups (Weber 1978; Arrighi, Hopkins & Wallerstein 1983: 296). An assumption of homogeneity of status-groups on this scale is thus unwarranted. When analyzing the literature from the perspective of the method of difference, we see blocked opportunity being utilized in the literature to assert that there are similarities across status-group boundaries. However, if an assumption of homogeneity within status groups based upon blocked opportunities is unwarranted, it then follows that its use to establish across-group homogeneity is also problematic.

The small-business literature reinforces racist stereotypes because it ignores the existence of diversity within status-group categories. It operates from the fixed attitude that there is a relationship between status-groups and some internal factor (organizing capacity) that determines the rate of small-business participation of its members. In this regard attention is shifted away from the social context within which groups are created and re-created and toward the internal characteristics of groups. This implies that social mobility is a result of characteristics of groups that are embodied in all of its members.

These characteristics appear primordial in that there is no explanation as to how they become group and individual traits.[9] The flip-side of this is that those groups with low rates of small-business participation lack these primordial characteristics. It is then not surprising to find within the literature a stress upon self-help as a mechanism of social mobility (Cummings 1980). This position ultimately asserts that groups succeed or fail as a result of their inner resources, which exist despite blocked opportunities. Cummings states that "a major contention of the essays in this volume is that the sources of immigrant social mobility and economic activity are to be found within the cultural and historical traditions of particular ethnic groups and embodied in the collective self-help institutions created by the group" (1980: 9). While he utilizes this position in order to attack notions of rugged individualism as the essential force of ethnic economic development, Cummings ends by reifying and glorifying the social conditions of ethnic groups in the United States.

STATUS-GROUPS IN THE WORLD-SYSTEM

How then do we get beyond the obvious contradictions that have remained so buried in the existing literature? One way out is to look more carefully at the historical circumstances that come with blocked opportunity and, as an extension, at the social context within which the status-group categories *ethnicity* and *race* are created. Important in this regard is the fact that "blocked opportunities" is utilized in the literature only within the context of the United States. This limited usage asserts that the periods prior to the time when groups arrived in the United States are not relevant to how their opportunities were structured upon their entrance into the United States. Here we arrive at the totally unwarranted conclusion that the past has no effect upon the present. It also allows for the equally unwarranted conclusion that present blocked opportunities have the same impact upon all those who have to confront them.

But it is certainly the case that even all nonwhites have not experienced the same types of blocked opportunities in the past. We need only call attention to the fact that during most of the nineteenth century, when people of African descent in America were an enslaved minority, the immigrants from China were neither enslaved nor a minority in their own country (colonial statues provides room for the development of an indigenous elite, while slavery largely prohibited such a development). India presents a more clear-cut instance of colonialism, but not of minority status or slavery. Korea also presents the case of colonialism, but not minority status or slavery. When looking at Japan during the nineteenth century, we find neither a minority, a colonial people, nor an enslaved people. While it is difficult to determine the degree to which such historical distinctions have affected the ability of a population to survive in the present, it is clear that such distinctions must be considered before assuming that "nonWhiteness" equals "blocked opportunities."

The significance of this point is that past social conditions can be more or less conducive to the development of tools to confront blocked opportunities (access to education; possibilities of earning an income which can result in saving; access to capital markets; etc.). Equally important is the fact that this point holds, not only across status-groups, but also within them.

Looking at status-groups within the context of the world-system provides us with a conceptual framework by which to explain differences in rates of small-business participation without resorting to racial stereotypes. Wallerstein (1974: 353) argues that status-groups develop from two directions. One is the response of local elites to a class-conscious lower stratum. In this case, common local traits (e.g., religion, language, physical distinctions) are utilized to make a sharp distinction between all of the locals—regardless of class—and nonlocals. The desired outcome is diminished internal conflict.

Status-groups also develop as a response by local elites to their subordinate position within the world-system. As in the former instance, the desired outcome is increased potential power for the local elite. Here, however, the concern is with the larger world context within which the state operates rather than with the state as the social context of action.

This perspective provides us with insight about possible confusions that can arise from treating status-groups as if they are entirely homogenized, or as if they are primordial groups. The roots of the confusions can be found in the differences between the objective and the subjective definitions of world classes. Wallerstein (1980) calls attention to the fact that, objectively, the bourgeoisie as well as the proletariat are classes formed in the world-system. But, despite that objective reality, it is clear that advantages exist in relying upon subjective (self-perception/other-perception) definitions.

The move is away from the objective world-class definition of the distribution of power and toward a status-group definition of that distribution. Wallerstein (1980) also asserts that nationalism is the most powerful force behind status-group formation in the modern world. In addition to nationalism, however, race and ethnicity have also proven to be effective bases of status-group distinctions within the modern world.

Race and ethnicity ("nation") have two important characteristics in common. One is that they define boundaries which, although subjective, quickly appear to create objective distinctions among people (Berger & Luckmann 1967). The other is that they, as do all status-groups, categorize populations in a way that includes a range of economic differentiation (Miles

1986: 26). The combination of the two characteristics gives the appearance of distinct and independent social categories that are economically, culturally, and "racially" homogeneous. Once this homogenization process occurs the stage is set for misinterpretations of social reality. This can be seen as we return to the discussion of differential rates of small-business participation among groups within the United States.

The data are overwhelming. The 1980 U.S. census data on males indicate that 17.4% of Koreans, 12.6% of Japanese, 9.8% of Chinese, and 8.6% of Asian Indians were business owners, while only 2.5% of blacks were business owners during that period (Willette & Shaycoft 1986). When we look at these status-group categories there is indeed a gap between blacks and Asians (a significant proportion of whom are recent immigrants).[10] But, the world-systems perspective allows us to hypothesize that the existence of variation is a result of the process by which these status groups have been lumped and, even further, that the process of classification is problematic because the social context (the world-system) within which these groups are created and re-created is not taken into account by those studying ethnic small business.

The reasoning behind utilizing "Asians" has been the desire to establish more comparable units of analysis (Waldinger, Ward & Aldrich 1985: 586). The issue of comparability is premised, however, upon the notion that immigrants from peripheral and semiperipheral countries (the areas from which the immigrants were coming)[11] are economically homogeneous, and face similar blocked opportunities as do people of African descent in the United States. Not only is the assumption made that they are economically homogeneous, but it is also assumed that they are proletarians, rather than bourgeois or petty bourgeois.

Given those premises, immigrants moving from peripheral and semiperipheral states to core states are easily viewed as proletarians, and nonwhite. If over time we observe that those immigrants are succeeding within the core society at higher rates than the proletarian, nonwhite populations that are indigenous to the core state (United States), it becomes logical to explain this distinction as the result of factors within the specific populations because, after all, both are proletarian and nonwhite, thus conforming perfectly to the requirements of the comparative method.

What needs to be looked at more carefully, however, is the extent to which the above descriptions of immigrants from the periphery and the semiperiphery to the core are correct. The U.S. census data, in fact, indicate that legal immigrants to the United States from the periphery and the semiperiphery, after 1965, tend to be educated and have savings and networks in the host country (Rheimer 1985: 107).

It is interesting that the Japanese are also placed within the lumped category "nonwhite," despite Japan's obvious core status. This is a clear indication of categorization based upon nonwhiteness rather than upon concrete life chance attributes. It is this type of aggregation, rather than the generally asserted cultural differences between groups, that accounts for much of the ethnic differences in rates of small-business participation.

It thus appears that shifting to new immigrant nonwhites only gives greater comparability as far as pigmentation goes, but it does not do so in regard to class position within the world system. In fact what needs to be done in order to establish comparable units of analysis is to make a detailed analysis of the manner in which the nonwhite immigrants who are succeeding in small business have gained their class position within their country of origin and then to find a similar social group within the United States with which to compare them. Only in this manner can we keep from being fooled into assuming that nonwhiteness or nationality makes for comparability. It is precisely the way in which subjective factors are given precedence over objective factors that allows for the types of race- and nation-based explanations that today have such a familiar ring of truth. It is also precisely in this process that racism is reinforced in the United States.

CONCLUSION

The literature on ethnic small-business participation in the United States places a great deal of emphasis upon the fact that some ethnic groups have higher rates of participation than others. While on the surface this approach is the traditional sociological one for explaining social variations, it ultimately serves the political purpose of deflecting attention away from institutionalized racism within society.

Because of the focus of the literature, the issue of black unemployment in the United States, for example, is implicitly characterized as a problem of the black population, rather than of institutionalized racism (Auster & Aldrich 1984: 44). Such is the case because it provides a context within which to compare cases that appear to be similar. But while the use of ethnic groups gives the appearance of comparable units this appearance has been achieved at the expense of ignoring the groups' historical roots.

This distortion, which operates at various levels, reinforces racism by shifting our attention away from the larger society and toward stereotypical "ethnic" groups that are isolated from the larger society. At one level all "nonwhites" are characterized as being in the same economic category and facing similar forms of discrimination within the United States. This premise will thus legitimatize comparisons among "nonwhites" as similar units of analysis.

Once nonwhites are legitimized as groups facing similiar types of discrimination and being in similar economic categories (poor), a second level of racism comes into play. When comparisons inevitably result in differences in regard to variables that have come to signify success within the society (e.g., family income, years of schooling, small-business proprietorship, percentage of ethnic group unemployed, percentage of ethnic group members employed by fellow ethnic group members) those nonwhite ethnic groups who score high become models for the rest of the society, but in particular for nonwhites; this naturally leads to assertions such as: "if they can do it, then any hard working group should be able to succeed." It should be recognized that the notion of hard work always accompanies those groups.

In the final analysis therefore differentiation within the lumped category *nonwhite* allows for an avoidance of the larger issue, that is, the manner in which inequality among nation-states is paralleled in the unequal distribution of wealth between the core and peripheral regions of the world-system. Hence the fact that all peoples from peripheral regions are not poor is easily lost sight of.

As an extension, issues of racism that are manifested in core countries toward recent migrants from peripheral regions and those identified with peripheral regions (i.e., "Third World" people) get lost in discussions about self-help of peoples from peripheral regions of the world. Pulling the group up by the boot strap becomes the symbol of the day and such statements as this become commonplace: "Don't blame the system. It's essential that all groups with peripheral identifications take care of their own; after all other peripheral groups have been able to succeed."

It is thus by viewing groups apart from their social contexts that racism takes on legitimacy within the society. An important social context from which groups that are compared in the ethnic small-business literature have been removed is the world-system. A serious assessment of ethnic small-business participation would require rejecting the assumption that all nonwhites are similar, merely because they are presently identified with peripheral regions of the world. This is especially true in regard to class background and the following related factors: (1) the amount of capital different groups have historically been able to accumulate; (2) the time period during which they arrived in the United States; (3) the type of social networks that were available to them; and (4) the treatment received from the state as well as from the population at large upon arrival.

An explanation of variations in small-business participation among ethnic groups needs to take into account a series of historical factors that transcend the boundaries of the United States and the cultures of the groups compared. Without this historical approach studies of ethnic participation in small business naturally result in the reinforcement of racism because they force the analysis toward group attributes isolated from social facts.

By establishing distinctions between groups in regard to their life chances prior to meeting in the United States (a task that can be accomplished by an analysis of those groups within the context of the world-system), superficial comparisons based upon nonhistorical (e.g. cultural) variables lose some of their explanatory centrality. This can be achieved by looking more carefully at the circumstances that have led to the recent movements of peoples to the United States, as well as a careful analysis of the attributes of those individuals who are to be compared in regard to social mobility within the society.

NOTES

The author would like to thank Sonia Ospina for her insights about this chapter.

1. Although the tendency is to focus on negative stereotypes, as is the case here, clearly stereotypes can also be positive.

2. Relying upon both Cox (1948: 318) and Van den Berghe (1967: 16), "race" and "ethnicity" are here viewed as essentially similar categories.

3. These assumptions about the long-term effects of slavery are merely assumptions that have never been seriously addressed. Their primary impact appears to be the blunting of discussion about the impact of present conditions upon the African population in the United States.

4. There is no question that this statement appears as a fundamental truth of American society. As we proceed, however, we will have cause to call this into question. The point that is being made here is not that there is no racism within society. "Race" is not necessarily the sole determinant of what people's life chances are within the society. Contrasts between the "whites" of Appalachia and the "non-whites" of Japan easily makes that clear.

5. Commonality is ultimately achieved by viewing groups apart from their historical context and utilizing the category "minority" to characterize both "blacks" and "Asians." Auster and Aldrich state: "Employment opportunities for minorities are often restricted because of their limited education, lack of training in the skills required in higher paying jobs, and poor facility in the majority group's language" (1984: 46). They also say: "Discrimination often limited minorities to particular quarters of a city" (1984: 47). There is no sense here that "minorities" are socially created, rather than primordial. In addition there is clearly no room for specific conditions which might make distinctions within this category of "minority."

6. Auster and Aldrich characterize "black" banks as of little help due to the incompetence of bank officials, "venality and misappropriation of funds," and faulty and inadequate records (1984: 48). These ideas are taken from Light (1972), who takes them from Glazer and Moynihan (1963), who take them from Frazier (1957). Frazier takes his ideas from Drake and Cayton (1945). No evidence for these assertions is provided by Auster and Aldrich, and little was provided by Drake and Cayton in 1945; nonetheless, these ideas persist. It would thus appear that the sins of 1945 will be with the group forever if the literature has its way. So, even when black organizations exist, it is assumed that there are internal problems which hamper their ability to aid each other.

7. This notion that the experiences of members of groups that are socially defined as similar will also be similar lacks an understanding of how such groups are created (primordially).

8. This similarity has been insisted upon in the pre-1970s literature as well as in the present literature. This problem is not unknown to those writing in the field. It is openly acknowledged by Auster and Aldrich, for instance, when they state that most theories do not explain the situation for blacks in the United States (1984: 48). Despite this disclaimer, however, the notion persists that this breakdown in regard to blacks does not then negate the validity of the overall relationship being asserted. It even does not prevent those writing from making statements about the causes for low rates of small-business participation among blacks that assume that there are no inconsistencies in the manner in which comparisons are carried out in the literature.

9. Bonacich (1973) in her discussion of "middlemen minorities" seems to indicate that the small-business spirit comes from the process of sojourning. She does not confront the question as to why sojourning operates for some groups and not for others, however. As a result, we are again left with the existence of some primordial feature of groups as the determinant of differences among them.

10. Rheimer states: "Congress did not foresee exactly how the 1965 act would work, especially in the case of Asian nations. Asian immigrants grew rapidly after 1965 and accounted for about 40 percent of the annual totals as the 1970s came to an end. . . . Altogether Third World peoples dominated the immigration statistics after 1965; Europe sent only about 15 percent of the total by the late 1970s and early 1980s" (1985: 243).

11. See note 9. Rheimer, relying upon U.S. census data, also states that "not all (immigrants from) Hong Kong or Taiwan had poor education or lacked English. Among the new immigrants were engineers, doctors, mathematicians, and scientists" (1985: 107).

REFERENCES

Arrighi, Giovanni, Terence K. Hopkins, and Immanuel Wallerstein (1983). "Rethinking the Concepts of Class and Status-Group in a World-System Perspective." *Review*, 6, 3, Winter, 283–304.

Auster, Ellen, and Howard Aldrich (1984). "Small Business Vulnerability, Ethnic Enclaves and Ethnic Enterprise." In Robin Ward and Richard Jenkins, eds. *Ethnic Communities in Business*. Cambridge: Cambridge University Press, 39–54.

Berger, Peter, and Thomas Luckmann (1967). *The Social Construction of Reality*. New York: Anchor.

Bonacich, Edna (1973). "A Theory of Middleman Minorities." *American Sociological Review*, 37, 5, October, 583–94.

Bonacich, Edna, and John Modell (1980). *The Economic Basis of Ethnic Solidarity: Small Business in the Japanese American Community*. Berkeley: University of California Press.

Cox, Oliver C. (1948). *Castle, Class and Race*. New York: Monthly Review Press.

Cummings, Scott, ed. (1980). *Self-Help in Urban America*. Port Washington: National University Press.

Drake, Saint Clair, and Horace Cayton (1945). *Black Metropolis*. New York: Harcourt, Brace & Co.

Frazier, Edward Franklin (1957). *The Negro in the United States*. New York: Macmillan.

Glazer, Nathan, and Daniel Patrick Moynihan (1963). *Beyond the Melting Pot*. Cambridge, Mass.: MIT Press.

Lieberson, Stanley (1980). *A Piece of the Pie*. Berkeley: University of California Press.

Light, Ivan (1972). *Ethnic Enterprise in America*. Berkeley: University of California Press.

———— (1980). "Asian Enterprise in America: Chinese, Japanese and Koreans in Small Business." In S. Cummings, ed., *Self-Help in Urban America*. Port Washington: National University Press, 33–57.

Miles, Robert (1986). "Recent Marxist Theories of Nationalism and the Issue of Racism." *The British Journal of Sociology.* 38, 1, 24–41.

Myrdal, Gunnar (1944). *An American Dilemma: The Negro Problem and Modern Democracy.* New York: Harper.

Rheimer, David (1985). *Still the Golden Door.* New York: Columbia University Press.

Sagarin, Edward (1975). *Deviants and Deviance.* New York: Praeger.

Skocpol, Theda (1979). *States and Social Revolutions.* New York: Cambridge University Press.

Van den Berghe, Pierre (1967). *Race and Racism.* New York: Wiley & Sons.

Waldinger, Roger, Robin Ward, and Howard Aldrich (1985). "Trend Report: Ethnic Business and Occupational Mobility in Advanced Societies." *Sociology,* 29, 4, November, 586–97.

Wallerstein, Immanuel (1974). *The Modern World-System. Vol. 1, Capitalist Agriculture and the Origins of the European World-Economy in the Sixteenth Century.* New York: Academic Press.

_____ (1980). "The States in the Institutional Vortex of the Capitalist World-Economy." *The International Social Science Journal,* 32, 4, 745–51.

Weber, Max (1978). *Economy and Society.* Berkeley: University of California Press.

Willette, JoAnne L., and Marion F. Shaycoft (1986). "The Inter-Ethnic Comparison of Business Owners and Non-Business Owners," unpublished paper delivered at the annual meeting of the American Sociological Association, New York City, September 1.

11

UNEVEN DEVELOPMENT AND THE ORIGINS OF SPLIT LABOR MARKET DISCRIMINATION: A COMPARISON OF BLACK, CHINESE, AND MEXICAN IMMIGRANT MINORITIES IN THE UNITED STATES

Terry Boswell and David Jorjani

A split labor market is defined as "a difference in the price of labor between two or more groups of workers, holding constant their efficiency and productivity" (Bonacich 1976: 36; see also 1972: 549).[1] Ethnic discrimination is generated within the working class when ethnic groups with different labor costs are forced to compete for the same jobs at different wage levels.[2] The source of the difference in the cost of labor for ethnic groups is the national differences in wages and the standard of living caused by the labor market consequences of uneven development on international migration patterns (Bonacich & Cheng 1984). Historically this has meant that migrants from poor rural nations in the periphery of the world-economy, such as peasant countries in southeastern Europe, Africa, or Latin America, have served as cheap labor in the core. Dominant workers will try to prevent capital from employing any workers, regardless of ethnicity, at a wage below the prevailing standard. This class conflict is transferred to an ethnic conflict in the labor market when cheap labor is identified with ethnicity (Bonacich 1972; Boswell 1986).[3]

Extensive research on split labor markets in the United States has demonstrated the importance of split labor market dynamics for explaining working-class racism (Bonacich 1972, 1975, 1976, 1981; Wilson 1978; Boswell 1986; Marks 1981; Hilton 1979; Howell 1982; Jorjani 1986). In this chapter we explore the causal link between world-systems dynamics and discrimination in split labor markets. At different periods in the development of the world-system, the combination of imperialism, proletarianization of peripheral labor, and commodification of world markets produces different types of migration. The type of migration affects the origin and subsequent reproduction of split labor market conditions.

Given the corrosive power of competitive commodity markets on discriminatory nonpecuniary "tastes" (Becker 1971), the causal link between the capitalist world-system and ethnic discrimination is not obvious and in many instances works in the opposite direction. Furthermore, transnational capital and global marketing have undeniably reduced the world's cultural heterogeneity. On the other hand, the development of the world-economy is decidedly uneven, producing and reproducing labor markets that are split between low- and high-wage workers of different ethnic backgrounds.

Uneven development has previously been treated in split labor market theory as producing an undifferentiated source of migration of low-wage peripheral workers to high-wage core labor markets. However, it is possible to distinguish different types of migration depending on the extent to which the peripheral area is incorporated into the world-system and the extent to which internal relations have been commodified. We first outline a model of three types of peripheral migration based on different levels of incorporation and commodification in the world-system. The history of the origins of split labor markets for three minority groups in the United States—blacks, Chinese, and Mexicans—is then described and compared in order to explain how the different types of migration produced differing forms of split labor markets and ethnic discrimination. The comparisons suggest that the world-systemic origins of migration have long-term effects on split labor market dynamics and the reproduction of ethnic antagonism.

THE WORLD-SYSTEM AND SPLIT LABOR MARKETS

In defining the relationship between the core and periphery, along with other factors, one can "define the core as a high-wage zone and the periphery as a low-wage zone" (Hopkins & Wallerstein 1979: 495). Since its origins in the "long sixteenth century" (1450-1640), the capitalist world-system has been driven by competitive capital accumulation to constantly expand and peripheralize external areas (Wallerstein 1976). With peripheralization, external areas are eventually incorporated into the world-system through some combination of colonization of states, commodification of exchange, transnationalization of capital, and proletarianization of labor.

At least initially, the origin of core split labor markets is the migration of low-wage peripheral workers to high-wage jobs in the core, creating an ethnic difference or split in labor costs. The ethnic split in labor costs is graphed in figure 11.1 in terms of the labor supply of immigrant minority and dominant workers. The figure shows that there is more elasticity in the supply of dominant labor (D) than minority labor (M). That is, for the same wage (W_1), the supply of minority labor is much higher than that of dominant workers ($Q_2 > Q_1$) and more importantly, for the same number of workers (Q_1), the minority wage is lower than the wage paid to dominant workers ($W_2 < W_1$). All else equal, capitalists hire whoever will accept the lower wage. Current dominant employees who find themselves competing with an immigrant ethnic minority group that has lower labor costs are faced with the prospect of either wage cuts or job losses. The obvious result is ethnic antagonism and discrimination.

Uneven Development and Peripheral Emigration

The extent to which the peripheral area is incorporated into the world-system will affect the possibility and pattern of migration of workers from periphery to core. Based on the historical period and degree of incorporation into the world-system, three main types of migration can be identified: (1) coercive migration, where colonial populations are forced to migrate to the core; (2) sojourning migration, where temporary migrants remain in the core labor market only as long as necessary to earn a certain amount of income; and (3) wage migration, where migrants seek high wages in the core after being pushed out of petty commodity production in the periphery by proletarianization. To be sure, specific migration conditions will differ for each nation and each ethnic group. The form of split labor markets also depends on a number of cultural factors such as preexisting ideologies of racism, cultural distinctiveness, and ethnocentrism that, for purposes of parsimony, will not be considered here. Since we are dealing only with the United States, we can basically assume that widespread racist ideologies

Figure 11.1
Ethnic Differences in the Cost of Labor

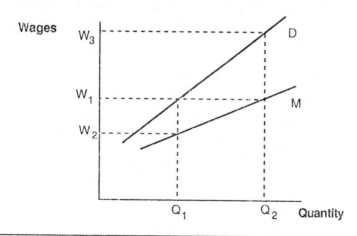

D = Dominant Labor Supply
M = Minority Labor Supply

and a high level of ethnocentrism already exist prior to and throughout the periods under investigation. Therefore, we can concentrate on the effects of the world economy.

Coercive Migration. Before an external area is incorporated into the world-system, imperialist capital typically requires coercion to acquire labor (Portes 1978: 11). Where populations in what Thomas Hall (1986: 391–92) calls the initial "contact periphery" have to be forced to become colonial labor, their labor supply elasticity is equal or more than that for dominant workers (rather than less as found in core split labor markets) (Berg 1961). The peripheral population is usually unwilling to enter the labor market because it is involved in noncapitalist modes of production (petty commodity, communal-tribal, etc.). As graphed in figure 11.2, the labor supply (S) in the contact periphery is likely to slope steeply backwards, be high cost (C_1), and be little used (Q_1). Imperialist coercion turns peripheral populations into colonial labor, forcing down the cost (C_2) of the colonial labor supply (CS) and increasing usage (Q_2). The increased profits of colonial coercion for imperial capital are represented on the figure by the *a-b-c* area.

Sojourning Migration. The world capital accumulation drive eventually incorporates colonial areas into the world-system by commodifying economic relations (Bonacich & Cheng 1984). The process of commodification and incorporation into the world-system makes the traditional petty commodity agricultural sector dependent on the imperial enclave, which in turn is dependent on the imperial core. The double-layered dependency in the peripheral society is what Portes (1978: 11–12) calls a "structural imbalance" that disrupts traditional culture, but does not necessarily eliminate noncapitalist modes of production. On the contrary, by reducing reproduction costs through subsistence production, the traditional noncapitalist sector lowers the cost of colonial labor to the imperial employer. Capitalist and noncapitalist modes of production co-exist, both producing for the same single capitalist commodity market in the world formation (Boswell 1984a).

Because economic relations have been commodified and monetized, coercion is no longer necessary to create a supply of colonial labor. A steady stream of workers will now voluntarily seek wages in order to acquire increasingly commodified consumption goods, but not to become permanent wage workers. Instead, in this second migration situation, workers from the traditional segment will have a sojourning relationship to the labor market, seeking wage employment only during off-seasons, in order to purchase land or for expedient purchases (Siu 1952).

Sojourners have a short-term orientation toward the returns to employment and will avoid jobs that entail long-term training or other commitments from which they do not benefit within the short time period of their employment. Likewise, employers will not invest in the human capital of workers whose job tenure is likely to be short. As a result, these short-term workers will be concentrated in jobs that do not have unions, on-the-job training, internal labor market career ladders, or seniority provisions.

Figure 11.2
Differences in the Cost of Contact Periphery and Coerced Colonial Labor

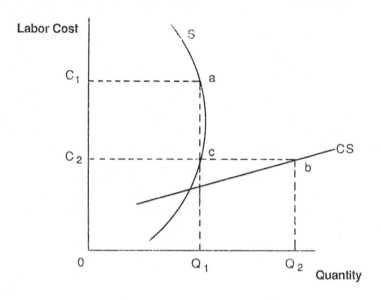

S = Supply of Labor in the Contact Periphery
CS = Supply of Coerced Colonial Labor

Therefore, when an immigrant ethnic minority group has a large proportion of sojourners, few of the immigrant workers will be found in the high seniority, best-paying career positions.

Wage Migration. The third type of migration, wage migration, occurs with proletarianization. Proletarianization represents the full extent of the commodification of labor power. In this case, the property of noncapitalist peripheral producers is expropriated, forcing the population into the labor market on a full-time, totally dependent basis. Wage migration, where low-wage workers migrate to higher paying areas, is simply an extension of labor market forces of supply and demand across national borders (Greenwood 1975; Vickery 1977). However, during the process of proletarianization, the variation in migration is mainly determined by the social conflict at the point of origin, not the attractiveness of higher wages at the destination (Fligstein 1981). Unlike sojourners, proletarians have no agricultural plots to return to and thus seek permanent employment in jobs that are the best-paying over the long term. Labor costs are lower for recently proletarianized ethnic immigrants only because of the destitution and oversupply of labor that proletarianization entails, not because of coercion, subsistence subsidies, or temporary orientation.

Expropriations that created a dependent labor supply have historically taken numerous forms, but the most common has been the result of the centralization of ownership in agriculture. The mass of the population in peripheral areas are usually peasants, sharecroppers, small farmers, or other semi-autonomous agricultural producers. Class struggle revolves around control over the land between the producers and landlords. Integration into the world commodity market intensifies the struggle as imperial (or *comprador*) landlords seek to replace subsistence production with production for the world market. The centralization of land-owning by landlords expropriates the small producers, forcing them into the labor market.

The three sources of migration that fuel split labor markets described above are outlined in figure 11.3. While the uneven development of world capital accumulation underlies all three migration trajectories, there is also a tiered temporal determination from the top to the bottom. In the earliest period described by the top line, colonization by core empires which leads to coercive migration also leads to increased integration of world commodity markets. The latter, which provides for sojourning migration between production modes (middle line), simultaneously leads to the expropriation of noncapitalist producers when coupled with imperial investment (bottom line).

THE ORIGIN OF SPLIT LABOR MARKETS IN THE UNITED STATES

It is important to point out that while proletarianization of colonial populations is a likely outcome of incorporation into the capitalist world-system, it is not inevitable. Coercive migration may persist for centuries (as in the case of the American slave trade) or the colonial population may be eliminated from the economy by core settlers through genocide or reservation systems (as in the case of the native American and aboriginal Australian populations). Nor should these three migration trajectories be seen as pure alternatives; a mixture of all three could easily occur. The extent that migration can be described as coercive, sojourning, or wage can best be determined by examining the history of the origins of ethnic split labor markets.

Historical Comparisons

For each of the three minority groups, blacks, Chinese, and Mexican, we compare the origins of split labor markets during the initial period of migration to the United States. A brief description of the history of initial immigration is presented for each group, with emphasis on the less well-known

Figure 11.3
Sources of Peripheral Migration to Core Split Labor Markets

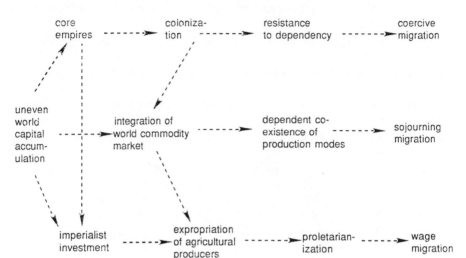

factors. The main sources of the historical descriptions unless otherwise noted are culled from the existing studies of split labor markets (Bonacich 1972, 1975, 1976, 1981; Wilson 1978; Marks 1981; Boswell 1986; Cheng & Bonacich 1984; Hilton 1979; Howell 1982; Jorjani 1986).

No more than synopses of migration history are possible here, and we concentrate on the most relevant periods. With blacks, we concentrate on the period following the Civil War until the 1960s. For the Chinese, we examine only the initial immigration from 1848 until Chinese immigration was banned in 1882; recent Chinese immigration falls outside the scope of this study. The first period of rapid migration, 1880–1945, is emphasized in the examination of Mexican immigration. The intent of the comparisons is to examine what type of peripheral emigration produced split labor markets for each ethnic minority group and what effect the different types of immigration had on split labor market dynamics.

Blacks. The role of coercive migration is obvious in the African slave labor in the United States (Genovese 1965). Imperial capital came into contact with noncapitalist modes at two points: with tribal populations in Africa and with (white) petty commodity farmers in America. Coercion was required both to integrate African labor into the world market and to sustain large-scale plantation, as opposed to either petty commodity or pure capitalist agriculture in America. The former was mainly accomplished by private agents of British merchant capitalists, the latter by the state acting in the interest of and in conjunction with British colonial and, later, American plantation owners.

As slaves, blacks did not directly compete with dominant workers in the labor market for paid positions, although the use of slavery removed some positions from competition and constricted the overall size of the labor market. Labor market conditions for most blacks did not begin until after the Civil War. Yet following the war, sharecropping and petty commodity farming consumed much of the black labor force, and a major black migration stream into the labor market did not begin until World War I and the boll-weevil infestation of the late 1910s (Wilson 1978: 66–67). From this time on, black rural migrants constituted a low-cost alternative to dominant workers in low-skill jobs, replacing the diminished supply of southeast European peasant immigrants whose migration was legally curtailed in 1917 and 1923 (Piore 1979: 158; Wilson 1978: 66).

Until the 1930s, blacks mainly left sharecropping and petty commodity farming for wage work because the latter provided a better income. Michael Piore (1979: 159–62) suggests that throughout this period and to a lesser extent continuing to the 1960s, black migrants out of the South were sojourners. Like the southeast Europeans before them, southern black migrants found northern cities less repressive but more inhospitable, a place to make money, not to live. Piore's claims are only weakly substantiated, especially those pertaining to the period following the 1930s, but it is clear that large numbers of blacks in the North were initially unsettled and in flux.

Starting in the 1930s, black migrants out of the South were increasingly forced to become proletarians by the unprecedented and uniquely American concentration and centralization of agricultural production (Fligstein 1981; Wilson 1978). New Deal programs targeted capitalization of agriculture in the South where black small farmers and sharecroppers were concentrated. Mechanization of agriculture began in earnest after World War I and continued to the point that, by the 1960s, migration of small farmers into urban labor markets was no longer a significant source of split labor markets in the United States. This was true of American agriculture in general and did not by itself constitute ethnic discrimination.

Chinese. Coercive coolie migration, a form of debt servitude, existed in Latin America but, despite popular conceptions, was not used in the United States (Coolidge 1909; Boswell 1986). Instead, Chinese migrants were sojourners drawn first by the California gold rush of 1849 and later recruited for wage work on the transcontinental railroads and, later still, for jobs in manufacturing and agriculture. The sojourners benefited from a major difference in living costs between California and China where they would return to resume peasant agriculture at a marked increase in status. Most Chinese migrants were from southern China where the population faced a significant push factor, but this was due to food and land shortages, not proletarianization. Nor was the state forcing migration. On the contrary, emigration was technically illegal in China until the 1860s (Zo 1978; Chen, 1980; Mei 1984).

The first Chinese migrants working in the petty commodity placer mines faced little ethnic discrimination until capitalist production began to replace the producers. In this case, the source of discrimination was not capitalists seeking to force producers into the labor market, but dominant independent miners seeking to defend their position against capitalist mining and water companies. Price standards set by the dominant producers for dealing with the companies were undercut by the sojourning Chinese. The dominant producers reacted directly with often violent discrimination during recessionary periods and indirectly through the local state apparatus which was largely under their control. Discrimination forced Chinese into the labor market (or alternative petty commodity production), reducing the elasticity of Chinese labor which, ironically, provided lower cost labor to the capitalist mining companies.

Despite the resistance and political power of the dominant producers, the mines were capitalized. In addition to the effects of concentration and centralization (which may be politically forestalled), the economic geology of mining requires ever more capital-intensive production as the grade of ore declines and the source of ore deepens. By the late 1860s, Chinese immigrants primarily came to be wage workers, not petty commodity producers. The railroad companies and large agricultural employers played a major role in recruiting Chinese immigrants and encouraging the state to reduce migration restrictions, but there is little evidence that imperial capital or the state directly forced emigration from China. However, one reason capital recruited Chinese labor besides cost was that imperialism made the Chinese state politically impotent, incapable of and often unwilling to protect migrants from harsh working conditions abroad (Zo 1978). Furthermore, the Chinese were denied by international treaty the right to become naturalized U.S. citizens, legally entombing them in the status of sojourners (Boswell 1986; Chen 1980; Bonacich 1984a, 1984b).

While the geographic dispersion of Chinese immigrants east of the Rockies was still minuscule (3 percent) in 1880, their occasional employment in eastern factories and southern plantations attracted national media attention (Boswell 1984b: 365–66). Anti-Chinese discourse became a focal point in re-unifying white workers and farmers in the Democratic party. A moral tone was added to appeal to the middle classes, leaving only big capital, primarily the railroads and large-scale western agriculture, in clear support of open immigration. Resistance by the latter was muted by increased immigration from primarily southeastern Europe and Mexico. The Exclusion Act was passed in 1882 which banned further immigration of Chinese workers (Saxton 1971; Boswell 1986: 365–66).

Mexicans. Acquisition of northern Mexico in 1848 created an internal colony in the American Southwest, but unlike subjects of overseas colonial conquests Mexican-Americans were granted U.S. citizenship. While state-organized violent discrimination and even genocide were practiced against the Indian population, the small number of Mexican-Americans, who were mainly family farmers, were relatively ignored. No widespread attempts to forcibly proletarianize Mexican-Americans occurred during this period. To be sure, isolated instances of land grabs and even village pogroms occurred (Acuna 1981), and debt peonage was occasionally practiced in the early development of capitalist mining (Boswell 1984b). But the small size of the indigenous Mexican-American population, coupled with their cultural isolation and concentration in family farming had little impact on the developing labor market. Not until the turn of the century did large numbers of Mexican immigrants enter the labor market, and it is on the Mexican immigrants, not the indigenous Mexican-American population, that we focus.

A dramatic increase in Mexican immigration to the United States began in the 1880s and accelerated after 1900 when railroads were constructed to connect the densely populated Mexican interior with the sparsely populated border area. At the same time, a "phenomenally rapid agricultural expansion in the (U.S.) Southwest created a pressing demand for cheap, unskilled, migratory labor" (Elac 1972: 6). The proletarianization policies of the Porfirio Diaz government displaced thousands of peons in the late 1800s. The Porfirian decrees of 1890 and 1894 were the culmination of four decades of land reform legislation (Jorjani 1986). The peons and *ejidadores* (communal Indians) were caught in the middle of the confrontation of the landed aristocracy (the *hacendados* and the Catholic Church) and the new liberal government. The liberal government of the early 1800s began monetization policies to transform the neofeudal economy into a capitalist economy, propelling Mexico into a phase of export-led growth based on foreign investment and world market integration (Brading 1980: 17).

The goals of the liberal government were twofold: politically, the new government tried to develop a rural constituency for liberal politics by redistributing lands held by the Church; and economically, the government promoted economic progress through imperialist investment (Bazant 1977). However, by the end of this liberal reform era (starting with Alvarez in 1855, and ending with Diaz in 1910) the ultimate benefactors of the expropriation of the church and other lands were the hacendados and *ranchos* who bought up the small peon holdings (Bazant 1977: 104–5). The increasingly landless mass of the rural population ballooned the labor pool and eventually revolted against the hacendados in 1911 when Diaz's rule ended (Brading 1980: 18). The immediate effect of the Mexican Revolution on migration was to cause a surge of migrants northward during its occurrence and subsequent upheavals. The long-term effect of the revolution has been increased protection of *ejidos* and periodic land reform, enacted by most all subsequent governments, that has slowed proletarianization (Cardoso 1980). Sojourning to the United States served to provide supplemental income to peons, ejidadores, and small farmers who faced continuing pressure from hacendados and from population increases.

The Mexican migrants were continually funneled by labor contractors into the agricultural businesses of the southwestern United States. They originally encountered little discrimination from the few dominant workers already there (Elac 1972:6). By the turn of the century, U.S. petty commodity farmers were overcome by the huge capitalist operations due to the advent of mechanized farming (Daniel 1981: 34–35). While preharvest operations and postharvest operations were continually becoming mechanized, the harvest phase was still labor-intensive. The restrictive immigration acts against the Chinese and Japanese and the rapid expansion of commercialized growing created a vacuum in the labor supply. Mexicans filled this shortage, displacing the few Japanese and Chinese, and the even fewer white U.S. workers (Elac 1972:6). With the Great Depression, waves of "okies" did come into direct competition with the Mexicans for jobs in Texas and California, but the competition was short-lived as the "okies" moved into war-related occupations during World War II (Wollenberg 1970: 152).

World War II marked a new era for Mexican immigration that has continued up to the present day. Due to the war and an increasing attractiveness of industrial jobs as compared to agricultural jobs for dominant labor, Mexican immigrants have more or less saturated low-paying agricultural wage labor in the Southwest. In Mexico, emigration was fueled by factory mechanization and capitalization of agriculture during the 1950s and 1960s which produced increasing numbers of unemployed and landless workers.

Attempts by the U.S. government to control undocumented immigration, such as the Bracero Programs of the 1940s and 1960s and Operation Wetback of 1954, channeled but failed to stop immigration. The limited ability of the state to exclude Mexican migration across the border enabled employers to legally discriminate in working conditions and use the Immigration and Naturalization Service (INS) to discourage or raid unions (Acuna 1981).

DISCUSSION

To what extent can the migration of blacks, Chinese, and Mexicans to the United States be described as coercive, sojourning, or wage? Only blacks faced coercive migration of any major consequence. Coercive migration of Chinese was widespread in parts of Latin America, India, and southern Africa but not North America. The exception was approximately 2,000-3,000 Chinese prostitutes, who made up the majority of the small number of female Chinese migrants until the late 1870s (Cheng 1984). Small numbers of Mexican peons were also imported for use in a few southwestern silver mines in the 1850s, but this was short-lived (Boswell 1984b).

In general, almost all the Chinese migrants and most of the Mexican migrants were sojourners. During the interwar period, blacks in the South also migrated to urban labor markets, to some unknown extent, in a sojourning fashion. Black sojourning migration resembled that of the European immigrant populations from the semicapitalized agricultural areas that they were replacing. The uneven development between industry and agriculture that was fueling sojourning migration at the world level was also the source of sojourning migration between the South and North in the United States. After the 1930s and especially after World War II, proletarianization forced blacks into the labor market without recourse to sojourning. After World War I and especially after World War II, blacks were increasingly wage migrants. The combination of boll weevil infestation, the Great Depression, mechanization of agriculture, and wartime and postwar industrial surge thoroughly proletarianized and urbanized the bulk of the black population.

Chinese immigrants on the other hand, began and largely remained sojourners. Like blacks, the first immigrants did not orginally enter the labor market. But unlike blacks, the Chinese could remain sojourners because they were returning to China where proletarianization in agriculture was little advanced. The project nature of early mining and railroad work also set a limited time period of expected employment for any one employer, thereby increasing the likelihood of return to China when the project was finished. The prohibition on naturalization had a like effect.

With the early Mexican migrants, centralization in agriculture was pushing Mexican peasants into the U.S. labor market, but most of the migrants were still sojourners. The Mexican migrants were seeking to maintain existence as agricultural producers by using U.S. wages to purchase land or otherwise supplement production incomes. Mexican migrants after World War II more resemble black migrants in the interwar years. Douglas Massey's (1987) recent research shows that Mexican migrants are still largely sojourners today, but with the mechanization of agriculture and formation of strong network ties, they are increasingly wage migrants. A male Mexican migrant, as experience in the U.S. increases, will increasingly settle, "irrespective of his legal status, origin, U.S. occupation, or whether he had children" (Massey 1987: 1394).

The Reproduction of Split Labor Markets

What difference does the world-systemic source of migration make for split labor market dynamics in the United States? This question cannot be fully answered here, but we can point out some of the more important consequences. The effect of coerced migration and slavery set the pattern for black-white interaction once blacks entered the labor market. To begin with, coercion against blacks continued to be socially legitimate and legal in most political and social circumstances. Systematic violence and social subordination were used by plantations attempting to control a low-cost labor force and by white workers attempting to continue the exclusion of blacks from direct labor market competition (Reich 1981; Trelease 1971).

The effect of continued discrimination was to perpetuate split labor market conditions even after blacks became fully proletarianized. To the extent that coercion reduced black incomes and confined them to low-wage, low-productivity positions, it reproduced the split in costs in the labor market between blacks and whites. In addition to the psychological and ideological functions, segregation in the South prevented the short-term decline in white wages that would have accompanied the rise in black wages (and long-term rise in white wages) if equal competition were allowed (Reich 1981). Segregation was also supported by racist capitalists. A segregated labor market protected racist employers who hired only white labor from employers who would hire low-wage black labor.[4] Thus the split labor market was relatively immune from the equalizing effects of competition and commodification.

The self-perpetuating split in the labor market was fractured in the North (but not completely broken) by employers after World War I when strikes and the cut-off of European immigrants threatened to dramatically increase white wages. The increased costs of union labor were not uniform across firms, reducing the ability of segregation to protect against competition from employers of lower-cost labor. The split in labor costs was not fully eliminated in the North due, not only to continued discrimination, but also to the fact that black workers were still migrating from the low-wage South.

Sojourners were discriminated against in all three cases. While this discrimination was historically important in reproducing the split in the labor market, it is not a necessary condition. Because sojourners expect a short-term duration, they willingly suffer low wages and poor working conditions, do not make long-term human capital investments, and have little interest in union (or community) benefits. With sojourning migration, split costs will be reproduced even with "pure" competitive competition (i.e., no coercion or other political interference). However, dominant workers are likely to be fiercely antagonistic and discriminate against ethnic sojourners simply because sojourners are temporary. At least in the case of the Chinese, the antagonism of permanent dominant workers was as high or higher than that expressed against coerced blacks due to the appearance of sojourners voluntarily accepting slavelike wages and working conditions (Boswell, 1986).

The difference between Chinese and Mexican sojourners is instructive. The Chinese were eventually excluded, while Mexicans have been largely segregated to low-paying positions. While cultural differences are relevant—ethnocentrism against the Chinese was much higher—the labor-market differences are also extremely important. To begin with, the practical differences in closing ports to Chinese immigrants versus patrolling an extensive border are quite large. Yet technically, the border is closed to most Mexican immigration and the Border Patrol, while having a proportionately small effect, is nevertheless a real and constant fear.

More importantly, political differences result from the circumstances of the split labor market competition. Dominant labor was attempting to exclude Chinese from relatively high-paying jobs in manufacturing, mining, and railroads (but largely ignored agriculture) (Chiu 1967). Mexican labor has been segregated into low-paying agricultural labor mainly due to dominant workers' abandoning agricultural labor for higher-paying jobs. There is consequently less political pressure from dominant labor for full exclusion. Also, those dominant workers most likely to directly compete with Mexican immigrants are Mexican-Americans. Finally, the political resistance by employers to exclusion of Chinese labor was mollified by the concurrent increase in southeast European labor, while no such alternative has yet to occur for Mexican agricultural labor.

Finally, turning to wage migrants, barring discrimination there is no obvious reason for the split in labor costs for the same jobs to perpetuate once the migration has been completed and the migrants have been absorbed into the labor force. Segregation may nevertheless continue, without coercion, via abandonment of low-paying jobs by dominant workers. Although of lesser severity as compared to coercive or sojourning migration, discrimination is, nevertheless, also likely to continue, perpetuating the split in the labor market even for permanently settled immigrants. As for blacks, the short-term shock of wage adjustment from eliminating discrimination is an incentive for dominant labor to discriminate. And of course, state-enforced discrimination, such as the lack of citizenship, has a similar effect. Like coercive migration, the long-term effect of wage migration is the perpetuation of split labor market conditions if discrimination continues, despite the initial cause of the split being no longer operative.

CONCLUSION

The origin of ethnic discrimination generated by split labor markets is to a great extent a function of the division of a world labor market into national segments. Except for sojourners, after initial immigration and absorption into the labor force, the perpetuation of split labor markets depends on the reciprocal effects of discrimination on the labor market.[5] With a decline in discrimination, the effects of the ethnicity of past immigrants on labor-market position, independently of class background or skill level, likewise decline in significance (Wilson 1978). On the other hand, with sojourning migration, a split is produced in the labor market even under "pure" competitive labor market conditions, that is, where no discrimination occurs. Ethnic sojourners are the quintessential economic source of split labor markets. Note that the sojourning migration we investigated occurs between different modes of production, mainly between petty commodity and capitalist labor markets, indicating the importance of differentiating modes even within the same world-system.

We can also look at the comparison of ethnic experiences in split labor markets from a long- term historical perspective. Proletarianization is one of the central continuing dynamics of the world capitalist system (Chase-Dunn, 1987). Consequently, coercive migration of noncapitalist labor will no longer be necessary and sojourning across modes of production will diminish. More salient than sojourners from noncapitalist modes will be temporary workers whose short-term orientation to the labor market is similar. If the distinction between permanent and temporary labor is defined along ethnic lines, ethnic antagonism and discrimination are likely to follow as evidenced by the reactions against "guest workers" in western Europe during recent economic recessions (Walliman 1984). Uneven development also insures that even in a fully proletarianized world labor market, differences in labor costs and thus split labor markets will be reoccuringly recreated by new waves of immigration from periphery to core. This need not result in ethnic antagonism and discrimination, but it likely will as long as dominant workers identify their interests in market and national, rather than class and world terms.

NOTES

1. The term *price* is used by Bonacich to include any labor costs borne by the employer, including wages and all auxiliary compensation. We use the term *cost* of labor rather than *price* in order to avoid confusing wage labor markets with petty commodity production.

2. Following Bonacich (1972: 548), we subsume racial groups under the broader category of ethnic groups for purposes of discussion.

3. In the case of a union, the unionized workers will try to restrict employment to union workers through a hiring hall and will violently protect their jobs from scabs. This only becomes an ethnic conflict if ethnicity and union membership are not cross-cutting. Historical examples of unions discriminating against minorities and minorities serving as strikebreakers point to the persistence and ferocity of the effects of split labor market conditions (Bonacich 1976; Wilson 1978).

4. Statistical discrimination is another important source of discrimination by employers (Reich 1981: 104–5). Statistical discrimination occurs when average skill differences are large enough between the dominant and minority ethnic groups for the employer to use ethnicity as a proxy for identifying skill differences. Following Bonacich (1976: 36; 1972: 549), efficiency and productivity are held constant in this study and we do not consider cases of statistical discrimination. Future research should incorporate statistical discrimination into split labor market theory.

5. There are, of course, other sources of racial and ethnic antagonism outside of the labor market, but our emphasis is on splits in the labor market. Also, while a split labor market is neither a necessary nor exclusive cause of ethnic antagonism, it is a sufficient cause and the primary source of antagonism within the working class in capitalist market societies.

REFERENCES

Acuna, Rodolfo (1981). *Occupied America: A History of Chicanos*. New York: Harper & Row.

Bazant, Jan (1977). *A Concise History of Mexico*. Cambridge: Cambridge University Press.

Becker, Gary (1971). *The Economics of Discrimination*. Chicago: University of Chicago Press.

Berg, Elliot J. (1961). "Backward-Sloping Labor Supply Functions in Dual Economies: The Africa Case." *Quarterly Journal of Economics*, 74, 468–92.

Bonacich, Edna (1972). "A Theory of Ethnic Antagonism: The Split Labor Market." *American Sociological Review*, 37, 5, October, 547–49.

———— (1975). "Abolition, the Extension of Slavery, and the Position of Free Blacks: A Study in Split Labor Markets in the United States, 1830–1863." *American Journal of Sociology*, 80, 1, November, 601–28.

———— (1976). "Advanced Capitalism and Black/White Race Relations in the United States: A Split Labor Market Interpretation." *American Sociological Review*, 41, 1, February, 34–51.

———— (1981). "Capitalism and Race Relations in South Africa: A Split Labor Market Analysis." In M. Zeitlan, ed., *Political Power and Social Theory*. Greenwich, Conn.: JAI, 239–77.

———— (1984a). "U.S. Capitalist Development: A Background to Asian Immigration." In L. Cheng and E. Bonacich, eds., *Labor Immigration Under Capitalism*. Berkeley: University of California Press, 79–129.

———— (1984b). "Asian Labor in the Development of California and Hawaii." In L. Cheng and E. Bonacich, eds., *Labor Immigration Under Capitalism*. Berkeley: University of California Press, 130–85.

Bonacich, Edna, and Lucie Cheng (1984). "A Theoretical Orientation to International Labor Migration." In L. Cheng and E. Bonacich, eds., *Labor Immigration Under Capitalism*. Berkeley: University of California Press, 1–56.

Boswell, Terry (1984a). "World Formation of World Mode of Production? Alternative Approaches to World-System Analysis." *Contemporary Crises*, 8, 4, October, 379–84.

———— (1984b). "Race, Class and Markets: Ethnic Stratification and Labor Market Stratification in the Metal Mining Industry, 1850–1880." Ph.D. diss., University of Arizona.

———— (1986). "A Split Labor Market Analysis of Discrimination Against Chinese Immigrants, 1850–1882." *American Sociological Review*. 51, 3, June, 352–71.

Brading, D. A., ed. (1980). *Caudillo and Peasant in the Mexican Revolution*. Cambridge: Cambridge University Press.

Cardoso, Lawrence A. (1980). *Mexican Emigration to the United States*. Tucson: University of Arizona Press.

Chase-Dunn, Christopher (1987). "Cycles, Trends or Transformation?: The World-System Since 1945." In T. Boswell and A. Bergesen, eds., *America's Changing Role in the World-System*. New York: Praeger, 92–137.

Chen, Jack (1980). *The Chinese of America*. San Francisco: Harper & Row.

Cheng, Lucie (1984). "Free, Indentured, Enslaved: Chinese Prostitutes in Nineteenth-Century America." In L. Cheng and E. Bonacich, eds., *Labor Immigration Under Capitalism*. Berkeley: University of California Press, 402–34.

Cheng, Lucie, and Edna Bonacich (1984). *Labor Immigration Under Capitalism: Asian Workers in the United States Before World War II*. Berkeley: University of California Press.

Chiu, Ping (1967). *Chinese Labor in California, 1850–1880: An Economic Study.* Madison, Wisc.: Logmark Edition, Society Press of the State Historical Society of Wisconsin for the Department of History, University of Wisconsin.

Coolidge, Mary (1909). *Chinese Immigration.* New York: Holt.

Daniel, Cletius E. (1981). *Bitter Harvest: A History of California Farmworkers, 1870–1941.* Ithaca: Cornell University Press.

Elac, John Chala (1972). *The Employment of Mexican Workers in U.S. Agriculture.* San Francisco: R&E Research Association.

Fligstein, Neil (1981). *Going North: Migration of Blacks and Whites from the South, 1900–1950.* New York: Academic Press.

Genovese, Eugene (1965). *The Political Economy of Slavery.* New York: Random House.

Greenwood, Michael (1975). "Research in Internal Migration." *Journal of Economic Literature,* 13, 2, June, 397–433.

Hall, Thomas D. (1986). "Incorporation in the World-System: Toward a Critique." *American Sociological Review,* 51, 3, June, 390–402.

Hilton, Mike (1979). "The Split Labor Market and Chinese Immigration, 1848–1882." *The Journal of Ethnic Studies,* 6, 4, Winter, 99–108.

Hopkins, Terrence K., and Immanuel Wallerstein (1979). "Cyclical Rhythms and Secular Trends of the Capitalist World-Economy: Some Premises, Hypotheses, and Questions." *Review,* 2, 4, Spring, 483–500.

Howell, Frances Baseden (1982). "A Split Labor Market: Mexican Farmworkers in the Southwest." *Sociological Inquiry,* 52, 2, Spring, 132–40.

Jorjani, David (1986). "Costs, Benefits and Solutions: A Split Labor Market Analysis of the Undocumented Mexican Worker Situation." Paper presented at the Emory Undergraduate Sociology Symposium.

Marks, Carole (1981). "Split Labor Markets and Black-White Relations, 1865–1920," *Phylon,* 43, 4, 293–308.

Massey, Douglas S. (1987). "Understanding Mexican Migration to the United States." *American Journal of Sociology,* 92, 6, May, 1372–1403.

Mei, June (1984). "Socioeconomic Origins of Emigration: Guang Dong to California, 1850–1882." In L. Cheng and E. Bonacich, eds., *Labor Immigration Under Capitalism.* Berkeley: University of California Press, 219–47.

Piore, Michael J. (1979). *Birds of Passage: Migrant Labor and Industrial Societies.* New York: Cambridge University Press.

Portes, Alejandro (1978). "Migration and Underdevelopment." *Politics and Society,* 8, 1, 1–48.

Reich, Michael (1981). *Racial Inequality: A Political-Economic Analysis.* Princeton, N.J.: Princeton University Press.

Saxton, Alexander (1971). *The Indispensable Enemy: Labor and the Anti-Chinese Movement in California.* Berkeley: University of California Press.

Siu, Paul C. P. (1952). "The Sojourner." *American Journal of Sociology.* 58, 1, July, 34–44.

Trelease, Allen (1971). *White Terror: The KKK Conspiracy and Southern Reconstruction.* New York: Harper & Row.

Tsai, Shih-Shan Henry (1983). *China and the Overseas Chinese in the United States, 1868–1911.* Fayetteville: University of Arkansas Press.

Vickery, William (1977). *The Economics of Negro Migration, 1900–1960.* New York: Arno.

Wallerstein, Immanuel (1976). *The Modern World-System*, Vol. 1, *Capitalist Agriculture and the Origins of the European World-Economy in the Sixteenth Century*. New York: Academic Press.

Walliman, Isidor (1984). "The Import of Foreign Workers in Switzerland: Labor-Power Reproduction Costs, Ethnic Antagonism and the Integration of Foreign Workers into Swiss Society." *Research in Social Movements, Conflict and Change*. Greenwich, Conn.: JAI 3: 153–75.

Wilson, William J. (1978). *The Declining Significance of Race*. Chicago: University of Chicago Press.

Wollenberg, Charles (1970). *Ethnic Conflict in California History*. Los Angeles: Tinnon-Brown.

Zo, Kil Young (1978). *Chinese Emigration into the United States, 1850–1880*. New York: Arno.

Asian-American Success in Hawaii: Myth, Reality, or Artifact of Women's Labor?

James A. Geschwender and Rita Carroll-Seguin

Much of the current research dealing with race and ethnicity has been seriously flawed in at least three aspects. First, there has been a tendency for many scholars to treat race and ethnicity as primordial concepts. They have failed to recognize that race and ethnicity are social constructs that emerge during the growth and expansion of the capitalist world-system and the subsequent labor migrations that take place within that system (Geschwender 1987). The second major flaw has been a tendency for many scholars to focus on race-ethnic relations, prejudice, and discrimination, rather than upon racial stratification, exploitation, and oppression as part of the process of capital accumulation. The third major flaw has been present even when scholars have attempted to analyze racial and ethnic stratification. This is the tendency to see the individual as the basic unit of analysis.

In contrast, the basic unit of analysis in studies such as this must be family or household (Curtis 1986; Fallers 1964; Hartmann 1981; Smith et al. 1984; Wallerstein et al. 1982). This is the unit that is the center of resistance to capitalist encroachment. This is the unit within which family members make decisions, allocate resources, distribute income, and, for the most part, share a common standard of living. The household or family may be located within what we call nationality communities (or racial or ethnic communities). As such, their decision-making processes are influenced by the legacy of the accumulated historical experiences of the national origins group. Thus, the family or household is not only the center of resistance to capital, but is also the bearer and teacher of tradition and culture.

These are not empty distinctions. This perspective leads directly to a concern with variations among groups in the role of multiple income earners within the family, and particularly with variations in the rate and type of female participation in the labor force. We shall illustrate the importance of this through an investigation of the Asian-American success myth as it applies to Hawaii. Much of the vaunted success of Asian-Americans, to the extent that it has occurred for some groups, is largely a consequence of much higher rates of female participation in the labor force and is not indicative of a favored position with respect to the opportunity structure.

Recent years have witnessed a great deal of research on the extent of economic mobility of Asian-Americans relative to that of Euro-Americans (Chiswick 1983; Chun 1980: 1–12; Hirschman & Wong, 1981, 1986; Huhr & Kim, 1986; Jaco & Wilbur, 1975; Jiobu, 1976; Wong 1982; Young 1977). Asian-Americans have been variously portrayed as a highly successful model minority that others would do well to emulate—an undifferentiated group that has, for various reasons, become at least as successful as Euro-Americans—and as a differentiated clustering of national origins groups that have had different historical experiences. It is generally argued that Asian-American peoples have acquired a higher level of education than that of Euro-Americans. Many currently have income levels that are, at the very least, equal to those of Euro-Americans. But this does not mean that they are not discriminated against in the sense that they receive a lower level of economic remuneration relative to their level of education than that received by Euro-Americans.

The Asian-American category includes a differentiated clustering of national origins groups that do not presently constitute a single racial-ethnic group. Each differs from the others in terms of time and manner of entry, initial reception, subsequent historical experiences, and current geographical distribution. Geographical distribution affects the degree of economic success. Each group is exposed to a different set of labor markets, each of which has its own unique configuration of opportunity structures. Consequently, any evaluation of the Asian-American success myth should control for geographic location. One technique for doing so is to select a research site that has relatively clear boundaries, a definable and distinct labor market, and a history that is both unique and easily analyzed. We believe that Hawaii fits the bill in all particulars.

METHODOLOGY

Hawaii is a relatively small state with a 1980 population of 964,691 composed of 331,925 Euro-Americans, 239,734 Japanese-Americans, 132,075 Filipino-Americans, 118,251 Hawaiian-Americans, 55,916 Chinese-Americans, and an assortment of smaller concentrations of persons of various ancestries. Contemporary Hawaii grew out of a plantation society in which Europeans came to Hawaii, alienated the land from the Hawaiians, and came to dominate the political and economic life of the society (Geschwender 1982). Chinese, Japanese, and Filipinos were sequentially brought in to work on the plantations when the number of available Hawaiians proved too small to meet growing labor needs. Over the course of time, each nationality group left the plantations and entered the larger society. Each has subsequently experienced a degree of economic mobility, the exact extent of which remains a subject of controversy. Asian-Americans in Hawaii (especially Japanese- and Chinese-Americans) are touted as an example of a model minority—a group that has not only equalled but exceeded the accomplishments of the former ruling racial group (Marden & Meyer 1978; Lind 1980a, 1980b; Geschwender 1980a, 1980b).

We shall attempt to evaluate the Asian-American success myth using data from the 1980 United States Census, Public Use Microdata Sample (5%-A sample). We shall concentrate on the three largest and historically most important Asian-origin communities in Hawaii (Japanese-Americans, Chinese-Americans, and Filipino-Americans). We shall compare their social location to that of Euro-Americans as a group. People are classified into groups according to their response to the racial identification question on the census. Because we are more concerned with national origins than race per se, we are using the term *Euro-Americans* to refer to those who labelled themselves as "white."

We have demonstrated elsewhere that not all national origins groups classified as Euro-Americans actually possess the same level of social standing or economic status in Hawaii's racial-ethnic stratification order (Geschwender & Carroll-Seguin, 1987). Portuguese-Americans, Spanish-Americans, and Puerto Rican-Americans entered Hawaii as agricultural laborers and, consequently, have been traditionally excluded from the category of *haoles*—the traditional, dominant racial-ethnic group in Hawaii. Thus we shall use information from the census ancestry question to arrive at the more narrowly circumscribed community of haoles—that is, those who remain after excluding persons of Portuguese, Spanish, or Puerto Rican ancestry from the category Euro-Americans. Data will also be presented describing the location of haoles within Hawaii's racial-ethnic stratification order.

DATA ANALYSIS

The relative position of national origins groups is usually portrayed by median family income. At first glance, it appears that Asian-Americans (at least Japanese- and Chinese-Americans) are better off than Euro-Americans. Japanese-Americans have a median family income of $29,640 as compared to $29,410 for Chinese-American families (respectively, 1.43 and 1.42 times as great as that of Euro-Americans—$20,650). Not all Asian-American groups are equally successful. The median family income of Filipino-American families ($20,380) is slightly lower than that for Euro-Americans. Even the apparent relative advantage of Japanese- and Chinese-American families may not be as great or as simple as these numbers suggest.

A large number of military personnel from other parts of the United States are temporarily stationed in Hawaii. If they are located there on census day, they are included in the Hawaii statistical profile. As temporary residents, they are not really part of the Hawaiian social structure. Their inclusion in the data presents a misleading picture of the racial stratification order in Hawaii because males in the military both earn less than, and differ significantly in national origins from, their civilian counterparts. More than one-fifth (22.9%) of all Euro-American families are headed by a member of the military as opposed to much lower proportions for each of the other national origins groups (Japanese-Americans, 0.7%; Chinese-Americans, 0.4%; and Filipino-Americans, 5.0%).

Civilian Families

The first column of figures in table 12.1 presents the distribution of mean and median family income of national origins groups with all families headed by military personnel removed. The Asian-American advantage over Euro-Americans remains but is greatly reduced. The median income of Japanese- and Chinese-American families is, respectively, 1.25 and 1.24 times that of Euro-American families. Filipino-Americans slip further behind with median family incomes that are 0.88 times as great as those for Euro-Americans. Median family income is a good measure of the typical standard of living for the various national origins groups. However, it is not necessarily a good measure of the differential opportunity structures to which the various groups are exposed. Groups can and do differ in the proportion of families that are headed by both parents, male parents, or female parents. More Euro-American families (19.5%) are headed by females than is the case for any other groups. The corresponding proportions for the other groups are, respectively, Chinese-Americans, 14.6%; Filipino-Americans, 11.2%; and Japanese-Americans, 11.2%

Given the real disadvantage that women face in the world of work, it would seem that a better reflection of the opportunity structure, as it is actually experienced by the various national origins groups, may be the median income of male-headed, civilian families. The second column of figures in table 12.1 presents these data. The Asian-American advantage over Euro-Americans is further reduced without being entirely eliminated. The median income of Japanese- and Chinese-American families is, respectively, 1.18 and 1.16 times that of Euro-Americans. The median income for Filipino-American families is 0.84 times that of Euro-American families. Thus it would appear that Japanese- and Chinese-Americans have been able to improve their standard of living to a level that is, at the very least, equal

Table 12.1
Family Income of Civilian Families by National Origins and Gender of Household Head: Hawaii, 1979

National Origins		All Families	Male Heads
Euro-American	N	3,086	2,485
	Median	23,715.00	26,110.00
	Mean	25,032.50	29,630.80
Haole	N	2,505	2,017
	Median	24,880.00	27,490.00
	Mean	28,048.60	30,734.10
Chinese-American	N	707	602
	Median	29,450.00	30,230.00
	Mean	31,533.60	33,196.90
Japanese-American	N	3,117	2,765
	Median	29,695.00	30,895.00
	Mean	31,553.60	32,635.70
Filipino-American	N	1,387	1,157
	Median	20,380.00	22,010.00
	Mean	23,150.80	24,368.20

Source: U.S. Census 1980, Public Use Microdata Sample, 5%-A sample.

to that of Euro-Americans. While the degree of their relative advantage is reduced, they still do quite well even if compared only to haoles—the ethnic group that has dominated Hawaii throughout much of the past two centuries. The median family income of Japanese-Americans is 1.19 times that of haoles among all civilian families and 1.12 times as great among those headed by males. The median family income of Chinese-Americans is 1.18 times that of haoles among all civilian families and 1.10 times as great among those headed by males. Filipino-Americans have not been as successful in either regard. They fall even further behind haoles than do all Euro-Americans. Their median family income is 0.82 times that of haoles among all civilian families and 0.80 times as much among those that are headed by males.

The use of family income as an indicator of the opportunity structures to which each national origins group is exposed is not without problems. It is clear that the family or the household is the appropriate unit for analyzing racial-ethnic stratification systems as this is the unit that allocates resources, distributes income, and shares a common standard of living. However, total family income is not a good reflector of the opportunity structure to which that family is exposed because it does not control for number of income earners. Euro-Americans have the lowest mean number of wage earners per household (1.5) of any of the national origins groups. The means for other groups are: Japanese-Americans, 1.9; Chinese-Americans, 1.9; and Filipino-Americans, 2.1. In the most typical case, it is the female spouse that provides a second income for the family (Chinen n.d.; Yamanaka 1985, 1986). Thus, it may prove informative to examine the oppportunity structure confronted by the male members of each of the national origins groups included in our analysis.

The Place of Males in the Racial-Ethnic Stratification Order

Table 12.2 presents data on the traditional stratification variables (education, occupation, and income) for males by national origins. Euro-American males over the age of twenty-five surpass all other groups in mean years of schooling completed, proportion of persons who have at least graduated from high school, proportion of persons with at least some college, and, except for Chinese-Americans, in proportion of persons with

Table 12.2
Education, Occupation, and Income of Males by National Origins: Hawaii, 1980

Stratification Dimension	Characteristic	Euro-American	Haole	Chinese-American	Japanese-American	Filipino-American
	% at least 12 yrs	79.8	84.4	78.3	74.8	47.0
	% at least 13 yrs	50.6	57.2	49.1	38.5	20.2
Education	% 16 or more yrs	28.3	33.0	30.7	19.4	6.2
	Mean yrs schooling	13.3	13.8	13.0	12.4	9.4
	N	4,816	4,015	1,054	4,656	2,323
	% management, prof. & specialists	35.8	39.8	36.0	25.8	7.9
Occupation	% tech., sales & admin. support	21.0	22.1	29.9	25.3	13.6
	N	3,849	3,250	794	3,690	1,489
1979 Salary & Wage Income	Median	$14,005.00	$14,005.00	$15,005.00	$15,005.00	$10,005.00
	Mean	$16,396.20	$16,923.80	$16,561.80	$16,213.50	$11,591.10
	N	3,608	3,043	781	3,579	1,643
1979 Total Income	Median	$14,010.00	$15,005.00	$14,030.00	$14,880.00	$9,010.00
	Mean	$17,762.00	$18,575.30	$17,169.60	$16,602.00	$10,989.40
	N	4,517	3,776	998	4,447	2,113
Conversion of Education Into Income	Dollar Value of Each Additional Year of Schooling	$1,247.89	$1,355.48	$1,037.51	$778.96	$434.60
	Percentage Increase Associated with Additional Year of Schooling	9.8	11.0	8.3	6.3	4.0

Source: U.S. Census 1980, Public Use Microdata Sample, 5%-A sample.

four or more years of college. Chinese-Americans are very close on all dimensions while Japanese-Americans have almost as many high school graduates but then lag somewhat in the proportion of those who go on to college—although they appear to have a very high completion rate among those who begin college. Filipino-Americans have considerably lower levels of educational achievement. Proportionately, only about 65 percent as many Filipino-American males as Euro-Americans have completed four or more years of college. Haoles are even better educated than the Euro-American community as a whole, exceeding all other national origins groups in proportion at each level of higher education.

Occupational status is sometimes seen as a reward received for increased levels of educational achievement and sometimes, more instrumentally, as a vehicle for earning income. Table 12.2 includes the proportion of employed males over the age of 16 in white-collar occupations by national origins. Euro- and Chinese-Americans have virtually identical proportions in the top strata of white-collar occupations (management, professional, and specialities). All other groups trail far behind. Haoles lead all groups with a 39.8 percent representation. Neither haole nor Euro-American males are as well represented in the lower white-collar strata of occupations (technical, sales, and administrative support) as either Chinese- or Japanese-Americans, although they are better represented than Filipino-Americans. Thus, it would appear the Chinese- and Japanese-American males are more likely than Euro-Americans to have white-collar occupations, but they tend to be more concentrated in those occupations at the lower end of the status heirarchy. Filipino-Americans simply do not do as well as any of the other groups.

The income data in table 12.2 are those for males over the age of 16 with income. Both Chinese- and Japanese-American males have a slightly higher median income than Euro-Americans (1.07 times as large). The median income of Filipino-American males is only 0.71 times as large as that of Euro-Americans. Median income provides a useful indicator of central tendency, but mean income is a better indicator of extreme values. An analysis of mean salary and wage income slightly alters the income distribution picture. Using the Euro-American mean as equal to 1.00, we find that Japanese-Americans earn slightly less and Chinese-Americans slightly more (with 0.99 ratio and 1.01 ratios, respectively) while Filipino-Americans earn considerably less (0.78). The median income of haoles ($14,005) is identical to that of all Euro-Americans, but their mean income ($16,923.80) is higher than that of any other national origins group—1.02 times that of Chinese-Americans. 1.04 times that of Japanese-Americans, and 1.46 times that of Filipino-Americans. Thus, it appears that there is a significantly greater concentration of males with higher levels of earnings among Euro-Americans—and especially among haoles—than among any of the Asian-American groups.

The picture is again altered slightly when we consider total income of males 16 and over with income, regardless of source. Japanese-Americans have a slightly higher median than Euro-Americans (1.06 times as much), Chinese-Americans earn about the same, and Filipino-Americans earn only 0.64 times as much. The median total income of haoles is greater than that of any other national origins group: 1.01 times that of Japanese-Americans, 1.07 times that of Chinese-Americans, and 1.67 times the Filipino-American median. Euro-Americans earn the most of any national origins group in terms of mean total income regardless of source. Chinese-Americans have a mean which is 0.97 times that of Euro-Americans, while the mean for Japanese-Americans is 0.93 times as great, and Filipino-Americans have a mean that is only 0.62 times as large. The haole relative advantage in terms of mean total income of males is even greater (1.08 times that of Chinese-Americans, 1.12 times the mean for Japanese-Americans, and 1.69 times that of Filipino-Americans).

Taken as a unit, the various indicators of male income suggest that Chinese- and Japanese-American males stand in roughly similar positions vis-à-vis the opportunity structure to those of Euro-Americans as a whole although they do not do as well as haoles. They do slightly better in terms of opportunity to earn salary and wages (i.e., to sell their labor power on the labor market), but do less well in terms of nonwage sources of income. Euro-Americans—and, especially haoles—appear to have significantly more capital and, consequently, more investment income. For the most part, Japanese- and Chinese-Americans seem to have overcome most of the disadvantages of their low entry status and have about caught up with Euro-Americans—but not with haoles—in terms of earning power. The same cannot be said for Filipino-Americans males who remain at a great disadvantage relative to all Euro-Americans, let alone, relative to haoles. It is clear that haoles—the community that has historically been located at the top of the racial-ethnic stratification order in Hawaii—continue to be the most privileged of all groups. In addition to the discrepancies in terms of typical income levels, there appears to be a greater concentration of males with very high incomes among Euro-Americans and, especially, among haoles than among any other national origins group.

Table 12.2 also presents data that demonstrate that males from the various national origins groups differ in their ability to convert education into income. Regression equations were run on wage and salary income using education as the predictor variable for each national origins group. When no factor other than years of schooling completed is considered, each additional year of schooling added $1247.89 to the earnings of Euro-American males ($1355.48 for haoles). Each additional year of schooling added only $1037.51 for Chinese-Americans, $778.96 for Japanese-Americans, and $434.60 for Filipino-Americans. Similar regression equations were run using the log of wage and salary income for the various national origins groups. This yields a figure that can be interpreted as the percentage increase in income associated with each additional year of schooling. Once again, Euro-Americans lead the way with a percentage increase of 9.8 (11.0 for haoles) as compared to Chinese-Americans, 8.3; Japanese-Americans, 6.3; and Filipino-Americans, 4.0. It would appear that Euro-Americans, and particularly haoles, earn significantly more than comparably educated Asian-Americans, although the latter differ considerably by national origins group in terms of rate of return to education.

There is an apparent parodox in that Asian-American males in Hawaii, regardless of national origins, to not have the same opportunities for economic success as Euro-Americans, yet Japanese- and Chinese-American families, on the average, seem to have a higher standard of living. Filipino-American males have fewer opportunities, and Filipino-American families have a lower standard of living than any other national origins group considered herein. Perhaps the resolution of this apparent parodox may be found in the fact that national origins groups differ in propensity for married women to be active in the labor force.

Wives in the Labor Force

Table 12.3 presents data on labor-force activities of married women with husband present by national origins. Asian-American married women are much more active in the labor force than either Euro-Americans in general or haoles in particular. The labor-force participation rate for Chinese-American married women is 10.0 percentage points higher than that for haoles and 11.7 percentage points higher than that for Euro-Americans. The corresponding advantages for Japanese-Americans are 15.1% and 16.8%, while they are 15.7% and 17.4% for Filipino-Americans. Differences in rate of full-time employment are equally dramatic. Chinese-American women are 10.6% more active than haole women and 11.4% more active then Euro-Americans. The corresponding advantages for Japanese-Americans are 17.4% and 18.2%, and they are 16.0% and 16.8% for Filipino-Americans.

It is not surprising in view of the foregoing to find that Euro-American and haole married women bring up the rear in terms of median annual earnings. Chinese-American married women earn 1.31 times as much as haole women and 1.18 times as much as Euro-American women. The corresponding figures for Japanese-American women are 1.48 and 1.55, while they are 1.12 and 1.18 for Filipino-Americans. The closeness in terms of earning of haole and Filipino-American married women despite great differences in rates of labor-force participation illustrates the tremendous differences between the two groups in terms of existing opportunity structures. The various national origins groups also differ in terms of the relative importance of wives' earnings relative to total family income. The earnings of married Chinese-American women comprise 1.21 times as high a proportion of total family income as do the earnings of haole wives and 1.25 times those of Euro-American wives. The corresponding figures for Japanese-American wives are 1.35 and 1.39, while they are 1.37 and 1.42 for Filipino-American

Table 12.3

Participation in the Labor Force by National Origins of Married Women, 16 or Over with Husband Present: Hawaii, 1979

National Origins	N	% in Labor Force	% Employed Full-Time	Mean Income	% Income is of Family Income
Euro- American	2,156	49.1	30.8	$4,525.51	15.0
<u>Haole</u>	1,727	50.8	31.6	4,756.60	15.5
Chinese- American	597	60.8	42.2	6,235.83	18.7
Japanese- American	2,768	65.9	49.0	7,020.62	20.9
Filipino- American	1,038	66.5	47.6	5,324.60	21.3

Source: U.S. Census 1980, Public Use Microdata Sample, 5%-A sample.

wives. It is evident that Asian-American wives, regardless of national origins, when compared to either haole or Euro-American wives, are more active in the labor force, are more likely to work full-time, earn more money, and contribute a greater share of the total family income.

Mothers in the Labor Force

Table 12.4 presents data that show the impact of the presence or absence of children upon presence in the labor force of married women with husband present, by national origins. The presence of young children is frequently cited as an impediment to participation in the labor force for mothers. We are not, herein, examining these data for the purpose of explaining differential rates of labor-force participation by national origins. Rather, we are attempting to ascertain whether the propensity for greater rates of labor-force participation among Asian-American women remains despite the presence of children. Euro-American women with either all of their children under the age of six or with children both under six and between six and seventeen, have, by far, the lowest labor-force participation rate of women from any national origins group with similar family circumstances. Differences range in size from sixteen to twenty-six percentage points. They also have the lowest labor-force participation rate among women with older children only, but the size of the differences between them and other groups are greatly reduced, ranging between ten and fifteen percentage points. There is a negligible difference between the labor force participation rates of haoles and those of all Euro-Americans.

Table 12.4
Labor-Force Participation Rates of Married Women, Husband Present by National Origins and Age of Children: Hawaii, 1979

National Origin		Children Under 6 only	Children 6 to 17 only	Both Children Under 6 & Between 6 & 17	No Children
Euro-American	N	280	512	222	1142
	% in Lab Force	43.2	61.5	45.0	45.7
	% Full-Time	21.1	38.1	31.5	29.9
Haole	N	235	405	164	923
	% in Lab Force	45.5	63.0	44.5	37.9
	% Full-Time	21.7	38.3	30.5	31.4
Chinese-American	N	76	154	65	302
	% in Lab Force	61.8	72.7	61.5	54.3
	% Full-Time	44.7	50.7	38.5	38.1
Japanese-American	N	261	747	198	1562
	% in Lab Force	68.2	77.1	70.7	59.6
	% Full-Time	50.2	57.7	49.5	44.5
Filipino-American	N	162	392	181	303
	% in Lab Force	69.7	76.5	66.3	51.8
	% Full-Time	46.3	57.4	44.2	37.6

Source: U.S. Census 1980, Public Use Microdata Sample, 5%-A Sample.

It is interesting to note that the presence of children, all of whom are under six, slightly reduces the labor-force participation rate as compared to that for all married women with husband present for both Euro-American and haole women, but that it increases the labor-force participation rates for all Asian-American groups. Virtually the same pattern exists if we shift our attention to the proportion working full-time, with Chinese-Americans being the only Asian-American group to exhibit a slight decrease. Thus, it is clear that already sizeable differences between European- and Asian-American married women in labor-force participation rates are further widened by the presence of young children. The presence of children between the ages of six and seventeen, but none under the age of six, is accompanied by increases in labor-force participation rate compared to that for married women without children for all married women regardless of national origins. However, the rate of increase differs among groups. The smallest absolute increase (15.7%) is found among Euro-American and Filipino-American women. The increases for Chinese-Americans and

Japanese-Americans were 18.4 and 17.5%, respectively. The increase for haole women (15.1%) was virtually the same as that for all Euro-American women.

Differences in proportions of mothers working full-time are even more dramatic. The proportion of mothers working full-time among those with all of their children under the age of six is more than twice as high among each of the Asian-American groups as it is among either Euro-Americans or haoles. The size of the difference is smaller but it still ranges between seven and fifteen percentage points among mothers with children both younger than six and between six and seventeen. The differences are in the same direction for mothers with children between six and seventeen only and range in size from twelve to nineteen percentage points. Thus it is clear that Asian-American women who are married with husband present are far more likely than either Euro-American or haole women to work outside the home for wages, and to work full-time, regardless of the presence or age(s) of children.

Working Wives and Husbands' Income

The participation of married women in the labor force has often been viewed as a reaction to economic pressures generated by low-earning capacities of males. We believe this to be an oversimplification. Patterns may have been historically initiated within groups in this manner, but it seems plausible to assume that they would then become firmly established within racial-ethnic communities as part of their strategy for group survival in a hostile environment. These patterns may remain as accepted, even expected, practice within groups long after the disappearance of the economic conditions that were responsible for their initial emergence. To the extent that the traditional argument is correct, we would expect to see married women's labor-force participation rates decline as husbands' income increases and that, within income strata, differences by national origins would be small or nonexistent. Deviations from that pattern would tend to support our alternative interpretation.

Table 12.5 presents labor-force participation data for married women by national origins and husbands' income with the latter being divided into quartiles. The labor-force participation rate for Euro-American wives increases from 31.3% in the lowest quartile of husbands' income to 62.8% in the third quartile before falling back to 52.0% in the fourth quartile. All national origins groups except Chinese-Americans (who peak in the second quartile) exhibit the same pattern of lowest labor-force participation rates in the first quartile, highest in the third, and then a fourth quartile that is more similar to the third than the first. The low, high, and fourth quartile labor-force participation rates for the other national origins groups are, respectively: haoles 34.3%, 66.2%, and 51.9%; Chinese-Americans, 39.2%, 71.1%, and 66.7%; Japanese-Americans, 45.2%, 79.3%, and 69.3%; and

Table 12.5

Labor-Force Participation and Earnings of Married Women with Husband Present by Husband's Income and National Origins: Hawaii, 1979

Husband's Income Level	National Origins	% in Labor Force	Percent Employed Full-time	% Wife's Earnings Are of Total Family Income	N
Lowest Quartile	Euro-American	31.3	17.8	11.8	556
	Haole	34.3	19.6	13.0	455
	Chinese-American	39.2	26.6	12.9	158
	Japanese-American	45.2	32.2	16.0	692
	Filipino-American	50.6	33.6	22.1	247
Second Quartile	Euro-American	53.7	34.2	21.3	492
	Haole	56.2	35.8	22.1	366
	Chinese-American	71.1	49.6	25.2	135
	Japanese-American	69.6	53.4	26.3	539
	Filipino-American	70.0	51.3	23.5	390
Third Quartile	Euro-American	62.8	40.6	17.2	436
	Haole	66.2	42.8	18.9	320
	Chinese-American	70.1	50.4	23.5	127
	Japanese-American	79.2	59.2	25.0	732
	Filipino-American	76.4	56.8	20.3	250
Highest Quartile	Euro-American	52.0	33.2	11.6	663
	Haole	51.9	32.5	11.5	578
	Chinese-American	66.7	45.4	15.3	174
	Japanese-American	69.3	51.1	17.9	802
	Filipino-American	68.2	46.6	15.5	148

Source: U.S. Census 1980, Public Use Microdata Sample, 5%-A sample.

Filipino-Americans, 64.4%, 82.9%, and 68.2 percent. In each quartile, Asian-American married women, regardless of national origin, exhibit strikingly higher labor-force participation rates than either haoles or Euro-Americans. The greatest excess of Chinese-American and Japanese-American labor-force participation rates over those of haoles (14.8 and 17.4 percentage points, respectively) are found in the highest quartile of husbands' income while the greatest excess for Filipinos is found in the lowest quartile.

The same pattern of lowest rates in the first quartile, increasing to a peak in the third, followed by a decline in the fourth quartile, characterizes proportions of wives working full-time in each national origins group. The respective lowest, peak, and fourth quartile proportions for each national origins group are: Euro-Americans, 17.8%, 40.6%, and 33.2%; haoles, 19.6%, 42.8%, and 32.5%; Chinese-Americans, 26.6%, 50.4%, and 45.4%; Japanese-Americans, 32.2%, 59.2%, and 51.1%; and Filipino-Americans, 16.8%, 56.8%, and 46.6 percent. Except for Filipino-Americans in the lowest quartile, Euro-Americans and haoles have lower proportions of wives working full-time than any Asian-American group in each quartile. The greatest differences between haoles and each of the Asian-American groups in proportion of wives working full-time come in the highest quartile of husbands' earnings.

Perhaps the most interesting column in table 12.5 is that which reveals the proportion of total family income supplied by salary and wage income of wives. In each of the four quartiles of husbands' income, married, Euro-American, and haole women provide a lower proportion of total family income than do their Asian-American counterparts. The one exception appears in the lowest income quartile where there is a negligible difference between Chinese-American and haole women. The full extent of the greater contribution of Asian-American wives becomes apparent if we create ratios setting the percentage contribution of haole wives equal to 1.00. For Chinese-American wives, the ratios between the degree of their contribution and those of haole wives in each quartile of husbands' income, moving from lowest to highest, are 0.99, 1.18, 1.24, and 1.33. The corresponding figures for Japanese-American wives are 1.23, 1.23, 1.32, and 1.56. For Filipino-Americans, the corresponding figures are 1.70, 1.10, 1.07, and 1.35. Not only do Asian-American wives make a greater contribution to total family income than haole wives, but the extent of their excess contribution tends to increase as husbands' income increases.

Wives' Earnings and Family Standing in the Stratification Order

Table 12.6 presents labor-force participation data for married women, by national origins, for quartiles of total family income. This allows us to examine the extent to which the economic standing of families of different national origins is a consequence of female labor-force participation and of wives' earnings. Within each income quartile, Euro-American and haole wives rank at the bottom in labor-force participation rate. The singular exception appears in the lowest income quartile, where Japanese-Americans have a labor-force participation rate of 31.6% as compared to 32.5% for Euro-Americans and 35.2% for haoles. The labor-force participation rate of haole wives most closely approximates that of Asian-American wives in the lowest income quartile although, even there, Filipino-American women are more active by 15.2 percentage points. The greatest difference in labor-force participation rates between haoles and Chinese-American or Japanese-American women appears in the highest income quartile (12.3 and 20.1 percentage points, respectively). The greatest difference relative to Filipino-American women appears in the third quartile (22.2 percentage points) before declining to 17.6 percentage points in the highest quartile.

A similar pattern emerges if we examine rates of full-time employment. Euro-Americans and haoles have the lowest proportion of haole wives employed full-time in each quartile. The rate for haole wives most closely approximates that of Asian-American wives in the lowest income quartile

Table 12.6
Labor-Force Participation and Earnings of Married Women with Husband Present by Total Family Income and National Origins: Hawaii, 1979

Family Income Level	National Origins	% in Labor Force	Percent Employed Full-time	% Wife's Earnings Are of Total Family Income	N
Lowest Quartile	Euro-American	32.5	16.4	12.7	566
	Haole	35.2	18.0	13.8	423
	Chinese-American	37.2	23.0	14.9	113
	Japanese-American	31.6	18.1	14.9	474
	Filipino-American	50.7	29.7	19.1	347
Second Quartile	Euro-American	48.9	29.8	16.0	550
	Haole	50.1	29.8	16.5	413
	Chinese-American	60.6	39.4	19.3	127
	Japanese-American	61.8	41.5	20.3	638
	Filipino-American	68.6	29.6	24.0	293
Third Quartile	Euro-American	58.3	39.8	17.6	485
	Haole	58.8	40.0	18.0	408
	Chinese-American	65.3	44.3	20.8	167
	Japanese-American	76.3	59.3	24.2	793
	Filipino-American	80.9	63.6	23.5	242
Highest Quartile	Euro-American	58.5	39.2	14.1	546
	Haole	58.9	38.5	14.1	475
	Chinese-American	72.2	54.6	18.7	187
	Japanese-American	78.5	62.0	21.7	860
	Filipino-American	76.5	59.5	17.4	153

Source: U.S. Census 1980, Public Use Microdata Sample, 5%-A sample.

although, even there, Filipino-American wives are more likely to be employed full-time by a margin of 11.7 percentage points. The greatest difference between haole wives and Chinese- and Japanese-American wives in proportion employed full-time appears in the highest income quartile (17.0 and 22.1% differences, respectively). The greatest difference between haole and Filipino-American wives appears in the third quartile (23.6 percentage points) before declining to 21.0 percentage points in the fourth quartile.

The earnings of Euro-American and haole wives make up a lower proportion of total family income than do those of Asian-American wives in all quartiles of total family income. The earnings of haole wives do not reach one-fifth of total family income in any income quartile. They increase from a low of 13.8% in the first quartile to a high of 18.0% in the third quartile before declining to 14.1% in the highest income quartile. The same basic pattern holds for each group except that the contribution of Filipino-American wives peaks in the second quartile.

Differences in the extent to which the various national origins groups depend upon the earnings of women to achieve various levels of affluence may be seen by creating ratios in which contribution at the same level as that of haoles equals 1.00. The resulting ratios for Chinese-American wives by income quartile starting with the lowest are 1.08, 1.17, 1.16, and 1.33. The corresponding figures for Japanese-Americans are 1.08, 1.23, 1.34, and 1.54, while they are 1.38, 1.45, 1.26, and 1.23, for Filipino-Americans. For both Japanese- and Chinese-Americans, the greatest excess reliance upon the earnings of wives relative to that characterizing haoles appears in the highest income quartile. It is clear that Asian-American families are far more dependent than Euro-Americans or haoles upon the earnings of women in order to achieve membership in the economic elite, or for that matter, in the upper half of families ranked by total income. This greater dependence upon women's earnings is evident at all socioeconomic levels, but appears to be especially important at, or near, the top.

The Relative Economic Importance of Wives

Thus, by whatever measure of female labor-force participation we use (proportion of married women with husband present who are in the labor force, proportion regularly employed full-time, proportion of total family income earned by wives, or the impact of presence of children of any age upon employment and earnings), the three most active national origins groups are the three Asian-American groups (Japanese-, Filipino-, and Chinese-Americans—usually in that order). Euro-American women are the least active in the labor force with participation rates that approximate those of haoles. It would appear that the differential female labor-force participation rates between national origins groups are closely related to the existing stratification order. They may, in part, have their origin in group strategies selected in order to cope with group disadvantages vis-à-vis the opportunity structure. These differential patterns of labor-force behavior may either reflect strategies designed to deal with present circumstances or be the historical legacy of situations existing in the past. Either way, they affect the present.

Euro-Americans and haoles are able to achieve a satisfactory standard of living for their families and significant overrepresentation among the economic elite with a much lower level of famale labor-force participation than that exhibited by Asian-Americans. On the other hand, women's earnings appear to be a major factor in helping Japanese- and Chinese-Americans to achieve a comparable standard of living and a similar overrepresentation among the economic elite. Even the labor of wives and daughters is not enough to bring Filipino-Americans up to the standard of living achieved by Euro-American families which, to a much greater extent, are able to rely primarily upon the earnings of the male head of household.

CONCLUSION

Our findings strongly suggest that Asian-Americans still do not have full equality of opportunity with Euro-Americans in Hawaii—and especially not with haoles. They have experienced a great deal of mobility over time and have improved their relative positions. Each Asian-American group has had a different set of historical experiences and now appears to occupy different positions vis-à-vis the stratification order. Chinese-Americans are the descendants of the first Asian group to come to Hawaii, and were the first to leave the plantations. As a group, they now enjoy a standard of living that is higher than that enjoyed by Euro-Americans. Chinese-American males, on the average, are about as well educated as Euro-Americans and appear to outearn them despite the fact that they receive less of an economic payoff for the education that they acquire. Chinese-American men also have smaller amounts of unearned income.

Japanese-Americans are the descendants of the second Asian group to come to Hawaii and were the second to leave the plantations. They also appear to enjoy a standard of living at least equal, and possibly superior, to that enjoyed by Euro-Americans. Japanese-American males are not quite as well educated as Euro-Americans, earn at about the same level (perhaps a bit less), receive a smaller economic return from education, and have less unearned income. Filipino-Americans are the descendants of the last Asian group to come to Hawaii and were the last to leave the plantations—in fact, they have not yet fully left. Filipino-American males do not have nearly the level of education of Euro-Americans, earn much less, receive far less of an economic return on their level of education, and have relatively low levels of unearned income.

We do not wish to imply with this chronology any support for the assimilationist perspective. The very real gains achieved by these groups are not the simple consequence of having become assimilated into the American culture. Rather, they are, in large part, the result of collective action and struggle (Geschwender 1981, 1982; Levine & Geschwender 1981; Geschwender & Levine 1983, 1986). Chinese-Americans left the plantations and moved into the cities at a time when the cities were still growing. Opportunities existed for them to move into economic niches where they would not threaten Euro-Americans. They shared their resources and advanced as the cities and region expanded and developed. Japanese-Americans struggled collectively both on and off the plantations but did not experience much in the way of advancement until after World War II. They organized politically, became a major force in the rising Democratic party, and used political power and patronage along with the education that was achieved, in large part, with the help of the G.I. Bill, to collectively move up economically. A large portion of gains that have been achieved by Filipino-Americans to date can be attributed to the growth of strong labor unions—a development to which Filipino-Americans contributed a great deal.

There has been struggle by, and gains achieved for, each of the Asian-American groups in Hawaii. However, we must be very careful not to be so impressed by the drama of the struggle that we fail to note that a very important dimension of the strategy for survival and collective advancement involved the proletarianization of women to an extent not seen in the Euro-American community. We cannot at this time trace the process of female proletarianization. But, we may note that it occurred among peoples who were uprooted from their homelands and transported long distances to a strange place where they were used as cheap labor and forced to work under oppressive conditions on sugar plantations. The entry of large numbers of Asian-American women into the labor force can best be seen as one of the many strategies that they devised in order to resist the encroachments of capital and to retain some control over their own lives (Glenn 1983).

The economic advances achieved by Asian-Americans have been un-equally shared among the various national origins groups. In addition, each has become internally differentiated by class. (Space concerns prohibit the presentation of data on this point, but each nationality group includes families living in wealth and families living in poverty.) We must be just as careful to avoid sweeping generalizations about all members of any one of the groups as we are to avoid generalizing about all Asian-Americans re-gardless of national origins. Nevertheless, we can close with three general thoughts. First, despite all of the progress that has been made, Asian-Americans in Hawaii still do not have an equal opportunity to achieve economically. It would seem that they experience some discrimination in the sense that their education does not bring the same degree of economic rewards that it does for Euro-Americans.

Second, much of the apparent affluence of Asian-Americans is the simple consequence of a much higher rate of female participation in the labor force. Asian-American families appear to need a much higher rate of female labor-force participation in order to achieve the same standard of living and degree of economic security that Euro-American (and particularly haole) families, with comparably qualified male heads, can achieve by relying mainly on the earning power of males. In other words, much of the vaunted success of Asian-Americans in Hawaii, and we suspect in American society as a whole, is achieved, not because of greater opportunities, but because of the increased labor of women. In short, Asian-Americans have risen, at least in part, by standing on the shoulders of women.

Finally, any analysis of racial-ethnic stratification must take the household or family as the basic unit of analysis. This is the collectivity that devises a strategy for survival. It makes decisions, allocates resources, distributes income, and shares a common standard of living. The general strategy and specific decisions are, in part, shaped in response to cir-cumstances existing at a particular time and place. However, the selection of a strategy and the making of decisions are also heavily influenced by the common historical experiences and shared traditions that have evolved within nationality groups. Patterns of behavior that people devise at one point in time to resolve their problems often become incorporated into the legacy passed on from generation to generation helping to shape subsequent behavior practices—culture, if you wish. Equally important is the fact that all nationality groups are class-differentiated. Differences in class location and class situation have a major impact upon the selection of a general strategy and the making of specific decisions. In short, the household or family, imbedded in a class situation, and located within a nationality group, must become the focus of our analysis of stratification and resistance.

REFERENCES

Chinen, Joyce (n.d.). "Working Wives and the Socioeconomic Status of Ethnic Groups in Hawaii." *Humboldt Journal of Social Relations,* 11, 2, Spring/ Summer, 165–86.

Chiswick, Barry R. (1980). "Immigrant Earnings Patterns by Sex, Race, and Ethnic Groupings." *Monthly Labor Review,* 103, 10, October, 22–25.

_____ (1983). "An Analysis of the Earnings and Employment of Asian-American Men." *Journal of Labor Economics,* 1, 2, April, 197–214.

Chun, Ki-Taek (1980). "The Myth of Asian-American Success and Its Educational Ramifications." IRCD Bulletin 15, A Publication of the Institute for Urban and Minority Education, Teachers College, Columbia University, 1–12.

Curtis, Richard F. (1986). "Household and Family in Theory on Equality." *American Sociological Review,* 51, 2, April, 168–83.

Fallers, Lloyd A. (1964). "Social Stratification and Economic Processes in Africa." In Melville Herskovits and Michael Harwitz, eds., *Economic Processes in Africa.* Evanston, Ill.: Northwestern University Press, 113–30.

Geschwender, James A. (1980a). "On Analyzing Race Relations Without Theory." *Contemporary Sociology,* 9, 2, March, 215–18.

_____ (1980b). "Reply to Lind." *Contemporary Sociology,* 51, 9, November, 737–39.

_____ (1981). "The Interplay Between Class and National Consciousness: Hawaii 1850–1950." In Richard L. Simpson and Ida Harper Simpson, eds., *Research in the Sociology of Work,* vol. 1. Greenwich, Conn.: JAI, 171–204.

_____ (1982). "The Hawaiian Transformation: Class, Submerged Nation and and Ethnic Minorities." In Edward Friedman, ed., *Ascent and Decline in the World-System,* vol. 5 of The Political Economy of the World-System Annuals. Beverly Hills: Sage, 189–226.

_____ (1987). "Race, Ethnicity and Class." In Rhonda Levine and Jerry Lembke, eds., *Recapturing Marxism.* New York: Praeger, 136–60.

Geschwender, James A., and Rita Carroll-Seguin (1987). "On the Creation of Ethnicity: The Portuguese and Haoles of Hawaii." Paper presented at American Sociological Association Meetings, Chicago.

Geschwender, James A., and Rhonda F. Levine (1983). "Rationalization of Sugar Production in Hawaii, 1946–1960: A Dimension of the Class Struggle." *Social Problems,* 30, 3, February, 352–68.

_____ (1986). "Class Struggle and Political Transformation in Hawaii, 1946–1960." In Richard G. Braungart and Margaret M. Braungart, eds. *Research in Political Sociology,* vol. 2. Greenwich, Conn.: JAI, 243–68.

Glenn, Evelyn (1983). "Split Households, Small Producer and Wage Earner: An Analysis of Chinese-American Family Strategies," *Journal of Marriage and the Family,* 45, 1, February, 35–46.

Hartmann, Heidi (1981). "The Family as the Locus of Gender, Class, and Political Struggle: The Example of Housework." *Signs,* 6, 3, Spring, 366–94.

Hirschman, Charles, and Morris G. Wong (1981). "Trends in Socioeconomic Achievement Among Immigrant and Native-born Asian Americans." *Sociological Quarterly,* 22. 4. Autumn, 495–514.

_____ (1986). "The Extraordinary Educational Attainment of Asian-Americans: A Search for Historical Evidence and Explanations." *Social Forces,* 65, 1, September, 1–27.

Hurh, Won Moo, and Kwang Chung Kim (1986). "The 'Success' Image of Asian-Americans: Its Validity, Practical and Theoretical Implications." Paper presented at American Sociological Association Meetings, New York, September 3.

Jaco, Daniel E., and George L. Wilber (1975). "Asian-Americans in the Labor Market." *Monthly Labor Review,* 98, 7, July, 33–38.

Jiobu, Robert M. (1976). "Earnings Differentials Between Whites and Ethnic Minorities: The Cases of Asian-Americans, Blacks, and Chicanos." *Sociology and Social Research,* 60, 1, October, 24–38.

Kim, Kwang Chung, and Won Moo Hurh (1980). "Social and Occupational Assimilation of Korean Immigrants in the United States." *California Sociologist,* vol. 3, 125–42.

_____ (1983). "Korean Americans and the 'Success' Image: A Critique." *Amerasia,* 10, 2, Fall/Winter, 3–21.

_____ (1985). "Ethnic Resources Utilization of Korean Immigrant Entrepreneurs in the Chicago Minority Area." *International Migration Review,* 19, 1, Spring, 82–111.

Kitano, Harry H. L., and Stanley Sue (1973). "The Model Minorities." *Journal of Social Issues,* 29, 2, 1–9.

Levine, Rhonda F., and James A. Geschwender (1981). "Class Struggle, State Policy, and the Rationalization of Production: The Organization of Agriculture in Hawaii." In Louis Kriesberg, ed., *Research in Social Movements, Conflict and Change,* vol. 4. Greenwich. Conn.: JAI, 123–50.

Lind, Andrew W. (1980a). *Hawaii's People.* Honolulu: University of Hawaii Press.

_____ (1980b). "An Error Compounded." *Contemporary Sociology,* 51, 9, November, 737.

Marden, Charles F. and Gladys Meyer (1978). *Minorities in American Society.* New York: Van Nostrand.

Smith, Joan, Immanuel Wallerstein, and H. D. Evers (1984). *Households and the World-Economy.* Beverly Hills: Sage.

U.S. Commission on Civil Rights (1980). *Success of Asian-Americans: Fact or Fiction?* Washington, D.C.: U.S. Government Printing Office.

Wallerstein, Immanuel, William G. Martin, and Torry Dickinson (1982). "Household Structures and Production Processes: Preliminary Thesis and Findings." *Review,* 5, 3, Winter, 437–58.

Wong, Morrison G. (1982). "The Cost of Being Chinese, Japanese, and Filipino in the United States 1960, 1970, 1976." *Pacific Sociological Review,* 25, 1, January, 59–78.

Yamanaka, Keiko (1985). "Labor Force Participation of Asian-American Women." Paper presented at the American Sociological Association Meetings, New York.

_____ (1986). "Labor Force Participation of Asian-American Women: Ethnicity, Work and the Family." Paper presented at the American Sociological Association Meetings, Washington.

Young, Jared J. (1977). *Discrimination, Income and Human Capital Investments and Asian-Americans.* San Francisco: R & E Research Associates.

Bibliography

Arrighi, Giovanni, Terence K. Hopkins, and Immanuel Wallerstein (1983). "Rethinking the Concepts of Class and Status-Group in a World-System Perspective," *Review*, 6, 3 (Winter):283–304.

Beechey, Veronica (1977). "Some Notes on Female Wage Labour in Capitalist Production," *Capital and Class*, 3: 45–65.

Beneria, Lourdes, ed. (1982). *Women and Development*. New York: Praeger.

———. (1985). *Women and Development: The Sexual Division of Labor in Rural Societies*. New York: Praeger.

Bonacich, Edna (1976). "Advanced Capitalism and Black/White Race Relations in the United States: A Split Labor Market Interpretation," *American Sociological Review*, 61, 1 (February):34–51.

Boserup, Ester (1970). *Women's Role in Economic Development*. New York: St. Martin's.

Curtis, Richard F. (1986). "Household and Family in Theory on Equality," *American Sociological Review*, 60, 2, (April):168–83.

Davis, Angela (1971). "Reflections of the Black Woman's Role in the Community of Slaves," *The Black Scholar, Journal of Black Studies and Research*, 3, 4: 2–16.

Etienne, Mona, and Eleanor Leacock, eds. (1980). *Women and Colonization: Anthropological Perspectives*. South Hadley, Mass.: Bergin and Garvey.

Fernandez-Kelly, M. Patricia, and Anna M. Garcia (1985). "The Making of an Underground Economy: Hispanic Women, Home Work, and the Advanced Capitalist State," *Urban Anthropology*, 14, 1–3: 59–90.

Fröbel, Folker, Jurgen Heinrichs, and Otto Kreye (1980). *The New International Division of Labor*. New York: Cambridge University Press.

Fuentes, Annette, and Barbara Ehrenreich (1984). *Women in the Global Factory*. Boston: South End.

Geschwender, James A. (1980). "On Analyzing Race Relations Without Theory," *Contemporary Sociology*, 9, 2 (March):215–18.

Glenn, Evelyn (1983). "Split Households, Small Producer and Dual Wage Earner: An Analysis of Chinese-American Family Strategies," *Journal of Marriage and the Family*, 45, 1 (February):35–46.

Glenn, Evelyn Nakano (1985). "Racial Ethnic Women's Labor: The Intersection of Race Gender and Class Oppression," *Review of Radical Political Economy*, 17, 3: 86–108.

Harris, J. S. (1940). "The Position of Women in a Nigerian Society," *Transactions of the New York Academy of Sciences*. New York.

Hartmann, Heidi (1981). "The Family as the Locus of Gender, Class, and Political Struggle: The Example of Housework," *Signs*, 6, 3 (Spring):366–94.

International Center for Research on Women (ICRW) (1980). *Keeping Women Out: A Structural Analysis of Women's Employment in Developing Countries*. Washington, D.C.: Agency for International Development.

Lieberson, Stanley (1980). *A Piece of the Pie*. Berkeley: University of California Press.

Mies, Maria (1986). *Patriarchy and Accumulation on a World Scale*. London: Zed.

Nash, June, and Maria Patricia Fernandez-Kelly, eds. (1983). *Women and Men in the International Division of Labor*. Albany, N.Y.: State University of New York Press.

Portes, Alejandro, and John Walton (1981). *Labor, Class and the International System*. New York: Academic Press.

Portes, Alejandro (1985). "The Informal Sector and the World-Economy," in M. Timberlake, ed., *Urbanization in the World-Economy*. Orlando, Fla.: Academic, 53–62.

Rosaldo, Michelle, and Louise Lamphere, eds. (1974). *Women, Culture and Society*. Stanford: Stanford University Press.

Smith, Joan, Immanuel Wallerstein, and Hans-Dieter Evers, eds. (1984). *Households and the World-Economy*. Beverly Hills, Calif.: Sage.

Takaki, Ronald, ed. (1987). *From Different Shores. Perspectives on Race and Ethnicity in America*. New York: Oxford University Press.

Tilly, Louise, and Joan Scott (1978). *Women, Work and Family*. New York: Holt, Rinehart and Winston.

Wallerstein, Immanuel (1976). *The Modern World-System*, I. *Capitalist Agriculture and the Origins of the European World-Economy in the Sixteenth Century*. New York: Academic Press.

⸻ (1981). "Race Is Class?" *Monthly Review*, 32, 10 (March):47–52.

⸻ (1983). *Historical Capitalism*. London: Verso.

Wallerstein, Immanuel, William G. Martin, and Torry Dickinson (1982). "Household Structures and Production Processes: Preliminary Thesis and Findings," *Review*, 5, 3 (Winter):437–58.

Ward, Kathryn (1984). *Women in the World-System: Its Impact on Status and Fertility*. New York: Praeger.

Wilson, William J. (1978). *The Declining Significance of Race*. Chicago: University of Chicago Press.

Young, Kate, Carol Wolkowitz, and Roslyn McCullagh (1981). *Of Marriage and the Market*. London: Routledge and Kegan Paul.

Young, Richard P. (1986). "History and the Politics of Race," *Socialist Review*, 16, 3/4, (87/88) (May-August):67–75.

Index

Affirmative action, 39, 51, 53–54; class contradictions of, 51–52

Ageism, 8

Agricultural businesses, funneling of Mexican migrants into, 178–79

Alpargatas factories, 117n. 48

Amoskeag Mill, 63–64, 70

Apartheid, 9

Argentina: exports of raw wool from, 102, 106; household production in, 99–102, 105–9; women's handicraft textile production in, 97–98

Asian women, and the world-economy, 57–72

Asian-workers, 46; as category of worker, 40; characteristics of, as workers, 11, 59; generic portrait of, 145; participation of, in small business, 156–57; success of, in Hawaii, 187–205

Association of Housewives of Siglo XX, 30

Baibieni y Antonini, 116

Bangladesh, textile industry in, 63

Belize, sugarcane production in, 19

Bell, Peter F., 75–82

Blacks, 40, 46; coercive migration of, 175–76; participation of, in small business, 154–56, sojourner migration of, 179–80; unemployment of, in the United States, 164; vulnerability of, to discrimination, 156–57

Bolivia: "March of Life" in, 29–30; New Economic Policy in, 29

Boswell, Terry, 169–83

Bracero Programs, 179

Brain drain, minoritization of the, 46–51

Brazil: employment of women in, 25; impact of divorce on women in, 20

Brotherhood of man, as phrase, 3

Cameroons: Kom women in, 133; organizations for women in, 126

Capital: impact of, on gender, 76–79; in the Third World, 75–82

Capital accumulation, 5, 75–76; as global process, 76; on a world scale, 76–79

Capitalism: and appropriateness of universalism, 4; cooptation of patriarchy of, in advance of, 16–18;

About the Contributors

PETER F. BELL is Associate Professor of Economics at the State University of New York at Purchase. He teaches political economy, has written and done research on Marxian theory, development, and Southeast Asian economics. His articles have appeared in book collections and journals.

TERRY BOSWELL is Assistant Professor of Sociology at Emory University. He is co-editor of *America's Changing Role in the World-System* and chair of the organizing committee of the 1988 PEWS conference on "War and Revolution." His current research includes a time-series analysis of the effects of world hegemony and long economic waves on the pattern of colonization and the intensity of war from 1650 to the present.

RITA CARROLL-SEGUIN is Research Associate in Sociology at the State University of New York at Binghamton. She is interested in stratification processes, in particular in the relationship between state activity, ethnicity, and household income strategies. Currently, she is writing *Global Transfer: Resettlement of South East Asian Refugees* (with Dr. Robert L. Bach).

JANE L. COLLINS is Assistant Professor of Anthropology at the State University of New York at Binghamton. She has conducted research on seasonal migration and labor dynamics in southern Peru and is the author of *Unseasonal Migration: The Effects of Rural Labor Scarcity in Peru.*

ANN E. FORSYTHE is a doctoral candidate in sociology at the State University of New York at Binghamton. She is currently director of New York Governor Cuomo's Task Force on Work and Family.

JAMES GESCHWENDER is Professor and Chair of Sociology at the State University of New York at Binghamton. He has written extensively in the areas of racial stratification, theories of ethnicity, and social movements and social change. His current work centers on Ethgender.

MARTHA E. GIMENEZ is Associate Professor of Sociology at the University of Colorado, Boulder. She studied law and sociology at the University of Cordoba, Argentina, and received a Ph.D. from the University of California, Los Angeles (1973). She is the author of numerous articles on population theory and Marxist feminist theory.

TERENCE K. HOPKINS is Director of Doctoral Studies in Sociology at the State University of New York at Binghamton and Board Member of the university's Fernand Braudel Center. Co-author with Immanuel Wallerstein and others of *World-Systems Analysis* (1982).

JOHN HORTON teaches sociology at UCLA. He is currently doing research on class, ethnic, and gender dimensions of "anti-growth" politics in Los Angeles interpreted as responses to the economic and demographic restructuring of the urban environment within the capitalist world-economy.

DAVID JORJANI is a graduate student at the School of Oriental and African Studies, University of London, and currently employed by Rafshoon Communications to research the origins of the Iranian Revolution for a forthcoming film. His other research interests include a study of the development of commercial codes in Middle Eastern international law.

KATHIE FRIEDMAN KASABA teaches Women Studies at the University of Washington in Seattle. She has been actively working with the Households and the World-Economy Project of the Fernand Braudel Center at the State University of New York at Binghamton. Currently she is writing a dissertation in sociology at SUNY-Binghamton about the bargaining power of New York sewing women in factories and households.

ROBERTO P. KORZENIEWICZ is Research Associate at the Fernand Braudel Center for the Study of Economies, Historical Systems, and Civilizations at the State University of New York at Binghamton.

EUN-JIN LEE received his M.A. from Seoul National University and is completing his doctorate in sociology at UCLA. His dissertation is an analysis of the regime of labor control in a peripheral country, South Korea.

NANCY LUTZ is Mellon Fellow in the Department of Anthropology at Cornell University. She received her Ph.D. in anthropology from the

University of California, Berkeley, in 1986, and specializes in the politics of language and culture in Indonesia.

AKBAR MUHAMMAD is Associate Professor of African and Islamic History at the State University of New York at Binghamton. He specializes and publishes on the social and intellectual history of Muslim North and West Africa, African-Arab relations, and Muslims in the Americas. Presently he is completing a book on women, ethnicity, and color, based on a fifteenth-century Arabic manuscript.

JUNE NASH is Professor of Anthropology at City College and the Graduate Center of the City University of New York. She is the author of *In the Eyes of the Ancestors: Belief and Behavior in a Maya Community*; *We East the Mines and the Mines East Us: Dependency and Exploitation in Bolivian Tin Mines*; *From Tank Town to HighTech: The Restructuring of Industry in a New England Industrial City*, and editor of several anthologies on Latin America as well as gender issues. She is currently distinguished visiting professor at the University of Colorado in Women's Studies.

JOAN SMITH is Professor of Sociology and a Research Associate at the Fernand Braudel Center at the State University of New York at Binghamton. Her work deals with the relationship between waged and unwaged labor in the world-economy. She has just completed a full-scale research project on this topic with Immanuel Wallerstein funded by the National Endowment for the Humanities.

IMMANUEL WALLERSTEIN is Director of the Fernand Braudel Center at the State University of New York at Binghamton and author of *The Modern World-System* and *Historical Capitalism*.

KATHRYN WARD is Associate Professor of Sociology at Southern Illinois University at Carbondale. She is author of *Women in the World-System: Its Influence on Status and Fertility* (Praeger, 1984) and other articles on gender in *Review, Work and Occupations, Social Science Quarterly, Sociological Quarterly*, and *American Sociological Review*. Her current research interests include the global debt crisis, the feminist critique of sociology, and the contemporary U.S. women's movement.

RICHARD WILLIAMS is Associate Professor of Sociology at the State University of New York at Stony Brook. His work is concerned with the social construction of identity.

Studies in the Political Economy of the World-System
(Formerly published as Political Economy of the World-System Annuals)
Series Adviser: Immanuel Wallerstein